P9-BYA-971

The Dynamics of
Conflict Resolution

The Dynamics of Conflict Resolution

A Practitioner's Guide

Bernard Mayer

JOSSEY-BASS
A Wiley Company
San Francisco

Copyright © 2000 by Jossey-Bass Inc., Publishers, 350 Sansome Street, San Francisco, California 94104.

Jossey-Bass is a registered trademark of Jossey-Bass Inc., A Wiley Company.

No part of this publication may be reproduced, stored in a retrieval system, or transmitted in any form or by any means, electronic, mechanical, photocopying, recording, scanning, or otherwise, except as permitted under Sections 107 or 108 of the 1976 United States Copyright Act, without either the prior written permission of the Publisher or authorization through payment of the appropriate per-copy fee to the Copyright Clearance Center, 222 Rosewood Drive, Danvers, MA 01923, (978) 750-8400, fax (978) 750-4744. Requests to the Publisher for permission should be addressed to the Permissions Department, John Wiley & Sons, Inc., 605 Third Avenue, New York, NY 10158-0012, (212) 850-6011, fax (212) 850-6008, e-mail: permreq@wiley.com.

Jossey-Bass books and products are available through most bookstores. To contact Jossey-Bass directly, call (888) 378-2537, fax to (800) 605-2665, or visit our website at www.josseybass.com.

Substantial discounts on bulk quantities of Jossey-Bass books are available to corporations, professional associations, and other organizations. For details and discount information, contact the special sales department at Jossey-Bass.

Manufactured in the United States of America on Lyons Falls Turin Book. This paper is acid-free and 100 percent totally chlorine-free.

Library of Congress Cataloging-in-Publication Data
Mayer, Bernard, 1946–
    The dynamics of conflict resolution: a practitioner's guide /
Bernard Mayer.— 1st ed.
        p. cm.
Includes bibliographical references and index.
    ISBN 0–7879–5019–X (hard: alk. paper)
    1. Interpersonal conflict.   2. Conflict (Psychology).   3. Conflict
management.   4. Negotiation.   5. Problem solving.   I. Title.
    BF637.I48 M39 2000
    303.6'9—dc21   99–050576

FIRST EDITION
HB Printing   10 9 8 7 6 5 4 3 2 1

Contents

Preface
Thinking About Conflict and Its Resolution

Understanding conflict is basic to its resolution. If we seek to end a conflict, we must start by understanding its nature. What makes a successful peacemaker or conflict resolver is not a set of processes, methodologies, or tactics; it is a way of thinking, a set of values, an array of analytical and interpersonal skills, and a clear focus.

The purpose of this book is to present a set of practical ideas to assist people to understand conflict and then to resolve it. Mediators and other conflict resolvers do not operate primarily in the world of theory but neither do they rely solely on specific procedures or intervention tools. Instead, effective conflict resolvers employ a combination of personal skills, substantive knowledge, and practical concepts. These concepts provide the link between theory and practice. It is this link that allows professions to develop out of crafts, specific experiences to inform general practice, and reflective practitioners to mature. The field of conflict resolution is at a stage of development that requires a focus on these frameworks.

In this book I focus on how conflict resolvers can productively think about conflict and resolution, rather than on what they should do. I present ideas that can assist people to be effective as negotiators, facilitators, mediators, and communicators. These concepts must be informed by our practical experiences and our values, but in turn they very much influence what we actually do when we are in conflict situations. I have drawn them from over two decades of experience as a mediator, facilitator, conflict resolution trainer, and dispute systems designer. In articulating the practical concepts I use in my work, I have found the process of self-reflection to be critical. I believe that our most creative moments as practical theorists come when we attempt to integrate the explanations of conflict and conflict resolution to which we are attracted with observations about what we actually do in real-life situations.

The experience I have had as a conflict resolution trainer has both crystallized my focus on practical concepts and convinced me of those concepts' importance in the development of the field. I have repeatedly observed people coming to seminars wanting to learn how to "do" mediation or facilitation or negotiation. The challenge has been to refocus them on how to *think* about conflict and its resolution in creative ways and how to put these *thoughts* into practice in the many different situations they face. When my colleagues and I succeed in helping people develop deeper ways of thinking about conflict resolution, we contribute to a far more important change in the way they do things than we do when we simply teach them processes or steps for handling conflict.

In this book I attempt to present in practical terms the concepts my colleagues and I use when facing different conflict situations and to provide practical examples of the ways these concepts apply across many different settings. I have been fortunate to have had the opportunity to work in a great variety of settings and with many different kinds of conflict, and I have tried to use the entire range of these experiences to illustrate these concepts. This does not mean that identical approaches should be taken to different types of conflict or that profound differences in the underlying structures of these conflicts do not exist. But I believe that if one discerns a dynamic that is operative in, for example, both international conflict and family conflict, there is an important lesson to learn from the very breadth of its relevance. The examples I use have therefore been drawn from my work with interpersonal, community, organizational, labor management, environmental, public policy, and international disputes. I also discuss conflicts that have been in the news.

I have approached this book with a strong belief in the value of collaborative problem solving, and my primary (although by no means exclusive) experience has been as a third-party neutral. My belief in the power and ability of people to solve their own conflicts is reflected throughout. But this is not primarily a book about collaborative negotiation, mediation, or dispute system design. Negotiation and mediation are basic life skills in my view, and no consideration of conflict resolution can be complete without a discussion of them. But I present them in the context of a broader consideration of conflict and resolution processes.

When I was first introduced to conflict resolution and mediation, I felt that two important strands of my life were suddenly brought together in a remarkable way. My first professional work was in child welfare and mental health. I worked as a psychotherapist and administrator in residential treatment centers for children, mental health centers, drug abuse treatment programs, and private practice. But I also came of age during the 1960s and was very active in a variety of movements for peace and social justice. The war in Vietnam and the civil rights movement in particular were major forces in my development. Work in the field of conflict resolution seemed to pull these different parts of my life together, the part that was interested in providing services to people in various stages of crisis and the part that was committed to social change.

Conflict resolution still has these twin thrusts, as a service to people who need assistance and as a force for social change, but it is easy to lose sight of them in the business of building a respected field of practice. In its earlier days it was easy to think of conflict resolution as a social movement, and to focus on demonstrating its relevance and effectiveness, creating new applications, and promoting a common set of practice principles and procedures. Now that the field is more accepted and institutionalized, it is easy to lose sight of the foundational values of our work. I believe this work continues to be about helping people keep control of their lives, even when in crisis, and about creating more powerful and democratic ways of dealing with important questions of social justice and peace. As we practitioners move from the initial excitement of creating a new field of practice to the less dramatic but equally important challenge of deepening the field's foundation and institutional structure, it is crucial that we retain a clear view of the core values of our work.

I have tried here to avoid being overly prescriptive about what conflict resolvers should *do* and instead have tried to concentrate on what the useful ways are of *thinking* about conflict and its resolution. I do not put these ideas forward as *the* right conceptual frameworks but rather as ways that I have found to be useful and poignant as I have worked as a conflict resolver and teacher. I hope that this will stimulate readers to deepen their own thinking or to put forward their own ideas, sometimes, perhaps, by way of disagreeing with mine.

I do not believe any of us can hold all these concepts in our heads as we engage in the day-to-day, hour-to-hour work of resolving conflicts. But I hope that some of these ideas will resonate with each reader and that he or she will take these into his or her practice. Other ideas may be useful as readers reflect on their own experiences and try to learn from them. Still others may not resonate at all and may either be rejected or, more likely, forgotten.

I do not try to present a single unified theory of conflict resolution, although I believe the concepts I present to be internally consistent. In fact, I am suspicious of such global theories because I think they too easily become straightjackets or dogmas. Instead, I lay the ideas out as a series of conceptual tools that build upon each other but also stand on their own. However, the following themes do recur because they are basic to how I think.

Conflict resolution is an interactive and dynamic process. No one approach is always appropriate or effective, and no one theory has a lock on how to understand conflict. At the heart of effective resolution is a set of constructive attitudes and good communication skills. Repeatedly, I find our attitudes toward conflict and communication determine the effectiveness of what we do. The art of conflict resolution lies in discovering the level at which a conflict is really operative, and the challenge is to find a way of working at that level. We can err by going too deep or staying too shallow. Although conflict resolution is not itself a movement for social justice, the values that guide us cannot be separated from a commitment to justice and peace. Unless our ways of understanding conflict and working toward resolution are consistent with such values, we will not be very effective. I believe conflict can be a constructive force in people's lives, and I believe it is essential to get beyond blame and helplessness if we are to be effective conflict resolvers. Finally, I believe that conflict resolution works best and operates most in keeping with its values when it helps people to solve their own conflicts in a collaborative, powerful, and just way. These beliefs are reflected in every chapter of this book.

Audience

I have written this book specifically for people involved in conflict resolution as a field of practice—mediators, facilitators, organizational consultants, trainers, public involvement specialists, community organizers, family therapists, and professional negotiators. But I have also tried to create a book that is accessible to others interested in conflict resolution. I do not assume a broad familiarity with conflict resolution literature or practice, and in setting the context for developing an expanded conceptual framework, I take the time to describe some fairly basic principles. I also try to focus on concepts that apply generically across different arenas of conflict and resolution. Though I have been profoundly influenced by many different thinkers over the years, this book is not a literature review. Rather, it is more about the practical concepts that have emerged from my work and that I have found to be powerful aids in my practice and teaching. Where I have specifically drawn on the ideas of others, I have of course cited their work.

Overview of the Contents

This book comprises two major parts. The four chapters in the first part present concepts that are helpful in understanding the process of conflict. Chapter One describes the nature of conflict—in particular, the different dimensions along which conflict occurs, the sources of conflict, what motivates people's participation in conflict, and the interaction between conflict as a means of expression and conflict as an attempt to achieve a particular outcome. Chapter Two focuses on the ways in which people engage in or avoid conflict and on the differences in how they try to get their needs met. It also presents a set of variables that can be used to understand people's conflict behavior. Chapter Three discusses the different types of power that people bring to bear in conflict and the sources of that power, and then describes the different ways in which power is applied in conflict. A distinction is made between integrative and distributive power, and the chapter concludes with a discussion of the relationship between power issues and social justice in conflict resolution. Chapter Four considers the important relationship between conflict and culture—in particular, the continuities and differences in how various aspects of conflict are handled by different cultures. Rather than focus simply on cultural obstacles, this chapter questions how people from different cultures transcend cultural barriers and differences when engaging in a conflict resolution process.

The chapters in Part Two discuss the resolution process. Chapter Five discusses the nature of resolution and asks what constitutes a genuine resolution of a conflict. It presents a model of the dimensions of resolution and examines the different purposes of various approaches to conflict resolution. It poses the key challenge that conflict resolvers face—how to find the right level of depth at which to pursue the resolution of conflict. Chapter Six examines the heart of conflict resolution—communication. It presents a way of understanding what constitutes effective communication, including listening, speaking with power, and framing conflicts in constructive yet poignant ways. It also considers how communication tools can be used to help people change the fundamental way in which they understand a conflict.

Chapter Seven looks at the negotiation process and examines the contradictory pulls that most negotiators face. It outlines the dimensions of negotiation and how negotiators function along these dimensions, and concludes with a detailed discussion of the different ways in which negotiators reach agreements and closure. Chapter Eight looks at the nature of impasse in conflict and presents a way of understanding impasse as a necessary and often constructive aspect of the resolution process. Chapter Nine discusses the essential contribution of mediation to the resolution process. It discusses the heart of what mediators bring to the table that helps alter the nature of a conflict interaction, and what mediators actually do to affect the course of a conflict. This chapter also discusses the contradictions between what mediators think about their role and what disputants want from a mediator.

Chapter Ten looks at the continuum of approaches to conflict resolution and at what each element on that continuum offers. In particular, it discusses prevention, procedural assistance, substantive assistance, reconciliation processes, decision-making services, and design and linkage procedures. Chapter Eleven considers the value base of conflict resolvers. It discusses these values in terms of how conflict is handled; how conflict resolution efforts fit into more general values about peace, democracy, and social justice; and the personal impact that conflict resolution as a field has on conflict resolvers.

It has been an exciting journey for me over my years of practice to arrive at the ideas discussed in these chapters and to commit to them by articulating them in writing. But it is also clear to me that this is a snapshot of a particular time in an ongoing process of discovery that I am on and that we are all on. I hope that by my sharing this snapshot with you, your journey will be enriched. Mine certainly has been.

Acknowledgments

It is a daunting task to acknowledge all the people who have helped me directly and indirectly with this book. Over the years, my ideas have of course been very much influenced by other writers and practitioners in the field and especially by my colleagues at CDR Associates of Boulder, Colorado, which celebrated its twentieth anniversary of conflict resolution practice and education just as I started this project. Through these years of a long and fulfilling professional relationship, I have felt as though I have been in an ongoing seminar with some of the most creative and able practitioners of conflict resolution anywhere. Where CDR's influence stops and my ideas begin is impossible to discern.

All my colleagues at CDR have been my teachers, my friends, and my supporters. I want to particularly thank my wonderful partners, whose dedication and capability have been a source of inspiration for twenty years: Judy Mares-Dixon, Mary Margaret Golten, Michael Hughes, Christopher Moore, Louise Smart, and Susan Wildau. In addition to allowing me to take the time to write this book, they have all reviewed parts of this manuscript and given me honest and valuable feedback. Most of my ideas have been developed in dialogue with them. Many other people have also reviewed parts of this book and provided terrific insights and suggestions: Peter Adler, Jonathan Bartsch, Daniel Bowling, Mark Gerzon,

Suzanne Ghais, Katherine Hale, Amy Miller, John Paul Lederach, Donald Selcer, Margaret Shaw, Arnie Shienvold, Paul Smith, and Michael Williams, and also my wife, Reggie Gray, and my brother, Tom Mayer.

The staff at Jossey-Bass, including Alan Rinzler and Mariana Raykov, have been very supportive and helpful, and I especially want to thank Leslie Berriman, my editor. Her patience, insight, and wisdom have been critical to me in completing this book. She saw the value of this project from the beginning and helped me understand how to take a concept and turn it into a book. I want also to thank Elspeth MacHattie for her excellent job of copyediting. Finally I want to thank my family. My children, Ethan Greene and Mark Mayer, have also been my teachers. This book reflects the many lessons I have learned from parenting them, and the joy they have brought into my life has sustained me always. Finally, my most special thanks to my wife, friend, and partner of twenty-seven years, Reggie Gray. With her I have learned how to face the depths of conflict and the joys of resolution. Her support, wisdom, and understanding have meant everything.

Boulder, Colorado   BERNARD MAYER
February 2000

The Dynamics of
Conflict Resolution

Part One

Conflict

Chapter One

The Nature of Conflict

We all are of two minds about conflict. We say that conflict is natural, inevitable, necessary, and normal, and that the problem is not the existence of conflict but how we handle it. But we are also loath to admit that we are in the midst of conflict. Parents assure their children that the ferocious argument the parents are having is not a conflict, just a "discussion." Organizations will hire facilitators to guide them in strategic planning, goal setting, quality circles, team building, and all manner of training, but they shy away from asking for help with internal conflicts. Somehow, to say that we are in conflict is to admit a failure and to acknowledge the existence of a situation we consider hopeless.

This ambivalence about conflict is rooted in the same primary challenge conflict resolvers face—coming to terms with the nature of conflict. As conflict resolvers, we may think of conflict on many different levels. How we view conflict will largely determine our attitude and approach to dealing with it. Conflict may be viewed as a feeling, a disagreement, a real or perceived incompatibility of interests, inconsistent worldviews, or a set of behaviors. If we are to be effective in handling conflict, we must start with an understanding of its nature. We need tools that help us separate out the many complex interactions that make up a conflict, that help us understand the roots of conflict, and that give us a reasonable handle on the forces that motivate the behavior of all participants, including ourselves.

Whether we are aware of them or not, we all enter conflict with certain assumptions about its nature. Sometimes these assumptions are very helpful to us, but at other times they are blinders that limit our ability to understand what lies behind a conflict and what alternatives exist for dealing with it. We need frameworks that expand our thinking, that challenge our assumptions, and that are practical and readily usable. As we develop our ability to understand conflict in a deeper and more powerful way, we enhance our ability to handle it effectively and in accordance with our deepest values about building peace. However, in order to simplify the task of handling complex conflicts, we need to complicate our thinking about conflict itself. This is an ongoing challenge for everyone concerned with conflict and its resolution.

A framework for understanding conflict is an organizing lens that brings a conflict into better focus. There are many different lenses we can use to look at conflict, and each of us will find some more amenable to our own way of thinking than others. Moreover, the lenses presented in this chapter are not equally applicable to all conflicts. Seldom would we apply all of them at the same time to the same situation. Nevertheless, together they provide a set of concepts that can help us understand the nature of conflict and the dynamics of how conflict unfolds.

What Is Conflict?

Conflict may be viewed as occurring along cognitive (perception), emotional (feeling), and behavioral (action) dimensions. This three-dimensional perspective can help us understand the complexities of conflict and why a conflict sometimes seems to proceed in contradictory directions.

Conflict as Perception

As a set of perceptions, conflict is a belief or understanding that one's own needs, interests, wants, or values are incompatible with someone else's. There are both objective and subjective elements to this cognitive dimension. If I want to develop a tract of land into a shopping center, and you want to preserve it as open space, then there is an objective incompatibility in our wants. If I believe that the way you desire to guide our son's educational development is incompatible with my philosophy of parenting, then there is at least a significant subjective component. What if only one of us believes an incompatibility to exist, are we still in conflict? As a practical matter, I find it useful to think of conflict as existing if at least one person believes it to exist. If I believe us to have incompatible interests, and act accordingly, then I am engaging you in a conflict process whether you share this perception or not.

Conflict as Feeling

Conflict also involves an emotional reaction to a situation or interaction that signals a disagreement of some kind. The emotions felt might be fear, sadness, bitterness, anger, or hopelessness, or some amalgam of these. If we experience these feelings in regard to another person or situation, we feel that we are in conflict—and therefore we are. As a mediator, I have sometimes seen people behave as if they were in great disagreement over profound issues, yet I have not been able to ascertain exactly what they disagreed about. Nonetheless, they were in conflict because they felt they were. And in conflicts, it does not take two to tango. Often a conflict exists because one person feels in conflict with another, even though those feelings are not reciprocated by or even known to the other person. The behavioral component may be minimal, but the conflict is still very real to the person experiencing the feelings.

Conflict as Action

Conflict also consists of the actions that we take to express our feelings, articulate our perceptions, and get our needs met in a way that has the potential for interfering with someone else's ability to get his or her needs met. This conflict behavior may involve a direct attempt to make something happen at someone else's expense. It may be an exercise of power. It may be violent. It may be destructive. Conversely, this behavior may be conciliatory, constructive, and friendly. But, whatever its tone, the purpose of conflict behavior is either to express the conflict or to get one's needs met. Again, the question of reciprocity exists. If you write letters to the editor, sign petitions, and consult lawyers to stop my shopping center, and I do not even know you exist, are we in conflict? Can you be in conflict with me if I am not in conflict with you? Theory aside, I think the practical answer to both of these questions is yes.

Obviously, the nature of a conflict in one dimension greatly affects its nature in the other two dimensions. If I believe you are trying to hurt me in some way, I am likely to feel as though I am in conflict with you, and I am also apt to engage in conflict behaviors. Also, none of these dimensions is static. People can go rapidly in and out of conflict, and the strength or character of conflict along each dimension can change quickly and frequently. And even though each of the three dimensions affects the others, a change in the level of conflict in one dimension does not necessarily cause a similar change in the other dimensions. Sometimes an increase in one dimension is associated with a decrease in another dimension. For example, the emotional component of conflict occasionally decreases as people increase their awareness of the existence of the dispute and their understanding of its nature. This is one reason why conflict can seem so confusing and unpredictable.

What about a situation where no conflict perceptions, emotions, or behaviors are present but where a tremendous conflict potential exists? Perhaps you are unaware of my desire to build a shopping center, and I am unaware of your plans for open space. Are we in conflict? We may soon be, but until conflict exists on one of the three dimensions, I believe it is more productive to think in terms of potential conflict than actual conflict. The potential for conflict almost always exists among any individuals or institutions that interact. Unless people want to think of themselves as constantly in conflict with everyone in their lives, it is more useful to view conflict as existing only when it clearly manifests itself along one of the three dimensions.

Can social systems—organizations, countries, and communities—as well as individuals be in conflict, particularly along the emotional or cognitive dimensions? Although there are some significant dangers to attributing personal characteristics or motivational structures to systems, practically speaking I think systems in conflict often experience that conflict on all three dimensions. Although we might better use terms like culture, ethos, public opinion, or popular beliefs to signify the greater complexity and different nature of these dimensions in social systems, conflict among groups clearly has cognitive and affective dimensions as well as a behavioral dimension. Is there an emotional and a perceptual aspect to the conflict between Iraq and the United States? Of course, and we cannot understand the nature of the conflict if we do not deal with these aspects. This does not mean that every individual member of each country shares the same feelings or perceptions or even that a majority do. Instead, it means that the conflict evokes certain reactions and attitudes from the dominant leaders and a significant number of people in each society. Similarly, when we look at conflicts between union and management, environmental groups and industry associations, Democrats and Republicans, it is important to understand the attitudes, feelings, values, and beliefs that these groups have toward each other if we are to understand what is occurring.

By considering conflict along the cognitive, emotional, and behavioral dimensions, we can begin to see that it does not proceed along one simple, linear path. When individuals or groups are in conflict, they are dealing with different and sometimes contradictory dynamics in these different dimensions, and they behave and react accordingly. This accounts for much of what appears to be irrational behavior in conflict. Consider this not unusual workplace dispute.*

> Two employees are assigned to work together on a project and soon find themselves in a conflict over whether they are each pulling their weight and passing along important information to each other. They engage in a fairly public shouting match, and they each complain to their supervisor. The supervisor sits them both down, and they agree on a workload division and certain behavioral standards, to which they then seem to adhere. Has the conflict been resolved? It may have been alleviated along the behavioral dimension. But each goes away from this meeting feeling victimized by the other and unappreciated by the boss. One of the employees decides that these feelings just result from the nature of the job and believes that the immediate conflict is over, but the other continues to see the conflict being acted out every time the other person comes late for a meeting or sends a terse e-mail. Thus progress has been made in the behavioral dimension, the emotional dimension is if anything worse, and there are contradictory developments along the cognitive dimension. This kind of result is not unusual in conflict, and

---

*All the examples from my own practice are either from public, nonconfidential forums or are heavily disguised to protect confidentiality.

it drives people to behave in apparently inconsistent ways. These employees may cease their overtly conflictual behavior, but the tension between them may actually increase.

What Causes Conflict?

Conflict has many roots, and there are many theories that try to explain these origins. Conflict is seen as arising from basic human instincts, from the competition for resources and power, from the structure of the societies and institutions people create, from the inevitable struggle between classes. Even though there is something to be said for most of these theories, they are not always helpful to us as we contend with conflict. What we need is a framework that helps us use some of the best insights of different conflict theories in a practical way.

If we can develop a usable framework for understanding the sources of conflict, we can create a map of conflict that can guide us through the conflict process. When we understand the different forces that motivate conflict behavior, we are better able to create a more nuanced and selective approach to handling conflict. The wheel of conflict, illustrated in Figure 1.1, is one way of understanding the forces that are at the root of most conflicts. This conceptualization of the sources of conflict has arisen out of my work and conversations with my colleagues at CDR Associates and is derivative of the circle of conflict developed by one of my partners, Christopher Moore (see Moore, 1986, 1996).

At the center of all conflicts are human needs. People engage in conflict either because they have needs that are met by the conflict process itself or because they have (or believe they have) needs that are inconsistent with those of others. I discuss the continuum of human needs later in this chapter. My major point for now is that people engage in conflict because of their needs, and conflict cannot be transformed or settled unless these needs are addressed in some way.

Needs do not exist in a vacuum, however. They are embedded in a constellation of other forces that can generate and define conflict. In order to effectively address needs, it is usually necessary to work through some of these other forces, which affect how people experience their needs and how these needs have developed.

There are five basic forces, or sources of conflict: the ways people communicate, emotions, values, the structures within which interactions take place, and history (see Figure 1.1). Let's examine each of these sources further.

Communication

Humans are very imperfect communicators. Sometimes this imperfection generates conflict, whether or not there is a significant incompatibility of interests, and it almost always makes conflict harder to solve. Human communication has inspired a large literature and multiple fields of study, and I will discuss communication as a resolution tool later. The main thing to consider here is how hard it is for individuals to communicate about complex matters, particularly under emotionally difficult circumstances. We should keep reminding ourselves just how easy it is for communication to

Figure 1.1. The Wheel of Conflict.

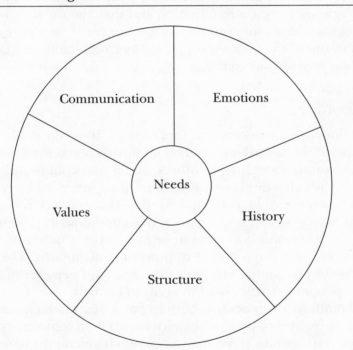

go awry. Conflict frequently escalates because people act on the assumption that they have communicated accurately when they have not. When they learn that others are acting on the basis of different information and assumptions, they often attribute this to bad faith or deviousness and not to the imperfections of human communication.

Many factors may contribute to communication problems. Culture, gender, age, class, and environment significantly affect individuals' ability to communicate effectively. People often rely on inaccurate or incomplete perceptions, tend to form stereotypes, and carry into their communications conclusions drawn from former interactions or experiences. They are also inclined to try to solve problems before they understand them. The greater the duress a person is under, the harder it is for him or her to communicate (and often the more important it is as well). Sometimes communication takes more energy and focus than someone is able or willing to give at a critical point, and it is easy to become discouraged or hopeless about communicating effectively in serious conflicts. Despite all these problems, people can and do muddle through when they communicate, and they can work on improving communication, even in very intense conflicts. Communication is one of the greatest sources of both difficulty and hope in dealing with serious conflicts.

Emotions

Emotions are the energy that fuel conflict. If people could always stay perfectly rational and focused on how to best meet their needs and accommodate those of others, and if they could calmly work to establish effective communications, then many conflicts would either never arise or would quickly deescalate. But of course that is not human nature, even if many of us occasionally pretend that it is. At times emotions seem to be in control of behavior. Sometimes they are also a source of power for disputants. They contribute to the energy, strength, courage, and perseverance that allow people to participate forcefully in conflict.

Emotions are generated both by particular interactions or circumstances and by previous experiences. When someone points a finger at us in conflict, we have a reaction based on the immediate context and meaning of that behavior, but we may also be reacting to all the times in the past when that gesture has been made at us in anger.

In conflict it is often possible and necessary to work specifically on the emotional content of disputants' experience. This usually requires creating some opportunity to express and release emotions and to experience someone else's understanding and empathy. We often talk about the need to ventilate, to let an emotion out through a direct and cathartic expression of it. Often, however, ventilation is neither possible nor desirable. A direct expression of feelings may escalate a conflict. Instead, it may be necessary for disputants to discuss feelings without demonstrating them, to work toward establishing a safe environment for the expression of emotions, to let emotions out in safe increments, or to express them to a third party rather than directly to the other person. Sometimes (although this may go against some popular beliefs of our culture), it is simply necessary to suppress feelings until a more appropriate opportunity for dealing with them presents itself.

Emotions fuel conflict, but they are also a key to deescalating it. Many emotions can prevent, moderate, or control conflict. Part of everyone's emotional makeup is the desire to seek connection, affirmation, and acceptance. A genuine expression of sadness or concern can be key to addressing conflict effectively. Another key in many conflicts is to find an adequate way of dealing with the feelings of all participants so that they are neither ignored nor allowed to escalate out of control. Sometimes it may be necessary to let a conflict escalate somewhat, enough to deal with emotions but not so much as to impair people's ability to eventually deal with the situation constructively. The art of dealing with conflict often lies in finding the narrow path between useful expression of emotions and destructive polarization. This is one reason why it is often helpful to employ the services of a third party.

Values

Values are the beliefs we have about what is important, what distinguishes right from wrong and good from evil, and what principles should govern how we lead our lives. When a conflict is defined or experienced as an issue of values, it becomes more charged and intractable. Because people define themselves in part by their core beliefs, when they believe these values are under attack, they feel they are being attacked. Similarly, it is hard for people to compromise when core beliefs are in play, because they feel they are compromising themselves or their integrity.

Although some conflicts are inescapably about fundamental value differences, more often disputants have a choice whether they will define a conflict in this way. When individuals feel unsure of themselves, confused about what to do, or under attack, it is particularly tempting to them to define an issue as a matter of right or wrong. This empowers and fortifies them even as it rigidifies their thinking and narrows acceptable options. Often it is easier to carry on a conflict if one can view oneself as honorable, virtuous, and the carrier of good, and opponents as evil, malicious, and dangerous. This stance, comforting though it may be, tends to escalate and perpetuate conflict.

Though values are often a source of conflict and an impediment to its resolution, they can also be a source of commonality and a restraint on conflict escalation. Usually, disputants can find some level on which they share values, and they often have values about interpersonal relations that support collaborative efforts. Recognizing when values are in play in conflict is critical to moving the conflict in a constructive direction. When individuals address values directly and express their beliefs affirmatively—that is, in terms of what they believe in rather than what they are against—they can address conflict more constructively.

Structure

The structure, the external framework, in which an interaction takes place or an issue develops is another source of conflict. The elements of a structure may include available resources, decision-making procedures, time constraints, communication procedures, and physical settings. Even when compatible interests might move people toward a more cooperative stance, the structure in which they are working may promote conflict. An example is the litigation process, one structure for decision making when people are in conflict. Litigation is well designed for achieving a decisive outcome when other less adversarial procedures have not worked.

However, it is also a structure that exacerbates conflict, makes compromise difficult, and casts issues as win-lose struggles. Voting is another interesting example. When voting is used to resolve serious differences about an issue, the issue tends to become polarized, and constructive communication can become difficult. Often, candidates for office try to seize the center of the political spectrum on many important issues and therefore exhibit little real difference on these issues. However, they also look for so-called wedge issues that can put them into conflict with their rivals and at the same time, they hope, into favor with a large segment of voters. However, this can increase the conflict among the public on such issues as affirmative action, abortion, gun control, welfare, or health care.

Other structural elements that often affect conflict include proximity of the disputants, distribution of resources, access to information, legal parameters, organizational structure, and political pressures. Sometimes these structural realities can be changed through a conflict resolution process. Often, however, part of what that process must accomplish is an acceptance of the structural elements that are unlikely to be altered.

History

Conflict cannot be understood independently of its historical context. The history of the people who are participants in a conflict, of the systems in which the conflict is occurring, and of the issues themselves has a powerful influence on the course of the conflict. History provides the momentum for the development of conflict. Too often we try to understand a conflict in isolation from its historical roots and as a result are baffled by the stubbornness of the players. Conversely, history is not a determinant of conflict, although sometimes it can seem that way. The long history of conflict in the Middle East, Northern Ireland, or the former Yugoslavia, for example, does not mean that present conflicts in these regions will never be settled. That form of historical determinism is dangerous and misleading. However, such conflicts cannot be solved without an understanding of the complicated systems of interaction that have developed over time and the degree to which the conflict itself has become part of the disputants' identity.

All these different sources of conflict—communication, emotions, values, structure, and history—interact with each other. People's history affects their values, communication style, emotional reactions, and the structure in which they operate. And history is constantly being made and therefore affected by these other sources.

The wheel of conflict is a construct, and the test of its power is how useful it is. I believe that these are the sources we need to analyze as part of comprehending conflict. To understand a conflict and to plan how to work with it, we need to think about where different people are stuck, where insights are needed, and where opportunities to improve a situation can be found. The wheel is a mechanism that helps us to do this. The value of such an analytical tool and of an understanding of the three dimensions of conflict described earlier is illustrated by the case of the ten cousins.

Ten cousins who lived in different parts of the United States and Canada jointly inherited a valuable piece of oceanfront property in New England. This property had belonged to their grandfather, who had decided to leave it directly to them partly because of his distress about the poor relationships among his three children, the cousins' parents. The property had been the site of many of the happiest moments in the cousins' childhood, but it was in disrepair, and the existing house and road probably needed to be replaced. The cousins ranged in age from twenty to forty-five and had extremely different financial situations, from quite poor to very wealthy. They had widely different views about what should be done, from selling the property and dividing up the equity to preserving it as a family center. For the property to be usable, a considerable investment would have to be made, which not all the cousins were in a position to do.

Complicating the picture were the tense relations in at least two of the three sibling groups. Also, the siblings and parents in one group had been out of contact with the rest of the family for most of the past fifteen years, largely because the mother did not get along with her siblings. Not knowing how to proceed, the cousins contacted me and, together with a colleague, I met with nine of them in a retreat setting.

How could we get a handle on the nature of this conflict? It was clear that all three dimensions of conflict were in play. There were behavioral issues that needed to be attended to, entrenched perceptions about the situation and each other, and a great deal of emotionality. However, even though work had to be done on the behavioral, or action, issues, the long-term success of the cousins' co-ownership depended more on their ability to work on the attitudes and emotions about each other that had been part of their family dynamics for so long.

It was not at first obvious where to focus our attentions given the complexity of this situation. Clearly, there were conflicting needs to be addressed. Some cousins wanted to maintain this property in the family and to "honor the grandfather's legacy and wishes." Others were worried about the time and resources this might demand. Most hoped to promote better family relations but were worried that the opposite might occur. But these needs were embedded in all the elements found in the wheel of conflict. There had been poor communication (and in some cases no communication) among the cousins for years. The property represented the complex emotions that all had about their family relations. It was a symbol of both the problems in the family and the best the family had to offer. The cousins had different values about sharing the property, developing it, equalizing contributions, taking into account different resources, and how families ought to interact. The structural problems were enormous. The cousins had no easy way of communicating, making decisions, or overseeing work on the property, and the disparity in their resources greatly complicated the picture. Furthermore, numerous local land use regulations limited their options for subdividing the property or building additional structures. Finally, history was a heavy presence. In many ways the cousins were continuing a multigeneration family saga. The conflicts among the parents were in danger of being replicated. There was also a positive history as well—the childhood memories that each had of their time at the property were almost all positive and were a motivation to seek a constructive resolution.

Because this situation was so complex and our time to deal with it relatively limited (three days), we decided that we could not deal with issues internal to sibling groups and that the strength of the cousins was the relatively positive attitudes they were expressing across sibling groups. We felt that the history needed to be addressed and that the major immediate focus needed to be on the structural barriers to moving forward. We therefore started by asking each cousin to share his or her memories of time spent on the property and his or her hopes and fears for its future. As an outcome of this discussion, they all decided they really wanted to keep the property if at all possible. They agreed to work on a plan for keeping the property, and they also agreed that everyone should have some access to it, regardless of his or her contribution. Once these general agreements were made, we then focused on the structural issues of how to communicate, make decisions, work with local authorities, and get information about different options. The cousins left with some general decisions made and an interesting communication and decision-making structure. They set up a steering committee with one representative from each sibling group. Our intervention thus flowed from our analysis of the structure and causes of this particular conflict. Without some way of organizing our thinking about this complex situation, we would have been lost.

Additionally, there are three dynamics that the wheel of conflict model does not include, because they cut across all the sources and are often best analyzed in terms of those sources. They are culture, power, and data. Culture affects conflict because it is embedded in individuals' communication styles, history, way of dealing with emotions, values, and structures. Power is a very elusive concept, one that can confuse our thinking or help us understand an interaction. Some sources of power are structural, but other elements are involved as well. I deal with power and culture more extensively in Chapters Three and Four. I do not view data themselves as a source of conflict, but how data are handled and communicated can lead to conflict. Therefore, data, or information, can be viewed as an issue within both communication and structure. (For an overview of the major theories of conflict and its origins, see Wehr, 1979; also see Frost and Wilmot, 1978; Kriesberg, 1982; Schellenburg, 1982; Schelling, 1960.)

The Continuum of Human Needs

At the center of the wheel of conflict model are the human needs that drive people's actions, including engagement in conflict. Many theorists, from Freud to Maslow, have characterized fundamental human needs. Several of them describe the different levels of needs that people experience. In the literature on conflict, a distinction is often made between interests and needs. Interests are viewed as more transitory and superficial, needs as more basic and enduring. Sometimes it is argued that resolutions that address interests but not needs are less meaningful, more Band-Aids than real solutions (Burton and Dukes, 1990).

Rather than conceiving of interests and needs as fundamentally different, which could be misleading and polarizing, I find it more useful to think of a continuum of human needs, roughly paralleling Maslow's hierarchy (1954). Interests then become a category of human needs that exists between the basic concern for survival at one end of the continuum and the striving for identity at the other (see Figure 1.2). Survival needs seem self-evident, so I focus here on interests and identity needs.

Interests

Interests are the needs that motivate the bulk of people's actions, and they can be viewed simply and superficially or in great depth. A challenge we face in the practical understanding of conflict is to determine what level of needs or interests best explains a conflict. When we have too superficial a view of the sources of a conflict, we cannot address it meaningfully. Conversely, when we address these sources at a level that is too deep, we make the conflict much harder to resolve and we may also fail to match the reality experienced by the disputants.

If a community is concerned about a proposal to place a chemical plant nearby, there are many levels at which we can understand the nature of the problem. For example, the needs of the community to minimize odors, noise, traffic, and toxic exposure may be contrasted to the needs of the plant operators for a practical, cheap, and convenient location. This may be a satisfactory level for analyzing the conflict, but if the motivational structures for either the community or the plant run deeper, it may be insufficient. The community may have fundamental concerns about the image this plant will create, its impact on the community's overall desirability and therefore on the attractiveness of the community to investors,

Figure 1.2. The Continuum of Human Needs.

Survival Needs	Interests	Identity-Based Needs
• Food	• Substantive	• Meaning
• Shelter	• Procedural	• Community
• Health	• Psychological	• Intimacy
• Security		• Autonomy

upwardly mobile families, and adult children of residents. Similarly, the plant may be concerned about its public reputation and the ease of attracting and retaining a workforce. If we fail to look at the deeper levels of interests, we are likely to end up working on the wrong issues and overlooking some important areas of mutual concern.

But we could go overboard on this and focus too deeply. We could concentrate on such fundamental concerns as business versus the environment, the nature of community, and the sense of self that both business leaders and community leaders have and how it is tied into their views of the chemical plant proposal. Although these might be real factors in the conflict, they are probably neither its practical source nor a useful basis for crafting an intervention. If we focused at this deeper level, we would not be addressing the conflict on the level that it is experienced by the participants, and we would be concentrating on a set of interests probably not amenable to a practical resolution process. The process of attaining the most useful level of depth in needs analysis is not an abstract one, and it does not take place in a vacuum. Only through interacting over time with key players can we understand the roots of a conflict in a practical and usable way. The art of conflict resolution is highly dependent on the ability to get to the right depth of understanding and intervention in conflict.

If we think of interests as midrange human needs, as the practical concerns that drive us in most conflicts, then for the most part it is on interests that we initially need to focus when we try to understand a conflict. It is also in the realm of interests that most conflicts can be resolved. If people can present their concerns to each other in a constructive way and are receptive to understanding each other's interests, they are most likely to make progress in working their way through a conflict.

In considering people's interests, we will find many types: short-term and long-term interests, individual and group interests, outcome-based interests and process interests, conscious and unconscious interests. Moore (1986, 1996) suggests three types of interests: substantive (concerns about tangible benefits), procedural (concerns about a process for interacting, communicating, or decision making), and psychological (concerns about how one is treated, respected, or acknowledged). Frequently, people are most vocal about one kind of interest but most genuinely motivated by another. We can often achieve progress in a conflict, even when disputants have incompatible substantive interests, if we are careful to address psychological and procedural interests.

The U.S. philosophy of government provides an interesting example of how these interests work. At the root of democracy is a commitment to addressing procedural interests, even when substantive interests cannot always be met. Many Americans' governmental values are related to these procedural interests. We in the United States remain loyal to our government, even if we disagree with its policies and have not voted for its leaders, because we fundamentally support the process by which they were selected. The basic deal in a democracy is that we may not always get our way but we will always have our say, and in return we will remain loyal citizens.

However we as conflict resolvers analyze the different types of interests that people bring to conflict, we need to work hard to understand everyone's interests (including our own) broadly enough and at the right level of depth in order to gain a practical handle on what is going on in a conflict.

Identity-Based Needs

Beyond interests are what we can call identity-based needs (Rothman, 1997). These are people's needs to preserve a sense of who they are and what their place in the world is. It is useful to think of four needs in this category: the needs for meaning, community, intimacy, and autonomy.

The need for *meaning* has to do with establishing a purpose for one's life, existence, actions, and struggles. Sometimes, pursuing a conflict is a great source of meaning for people. In that case the resolution of the conflict entails a significant loss of meaning. Unless they can find a new source of meaning, this loss may be devastating and may cause them to hold onto a conflict regardless of how well the proposed solution addresses their interests. I once acted as a mediator in an age discrimination case involving someone who was about to retire. When I asked him about his retirement plans, he told me that he was going to pursue his case until he was fully vindicated. Despite the fact that he could have obtained much in a settlement with the company and that his prospects through legal challenges were limited at best, I knew this mediation was going nowhere. For many of the people living in the Israeli-held West Bank, the issue is not simply security, economics, or even self-determination. It is the meaning that the struggle itself has given their lives. This is one of the sources of intractability in the Middle East.

Community refers to that aspect of people's identity that derives from feeling connected with groups with which they can identify and in which they feel recognized. Community can arise from actual communities. The nostalgic yearning of some for small-town American life is in part an expression of this need. Similarly, the desire many people have for participating in the communal life of their neighborhood is connected to establishing identity. But community can come from other group affiliations as well, with a company, for example, or with a social action organization; a church, synagogue, or mosque; an athletic or artistic subculture; a profession; or an ethnic group. Community can be experienced in both positive and negative ways. Individuals may identify with others on the basis of what they all share or what they are all against. As an identity-based need, community is not simply about feeling part of a group; it is about having a social home in an impersonal world—a home where people feel connected, safe, recognized as individuals, and appreciated. When people are in conflict in order to solidify a sense of community or to protect their community against the forces of disintegration, they are in part struggling to preserve their identity.

Intimacy is the need for a different kind of connectivity. It goes beyond needing to be recognized and involves wanting to be special, unique, and important to other people. Most intimacy needs are met in family and friendship structures. Intimacy implies some form of reciprocity. Often people cling to the symbols of intimacy or to a pretense of intimacy but actually feel quite alone. In divorce, it is often the loss of intimacy (or sometimes the fact that a facade of intimacy has been shattered) that causes so much pain and that challenges people's sense of themselves—their identity. One of the problems in a divorce mediation is that it is usually impossible (and often not desirable) to try to deal with the parties' needs at this level. This means that people may feel unfulfilled by the mediation process, even when a fundamentally sound agreement has been reached. A longer healing process is usually necessary to deal with loss of intimacy.

If intimacy and community are aspects of individuals' fundamental need for connection, *autonomy* is the flip side of the coin. At the same time as people need connection, they also need a sense of their independence, freedom, and individuality. In relationships they often struggle with how to find a deep sense of connection and of autonomy at the same time. This struggle to establish needed ties and their boundaries is a source of much of individuals' internal conflict, and it is also at the heart of many interpersonal conflicts. A common example is the many conflicts parents and adolescents have that are ostensibly about immediate issues such as chores, curfews, or school but are often more about dependency and autonomy. We can also see this need expressed in the struggles of many ethnic groups to be associated with an autonomous political entity. When people or groups feel that they do not have meaningful autonomy, independence, or freedom, this fundamental identity-based need is not being met and serious conflict is likely.

Some conflicts cannot be solved without addressing identity-based needs. These disputes are often not amenable to a negotiation process. They usually require an incremental process of change in which people, groups, or organizations gradually achieve a different level of understanding and a better ability to communicate. They also often call for a social change effort or a personal growth experience of some kind. Conciliation efforts in which the focus is more on the relationship among disputants and less on achieving a specific agreement may succeed in addressing these deeper needs.

It is not useful to argue whether it is less valuable or meaningful to work on interests than to address identity-based needs. Sometimes, we must work on conflict in a sequenced way because only through progress at a more accessible level can progress be made at a deeper level. Sometimes, deeper levels of needs are simply not involved in significant ways. If a resolution process genuinely addresses needs people have in a way that is meaningful to them, then important work has occurred.

In the case of the cousins described earlier, how deep to go into their needs was a major consideration. For some, the ocean-front property seemed to represent their need for community and even meaning. For others it was more a valuable potential resource and a beautiful vacation home. My colleague and I decided to touch briefly on the identity-based concerns, because they needed to be acknowledged, but given the immediate needs and availability of the group, we focused on their interests, because agreement here was the necessary next step for them.

The Desires for Expression and for Outcome

In many conflicts people act in a way that seems to go against their interests. Sometimes they seem more interested in having their day in court than in arriving at a solution that gives them what they need. They are sometimes more interested in expressing their feelings than getting results. Conversely, people sometimes dismiss attempts to explore what they are experiencing as inappropriate or "touchy-feely."

Lewis Coser proposes two components of conflict in his classic work, *The Functions of Social Conflict* (1956). One, which he labels "unrealistic," is people's need for some form of energy release. The other component, which he labels "realistic," is people's desire for a result that will meet their needs. The unrealistic component will not be satisfied by a good solution, but instead requires listening, ventilation, acknowledgment, validation, a day in court, or some means of expressing or releasing the feelings and energy associated with a conflict. The realistic component requires a satisfactory solution, one that addresses people's essential interests.

Coser's labels are sometimes confusing to people because both components are in some sense realistic. Instead, we might think of them as being the expressive and the outcome-oriented aspects of conflict. One component involves the need to deal with the anger, hurt, tension, frustration, sadness, and fear that disputants may be feeling. The other involves their concerns about arriving at a satisfactory outcome. Efforts to deal with the expressive part of conflict by proposing solutions or negotiating agreements will not succeed. Similarly, efforts to address the outcome-oriented component by encouraging the expression of feelings and by acknowledging the stress that someone may be experiencing will also fail. We all have experienced a time when our emotions were too intense for us to focus on a rational solution to a problem. But most of us have also experienced a time in a conflict when what we really wanted was a good solution, not more exploration of feelings or clarification of values.

We might think of the expressive element as the outer part of the wheel of conflict, and the outcome-oriented element as the inner region. Often (although not always) people must find a means of dealing with the expressive aspect of conflict—sometimes directly in the conflict interaction, sometimes elsewhere—before they can effectively focus on an outcome that will adequately address their needs.

The movement between the expressive and outcome-oriented aspects is not a linear process in which people always start in one place and work their way to another. They go back and forth; events throw them from a focus on their emotions to a focus on results, and both are frequently mixed together in ways that are hard to discern. Yet, as complex as the interactions between these two elements of conflict are, the distinction between them is often obvious, and people instinctively respond to them with different strategies.

Sometimes a symbolic act indicates that people are ready to let go of some of the expressive aspects of a conflict and become more outcome focused. The drama of the handshake between Yitzak Rabin and Yassir Arafat on the White House lawn was a symbol of a movement from the outer rim of the wheel to its inner core, saying as it were, "We can put our feelings and our pasts behind us and try to find a solution that will address the needs of both of our peoples."

Why Think About Conflict?

The premise of this book and the field of conflict studies in general is that conflict and conflict resolution are useful areas of focus in order to better understand human behavior. There are certainly alternative ways of analyzing these kinds of interactions. Professionals concerned with how people handle their differences can focus on decision making, negotiation, communication, stimulus response, power exchanges, and so forth. Why should those of us who have identified ourselves as professional conflict resolvers focus on conflict? Does this not direct our attention to the negative aspect of the interchange, to the part that has people at odds rather than the part that concerns the mutual interests people share?

Conflict is not in itself a bad thing. There are many reasons why it is a necessary part of the growth and development of individuals, families, communities, and societies. Conflict can help build community, define and balance people's needs as individuals with their needs as participants in larger systems, and help them face and address in a clear and conscious way the many difficult choices that life brings to them. Working through a conflict can be an important bonding and growth producing experience. The strength of social systems lies in part in how they prevent serious conflicts and, when conflicts do arise, how they address them so as to maintain system integrity and preserve the well-being of their members. By facing major conflicts, addressing them, reorganizing as necessary to deal with them, and moving on, social organizations adapt to changes in their environment. Understanding the dynamics of conflict therefore provides conflict resolvers and related professionals with a basic tool for addressing the essential forces that shape the development of individuals and social entities.

It is easy enough to say that conflict is inevitable and is not in itself good or bad, yet for many people, accepting this premise is an uphill battle. There may be an important lesson for us in the resistance that people have to acknowledging conflict in their lives. This may be something other than dysfunctional conflict avoidant behavior. Maybe there is an inevitable shift in the way people interact with each other once they acknowledge the presence of conflict, and therefore people have good reason to approach that admission with caution. If this shift in focus, energy, attitude, or behavior is a natural consequence of the emergence of conflict, and if conflict is itself necessary, inevitable, and often healthy, this poses a fundamental dilemma for all of us as individuals existing in groups. We had therefore better strive to comprehend the nature of conflict in all its complexities. Understanding conflict becomes the vehicle for understanding the many contradictions that are necessarily present in our efforts to be social beings.

Furthermore, something can almost always be done about conflict. This does not mean that it can always be resolved, but a productive response can usually be made to move conflict along a constructive path. Sometimes this response may be to escalate a conflict so that it emerges into people's consciousness or takes on a higher priority for resolution. Sometimes the response may be to do nothing and let events develop, allowing the conflict to mature. Sometimes it may be to help people understand their needs and express their feelings at a deeper, more meaningful level. Sometimes it may be to find some Band-Aid to stop the bleeding. Sometimes it may be to look for creative solutions that all parties can accept. There is no single correct response to conflict, but that does not mean that there are not wise and unwise responses to any particular conflict. Our success as individuals, communities, organizations, and societies is in no small measure related to our developing wisdom about how we can respond to the many conflicts that we face.

Chapter Two

How People Conflict

In order to understand conflict, we must pay attention to the dramatic differences in the ways individuals approach it. How people handle conflict is basic to whom they are, to how they try to make their way in life, and to how they relate to others. People's approach to conflict derives not only from what they have been taught about conflict and how they have experienced it but also from their personalities, their culture, and their particular role in a dispute. Although many frameworks may be useful in understanding these differences in the ways individuals approach conflict, I believe that four factors are especially significant: *values* and *beliefs* about conflict, approaches to *avoiding* and *engaging* in conflict, *styles* of conflict, and the *roles* people are drawn to play in conflict.

Values and Beliefs

Individuals' values and beliefs about conflict often affect their behavior as much as do their concerns about the issues causing the conflict. Many of these beliefs are rooted in the culture in which individuals have been brought up and the era in which they have come of age. But even within a particular culture, or family for that matter, we find tremendous variation in individuals' specific beliefs about conflict. The most influential beliefs deal with whether conflict is acceptable, how people should behave in conflict, and what kinds of outcomes are possible or acceptable. Let's consider these three areas of belief.

Is Conflict Acceptable?

Some people believe that conflict is a natural part of their lives and that it is perfectly acceptable to be in conflict. A willingness to take on conflict may be tied to their sense of self-esteem, or they may feel that if they are not engaged in some conflict, then they are not dealing with life's issues. For others, conflict is a sign of failure, of personal, organizational, or societal malfunction. These views are often connected to values about direct dealing and to beliefs about whether conflict is resolvable. A related issue is whether people believe there can be a conflict in which no one is wrong. If on the one hand people think that two individuals (or two societies) can have a major difference about an issue without either party's being wrong or bad, then it is easier for them to view conflict as acceptable. If on the other hand people think that at least one party in any conflict must be wrong, then the existence of conflict is more likely to threaten their relationships. This belief also makes it difficult for them to think of anything short of complete victory as an acceptable outcome.

How Should People Behave in Conflict?

All of us have values about the behavior that is acceptable in conflict. Sometimes disputants have one set of beliefs about how they should behave and another set of beliefs about how others should act. These values bear on how direct one can be about concerns, feelings, hopes, and ideas and on whether it is all right to be deceptive, to lie, or to mislead. People exhibit a wide range of attitudes about how to employ power, threats, or rewards. Some place a great deal of value on taking personal responsibility for mistakes, whereas others are more likely to value assertiveness and not looking like a victim.

These and many other values that people have about how to behave in conflict exist in a fairly complicated and often contradictory mix. Everyone at times struggles between contending values. For example, many people value being fair-minded, trusting, sensitive, and accommodating, but at the same time most do not want to be naïve or weak. People want to be both firm and flexible, optimistic and realistic, accommodating and tough. Sometimes these contradictory pulls are resolved as people work their way through a conflict, but often they constitute a major problem that interferes with disputants' ability to handle conflict in a measured, consistent, and powerful way.

Is Conflict Solvable?

People have widely variable views about whether conflict can be solved and people can change. The more that disputants believe conflict is solvable, the more likely they are to aim for a full resolution of their differences, a genuine transformation of the conflict, and the restoration of a positive relationship. If they do not believe that significant conflict can be resolved or that people can genuinely change as a result of experience, they are more likely to look for *fixes,* superficial solutions or ways to circumvent the conflict. This is like a self-fulfilling prophecy in that the more people believe conflict can be successfully addressed, the more likely they are to pursue this resolution as a goal. The more they believe that genuine conflict doesn't ever go away, the more they are likely to look for short-term solutions or ways of containing rather than resolving conflicts.

Some people tend to have set and unvarying beliefs about conflict. Others tend to have values that can vary according to the particular conflict and its context. For example, many people have one set of values about conflict in their personal lives and another about social or organizational conflict. As a result, they often have completely different approaches to conflict in these different arenas.

People are often unaware of their own values about conflict, not to speak of the values of others. Probably far more often than we realize, conflict behavior is as much motivated by disputants' values about conflict as by their desire to achieve a particular goal, as in the following case.

> Perhaps I did not want to make a decision in this arbitration, but I found myself particularly frustrated by what appeared to be the self-destructive intransigence of one of the disputants. I was the chair of a panel that was hearing a case about a public housing resident's potential eviction. Before

the final decision was delivered, the housing authority made a settlement offer that appeared to meet the needs of the resident, but he declined it. I asked the resident what he did not like about the proposal. "My father lent me the money to go through this hearing," he told me, "and he would kill me if I wimped out now." He valued "hanging tough" in this conflict, particularly in front of his father, and that was his primary motivation for turning down an offer that he acknowledged was a good one, far better than the eventual (and fairly obvious) outcome of arbitration.

Avoiding and Engaging in Conflict

The emotional and behavioral jump from avoiding conflict to engaging in it is often enormous. As a result, we sometimes observe what appear to be significant discontinuities in behavior, attitude, and interactional style when a conflict becomes manifest. We have all seen people who appear calm, easygoing, or accommodating until suddenly some switch seems to be thrown that unleashes a much more confrontational, emotional, or rigid approach. It may be that some personal value or deep emotion has been touched, but for many this change is largely a result of the different styles they exhibit when they are avoiding a conflict and when they are engaging in one. Of course, there are some for whom the jump from avoidance to engagement is not so dramatic, and they are less likely to change their behavior or approach as they engage a conflict. But for most, there is some emotional and behavioral shift that occurs when crossing the subtle barrier that separates avoidance and engagement.

All individuals have times when they chose to avoid conflict and times when they chose to engage. Both avoidance and engagement are key parts of the conflict process, but they involve very different stances toward it. In avoidance people's efforts are focused on preventing a conflict from surfacing, denying a conflict's existence, or staying out of an existing conflict. In general they are limiting their investment of emotion and energy in the conflict process. In engagement people's energy is directed toward participating in a conflict, asserting their needs, expressing their feelings, putting forward their ideas, and promoting particular outcomes. People sometimes go back and forth between avoidance and engagement many times during the course of a conflict, particularly when long-term relationships are involved.

Often the switch between avoidance and engagement produces a change in energy level. I have seen people resist engaging in a conflict with all the tools at their disposal, but once they engaged, they did not want to give it up. They can appear like the person who resists diving into the cold water, but once in, that is where he or she wants to stay. Sometimes when people withdraw from engagement and go back to avoidance, they feel a loss of meaning. The energy and vitality sometimes generated by engagement in conflict can be as hard to give up as the relative comfort and security of avoidance.

Some people are much more comfortable engaging a conflict quickly and if necessary repeatedly. Others will go to great lengths to avoid conflict, to disengage as quickly as possible, and to prevent its recurrence. Of course the specifics of the conflict have a lot to do with the pulls people experience toward avoidance and engagement. Most of us can think of conflicts that we would prefer to avoid at almost all costs, and others that we are very willing to engage, that seem almost fun.

Kenneth Thomas (1983; also see Thomas and Kilmann, 1974) has suggested five general strategies people use to approach conflict. These strategies reflect a varying relationship between satisfying one's own interests and addressing the interests of others. *Collaboration* involves an effort to solve both sets of interests; *accommodation* focuses more on satisfying others' interests; *competition* emphasizes one's own interests; *avoidance* involves a low commitment to addressing either set of interests; and *compromise* is directed toward sharing losses and gains jointly. This model has been very useful to conflict resolution practitioners because it provides a simple way of analyzing the different approaches that people take to conflict. It also provides a way for all of us to assess our own natural tendencies in conflict.

But there are limits to this model, especially in that it does not take fully into account just how variable approaches to conflict can be under different circumstances. In many conflicts, people move around among all these strategies. I think it is useful to consider how people avoid conflict and how they engage in conflict separately rather than to see both reactions as orientations toward conflict.

How People Avoid Conflict

There are eight major approaches to conflict avoidance that I have repeatedly observed.

Aggressive Avoidance ("Don't Start with Me or You'll Regret It")

Aggressive behavior is sometimes an effort to avoid conflict. Even though it often seems provocative of conflict (and often does create conflict), for many people aggressive behavior is best understood as an effort to intimidate others and thus keep them from engaging in a conflict.

Passive Avoidance ("I Refuse to Tango")

Staying removed from and nonreactive to a situation is another way to avoid engagement. There are many passive ways of avoiding a conflict, such as withdrawing from a relationship, avoiding contact, remaining silent at crucial times, creating distractions, changing the subject, or disappearing from the scene. Passive approaches seek to avoid conflict through inaction of some kind.

Passive Aggressive Avoidance ("If You Are Angry at Me, That's Your Problem")

We have all encountered people who are masters at provoking others without owning up to their own actions in any way. By getting others to react as they remain above the fray, they often try to have it both ways, both to have a conflict and to avoid it. Sometimes they will use hit and run tactics: for example, they will make an emotionally charged statement without allowing for a direct response, thereby relieving some of their own tension but preventing genuine conflict engagement. Or they may make a complaint or raise an issue but refuse to be part of any problem-solving effort.

Avoidance Through Hopelessness ("What's the Use?")

One of the easiest ways to avoid a conflict is to view the situation as beyond repair or to deny that one has any power to affect a problem. If there is no hope, then what is the point of engaging in conflict?

Avoidance Through Surrogates ("Let's You and Them Fight")

Another approach many take is to let others fight their battles or to set others up to engage in a conflict while they remain on the sidelines. Sometimes people avoid a conflict about a sensitive issue by engaging over a less sensitive one. Likewise, sometimes people will engage in a conflict with a person who functions as a surrogate for a more intimidating adversary.

Avoidance Through Denial ("If I Close My Eyes, It Will Go Away")

The simplest (and most primitive) approach is frequently the most prevalent. Often people deny that a conflict exists, hoping that in some way the denial will become the reality. Sometimes the existence of a conflict is acknowledged, but its scope or magnitude is minimized.

Avoidance Through Premature Problem Solving ("There's No Conflict; I Have Fixed Everything")

Trying to solve a problem before the timing is right, the conflict is understood, feelings have been expressed, values have been articulated, and people have been heard and acknowledged can be a very powerful way of avoiding conflict. Sometimes all someone wants is a solution, but to the extent that the conflict possesses a significant expressive element (the outer part of the wheel of conflict, as described in Chapter One), then problem solving can be equivalent to conflict avoidance. Also, premature solutions may easily be misdirected or superficial and therefore may avoid addressing the real issue.

Avoidance by Folding ("OK, We'll Do It Your Way; Now Can We Talk About Something Else?")

People sometimes avoid engaging by caving in, by accepting more responsibility than they really feel or by conceding on all the issues. Sometimes disputants will sacrifice very important needs in order to avoid engaging in a conflict or even seeing whether a conflict really exists. We all sometimes do this in simple interactions.

Haven't most of us felt at some time that we would rather lose a dispute about which movie to go see than take responsibility for the final choice?

In an important variation on this, people may make premature or insincere apologies at least in part to avoid engaging in a conflict. An apology under such circumstances can be very close to saying: "What more do you want? I have apologized. Do I really have to listen to you go on and on?"

Of course these eight approaches to avoiding conflict are often combined in different ways. Someone may first try a passive aggressive approach and then, when this does not work, attempt an aggressive outburst to forestall further engagement. In the end he or she may resort to folding or denial, as the avoidance approach of last resort. It is not unusual to see both parties to a conflict participate in a sort of collusion of avoidance, as in the case of these two accountants.

> Doug and Alex seemed happily mired in their conflict. Both were accountants, with adjoining offices in a midsize corporation. They could not stand each other, and they made this very clear to their supervisors, colleagues, friends, and anyone else who would listen. Once they even had a screaming match, heard by their whole department. But they never raised their issues directly with each other. They exchanged curt e-mails and communicated their feelings in many nonverbal ways, and their talk with each other was often dripping with sarcasm and innuendo, but they always danced around their actual differences. Their supervisor asked me to look into the possibility of mediation with them. Both were more than happy to share their tales of woe with me separately, but they adamantly refused to sit in the same room with each other. They said it was hopeless, talk was cheap, and that they would be better off just ignoring each other. It was amazing how similarly they viewed the situation. Their discussions with me did help to temporarily defuse the situation, and they did agree to try to minimize involving others in their conflict. But they were allies in avoidance. Eventually, they were both transferred to different departments.
>
> They employed many different avoidance strategies, including hopelessness, use of surrogates, aggressive avoidance, and at times folding. But both of them were especially adept at the passive aggressive approach—making

their feelings clear through innuendo and gesture but refusing to take on the conflict directly. Given the eventual outcome, avoidance may have been their best strategy. For me, it was an example of how resolution efforts cannot proceed when people are deeply committed to avoidance.

There are times when avoidance is appropriate and necessary. Sometimes timing or priorities make it desirable. It may also be the best alternative when someone does not have the power or the emotional resources to get his or her needs met through a conflict. And sometimes conflict should be avoided because it is physically or emotionally dangerous. At other times avoidance is a problem that can lead to later escalation of conflict or to sacrificing important needs.

How People Engage in Conflict

There are those who never give up trying to avoid conflict. That is their approach to it. But most people, when faced with an ongoing conflict, will eventually engage. When disputants engage in conflict, they do so with an attitude or approach to meeting their needs that is based on both their general assumptions about conflict and the particular circumstances they are facing. There are five basic ways in which people engaged in conflict go about trying to meet their needs. As Ury, Brett, and Goldberg (1988) suggested, they may work through the exercise of power, through the exercise of rights, or through an interest-based process. In addition, they may attempt to meet their needs through an appeal to fairness or through indirection (manipulation).

Power-Based Approaches

Power-based approaches to conflict are often destructive, sometimes violent, and seldom lead directly to improved relations. However, they are not always harmful. Strikes, public protests, letter writing campaigns, boycotts, and efforts to obtain political power may all be thought of as legitimized exercises of power that can produce very positive results. Sometimes individuals or groups must develop their potential to exercise power and demonstrate their willingness to use it before less confrontational approaches can be effective. Most social movements in our country have begun by promoting their causes through the (sometimes violent) exercise of power. The labor movement organized a series of worker actions. The civil rights movement employed nonviolent direct action campaigns, as did the women's suffrage and environmental movements. Sometimes these led to direct reforms, but often their main result was to create a framework for a different approach to conflict. Until environmentalists demonstrated that they could effectively assert their power through direct action, political campaigns, boycotts, and legal actions, they were not significant players in policy formation. Once they began to show that they were a force to be reckoned with, laws were passed and policies established that created a framework for a rights-based approach, and environmentalists were increasingly invited into policy development and problem-solving processes. Today it is hard to imagine a major environmental conflict being resolved without some involvement of environmental activists.

Rights-Based Approaches

Because power-based approaches are often disruptive, costly, and hard on relationships, social structures usually try to implement alternative mechanisms for dealing with conflict. This is particularly the case once it becomes clear that power is sufficiently distributed among the contending parties to make the process costly and the outcome doubtful. The usual response when this happens is the creation of a rights-based framework, through which disputants can attempt to get their needs met by asserting their privilege or claim under some established structure of law, policy, regulation, or procedure.

When it was clear that the environmental movement was a force to contend with (and that environmental issues could not be ignored), a number of federal, state, and local laws and implementing regulations were passed (such as the National Environmental Policy Act, the Clean Water and Clean Air Acts, and the Endangered Species Act). Supplemented with implementing regulations and court decisions, this legislation became the foundation for a rights-based framework for conducting environmental conflicts. As a result many environmental conflicts now take place through debates and struggles over legal rights, requirements, and prerogatives. Similar developments have occurred in the area of labor relations, family policy, civil rights, and special education.

Rights-based conflict is fundamentally different from power-based conflict. In a power-based struggle the essential message is, "Do what I want because I have the power to reward you or punish you in some way." In a rights-based struggle, the message is, "The law requires you to do what I want." The structure of rights-based conflicts tends to focus us less on what we need and more on what we have the right to get. This is both a strength and a weakness. On one hand it discourages destructive power struggles and sets parameters around both the process and potential outcome of conflict. On the other hand it tends to distract people from considering what their needs really are, and it can emphasize form over substance. Rights-based approaches can be costly, time consuming, and unpredictable as well. Much of the current cynicism about lawyers and courts arises from a sense that an alienating and somewhat out-of-control rights-based approach has taken over and complicated too many areas of conflict resolution and decision making in our society. At the same time, however, a major strength of any democracy is the existence of a popularly accepted rights-based approach to resolving conflicts. When people refer to *the rule of law*, this is essentially what they mean.

Rights-based approaches are not solely the product of legal systems or governments. Organizational policies and procedures, business agreements, ground rules for group interactions, and the bylaws of neighborhood associations all set up rights-based structures. Families set up such structures as well. Anytime we tell our children that they can watch TV one hour per day and that they must alternate who gets to choose the program, we have set up a rights-based framework.

Although power- and rights-based approaches are very different, they are not mutually exclusive. For example, there are many rights-based frameworks for conducting power struggles. There are laws that govern strikes, boycotts, and the exercise of parental authority. Developing one's ability to engage in rights-based efforts, or threatening to do so, can in fact be a power play ("I'll sue if you don't do what I want"). The conflict between abortion rights and antiabortion advocates would seem to be a classic power-based struggle, but there have been a number of efforts, as in the following example, to turn it into a rights-based conflict.

> Several years ago some colleagues and I were involved in an effort to negotiate rules for picketing outside an abortion clinic. The antiabortion groups wanted to protect their ability to exercise their First Amendment rights, but more important, they wanted to make sure they were visible and accessible to clinic clients. The clinic representatives wanted to make sure that clinic staff and patients were not threatened, intimidated, or scared away. The discussion focused on whether there were ways in which both sets of interests could be met, rather than on either what the law dictated or how each could force the other to change practices. This was in effect an effort at using an interest-based negotiation to establish a rights-based approach to governing a power-based political activity. It did not work. In the end both the clinic representatives and the antiabortion groups decided they would be better off using political and legal channels to establish a legal framework governing picketing at abortion clinics.

Interest-Based Approaches

Interest-based problem solving involves asserting one's needs or concerns and working toward a resolution that adequately addresses them. This normally also entails trying to understand and address the interests of others. (I discuss this approach in more depth in Chapter Seven, when I consider the negotiation process). Interest-based approaches, though often collaborative, are certainly not always so. For example, I have seen many divorcing couples engaged in furious fights over who should have the children at a particular time, and these fights have been almost entirely interest based. Instead of resorting to overt power tactics or arguing about the divorce agreement, the disputants have focused on why it is important that the children be with them at that time and how they think their proposal would best meet the children's needs. Nonetheless, some of these interchanges have been destructive, angry, and hurtful.

The essence of the interest-based approach is not that the disputants are necessarily collaborative or nice but that they try to deal with the conflict by discussing the various needs they have as opposed to trying to impose a solution through the application of power or the assertion of rights. The goal of many collaborative problem-solving efforts is to transform a power- or rights-based approach to an interest-based one. This was, for example, the purpose of the Child Protection Mediation Project.

> When a day-care provider reported a number of bruises on the back of a five-year-old, the child protection intake unit of the local child welfare agency was called. Its representatives placed the child in protective custody, notified the parent, Mrs. J., and told her to come to the agency's offices the next morning. After gathering background information the caseworker explained the child protection laws to the parent and discussed with her what options she had. The caseworker said that if the mother agreed to attend parenting classes and regular meetings with a counselor, the child could be returned home. Mrs. J. said she would do whatever she had to, but then she missed her first two appointments. The caseworker referred the case to the Child Protection Mediation Project (discussed by Golten and Mayer, 1987; Mayer, 1985), a CDR project that I codirected.
>
> In the ensuing mediation Mrs. J.'s concerns about attending classes and counseling while trying to hold down a job and take care of two children were discussed. She also shared her belief that everyone in the classes and counseling sessions would treat her as if she were a "bad person." The caseworker discussed her own need to have assurances that Mrs. J. was learning better ways to discipline her children, and her need to know that the child was not in danger. Mrs. J. agreed that she could use support in figuring out how to deal with her sometimes aggressive young child. The two worked out an agreed-upon schedule for attending a parent support group, and the mother also agreed to meet with the caseworker after her shift as a supermarket cashier ended.
>
> By engaging in a mediated discussion that focused on the concerns and needs of the parent, the worker, and the child, the parties reached an agreement based on their interests rather than on what Mrs. J. thought she had to do. Although this solution was fairly similar to the one originally negotiated, it proved more durable.

Principle-Based Approaches (Appeals to Fairness)

People often try to get their way in conflict by asserting a moral right to a certain outcome or course of action. They are trying to meet their needs through an appeal to what is fair, reasonable, moral, or just. We can call this a principle-based approach. It is similar to the interest-based approach because principles are related to interests. However, instead of focusing on interests (what their needs are), people are focusing on what is the "right" thing to do, and they are invoking some external standards of fairness or justice. In appealing to this external set of standards, a principle-based approach is also similar to a rights-based approach, but the natures of the standards in the two approaches are very different, and this leads to different ways of engaging in conflict.

The essence of an appeal to fairness is the invocation of some specified or implied standard of conduct. If I say that it is only fair that I get to have something, I am implying that there is some standard of fairness that says it is mine. The heart of my approach in this case is not to assert what my needs are or to argue that I have a right to something because of some established rule; instead I am asserting a value, which may or may not be formally codified.

Manipulation-Based Approaches (Indirection)

The final approach is through indirection or manipulation. There are of course countless ways of doing this. At times this approach may be a form of conflict avoidance, but often it is the result of a decision to deal with a conflict. Like all of these approaches, manipulation can be destructive or constructive. If I lie, cheat, mislead, and in general behave in an untrustworthy way, the potential for conflict escalation and long-term destructive consequences is great. But manipulation is not always destructive, especially when compared to the alternatives. In the Uncle Remus story of the Tar Baby, when Brer Rabbit is caught and threatened with a gruesome end by Brer Fox and Brer Bear, he resorts to manipulation. He handles his conflict with Brer Bear and Brer Fox by convincing them that the worst possible punishment he could receive is to be tossed into the Briar Patch, which in reality is his favorite spot on earth. Can we really say that is a destructive approach to handling that particular conflict? Exploited and unempowered people often have no alternative for addressing their needs in a conflict except to use indirection or manipulation.

Manipulation is a very common way in which people handle conflict, and to some extent it is probably present in most conflicts. The essence of manipulation is to try to get others to meet one's needs without directly confronting the issue oneself or putting one's needs or desires clearly on the table.

People blend and mix these different approaches in many ways, but there are fundamental differences among them, and at any given time, a single approach tends to be the essence of an individual's engagement in conflict. Consider, for example, the different ways in which a parent might try to enforce a bedtime on a child and how the child might try to resist.

Power Based:
Parent: Go to bed or I will take you to bed.
Child: If I can't watch this program, I'm going to hold my breath.

Rights Based:
Parent: We agreed that you could watch one late program a week, and you did that Monday.
Child: You said that if I cleaned up my room, I could stay up late.

Interest Based:
Parent: Go to bed; you need your sleep.
Child: But I want to watch the end of this program.

Principle Based:
Parent: I should not have to argue with you about bedtime.
Child: You're being unfair.

Manipulation Based:
Parent: Let's have some ice cream while I read you a bedtime story.
Child: OK, I'll be right there. *[Keeps watching the TV.]*

There are consequences for any approach that is taken, and there is a problem if a social structure does not achieve a good balance among them. It is easy for those of us in the business of collaborative conflict resolution to promote an interest-based approach, but at times it is in fact the application of power, rights, fairness, and even manipulation that is needed. It is true that overreliance on power, rights, fairness, or manipulation can escalate conflict and damage relationships. However, when unempowered disputants engage in an interest-based conflict process without having taken the steps possible to develop their power or assert their rights, they are very vulnerable.

Often problems arise when disputing parties use incompatible approaches to conflict. If an employee raises personal job scheduling needs with a manager who responds by citing the provisions of the employment contract, a communication breakdown may easily ensue. Often each feels unheard and believes the other is being unreasonable.

Styles of Conflict

If we know someone fairly well, we can often predict fairly well, without even knowing what the issues are, how that person will handle a conflict with someone else. Most people have a characteristic approach to dealing with conflict. But this does not mean that everyone has one set response for all conflict situations. One of the most important differences among people is in the flexibility of their response to conflict. Some have a fairly rigid or limited response, whereas others can vary their style from situation to situation. Flexibility of response is one important predictor of how well people will handle conflict in their lives.

There are several basic variables that I find helpful in defining the styles that people use in conflict. Each variable may be thought of as a continuum, and people tend to occupy different segments of that continuum in different types of conflicts. For example, one conflict style variable is direct versus indirect. Some people are very blunt, outspoken, and clear about their feelings and their desires. Others are more circumspect and abstract. Most people can probably employ at least a little of both tendencies if the context requires, even though they may prefer being closer to one end or the other of this spectrum. People vary their styles, so understanding how someone approaches conflict is not a simple matter of categorizing him or her in accordance with these variables but of understanding the range of styles the person is apt to use and the circumstances that evoke different styles.

The following variables may be divided into three groups: those relating to individuals' cognitive style (their way of understanding conflict), to their attitudes or feelings about conflict, and to their behavior in conflict. These groups are analogous to the three dimensions of conflict (cognitive, emotional, and behavioral).

Each variable can be thought of as a continuum between two polar characteristics.

Cognitive Variables

Cognitive variables describe differences in the ways people make sense of conflict, how they present their ideas and needs, and how they approach the problem-solving process.

Analytical Versus Intuitive

The analytical style is characterized by the use of logical reasoning and data analysis. Individuals attempt to weigh costs, benefits, and choices and to consider issues one at a time. Individuals using the intuitive approach rely more on perceptions, insights, and feelings as guides to how to proceed.

Linear Versus Holistic

In the linear style, people take issues one at a time, and consider facts, options, costs, and benefits sequentially. In the linear style of communication, one person speaks at a time and one subject is considered at a time. People employing the holistic style consider many issues simultaneously and move easily around among a focus on interests, an expression of feelings, a consideration of solutions, and a discussion of issues. In holistic communication, several people may speak about different things at once.

Integrative Versus Distributive

The integrative style promotes a focus on common interests and opportunities for joint gain. People have a tendency to think in terms of maximizing everyone's satisfaction. Disputants with a distributive style focus more on how to divide existing benefits among disputants and are usually particularly oriented to determining how to maximize their gain.

Outcome Focused Versus Process Focused

Many people are primarily focused on outcome in conflict. They want to figure out what is going to be done and when. Others' style is to be far more concerned about the process of the interaction.

Proactive Versus Reactive

Individuals using the proactive style anticipate potential conflicts and deal with them in a planned and organized manner. Those who have a more reactive approach prefer to wait for a conflict to develop before they face it and then to respond intuitively and immediately.

Emotional Variables

Emotional variables describe people's attitudes about conflict and how they handle these feelings in conflict.

Enthusiastic Versus Reluctant

People have widely different tolerances for being in conflict. Some are *conflict junkies,* who feel most alive and engaged in the middle of conflict. I can recall many meetings when someone (sometimes me) has decided to liven things up by starting a conflict. Some individuals seem to feel that any current or potential conflict must be raised at every opportunity. Most, however, are at least somewhat reluctant or fearful about being in conflict. People will sometimes go to great extremes to maintain their distance or minimize their participation in a conflict and to avoid having any direct interaction with anyone with whom they are in conflict.

Emotional Versus Rational

The emotional and the rational are not necessarily opposite as personality traits. In conflict, however, some people are more likely to be emotionally expressive and to focus on their feelings, whereas others are more likely to concentrate on employing a logical process to solve the conflict.

Volatile Versus Unprovocable

Some people in conflict seem to remain consistently calm, even, and unprovocable, and others always seem on the edge of a temper tantrum or emotional breakdown. Individuals often become considerably less volatile as they mature or develop their interpersonal skills. Also, the things that provoke people in conflict are themselves variable. For example, criticism of their personality, motives, or values will make some people volatile, whereas ignoring or discounting their suggestions is much more likely to make others react.

Behavioral Variables

An enormous number of variables could be identified that describe people's different styles of behavior in conflict, behavior that ranges from their overall demeanor to their particular responses to different situations. Here are some variables that I have found are often critical to the way a conflict unfolds.

Direct Versus Indirect

Some people assert their needs, issues, or feelings directly and openly, and others express them indirectly, through surrogate issues, metaphors, or third parties. There are people who feel that openly sharing their concerns or feelings is a personal violation and profoundly embarrassing, but there are also people who look to conflict as an opportunity to unburden themselves and who value directness in their communication.

Submissive Versus Dominant

Submissive and dominant behaviors have less to do with whether people get their needs met than with the roles they play in a conflict. At one end of this continuum are those who are always content to let others take the lead in a conflict process, even when they are in extreme disagreement with these others. At the other end are those who must be the driving force of the interactive process. Sometimes the submissive style is actually the most powerful in controlling the course and outcome of a conflict because it can induce others to work very hard to obtain the submissive disputants' agreement.

Threatening Versus Conciliatory

Some people try to get their way by intimidating others, threatening consequences, and using whatever sources of coercive power they have. Others try to placate, repair relationships, and avoid the direct application of coercive power at all costs.

For a behavior or attitude to be a conflict style, it has to be a characteristic behavior, not simply a product of the particular circumstances. However, that does not mean that circumstances and the styles of others do not affect individuals' approaches to a conflict. We may observe individuals who seem to vary their styles to fit the circumstance to the point where we wonder whether they have any continuity of style at all. Often they have more consistency than we may initially observe, but it is a consistency that can be understood only in context. For example, I have worked with people who appear to be calm, submissive, and even meek when there is no pressure to make an immediate decision. But when circumstances require a decision, they become emotional, dominating, and demanding. They do have a consistency of style, but understanding it requires analyzing style in relation to different situations.

The stylistic variables I have outlined here are not independent of one another. They are also not by any means an exhaustive catalogue of conflict styles, but they are significant descriptors of the different tendencies people exhibit in handling conflict. The existence of these variables raises a number of important questions, two of which are of particular concern to conflict resolvers.

First, do groups, organizations, communities, and societies have conflict styles? Does the United States have a conflict style? Does the United Autoworkers? Microsoft? New York City? A particular class in a school? Your family? As parties to conflict these entities do exhibit styles of conflicting, but this does not mean that all the individuals who make up each entity share these approaches themselves. Although the descriptions of the variables given here might have to be slightly altered to apply to groups or organizations, the variables themselves are very relevant. As a general rule the larger a group, the harder it is to identify a style without stereotyping or making unsupportable generalizations. But that does not mean we cannot find some predominant characteristics or themes in how any particular group, organization, community, or system handles conflict.

The second question is more complicated. Are there good and bad conflict styles? An extreme in any style may be harmful to the individuals or groups exhibiting it and to those with whom they interact. But I believe it is less productive to think about whether conflict styles are good or bad than to consider whether they are effective or nonproductive in any given circumstance. Extremes of style aside, most of these approaches have been effective at different times. The most important question here is how adaptable and flexible people can be in the style they bring to any given conflict. When people can alter their style to adapt to a particular situation, they are more likely to be effective than they are when their approach is extremely limited.

Roles People Play in Conflict

Conflicts call on individuals to play certain roles, roles that are different from the designated roles people occupy by virtue of their profession or position. Moreover, individuals cannot always choose the role they play in conflict. Often they are forced into a role they do not like, and this can cause a great deal of discomfort. Other roles seem natural and even inviting to them.

The roles that we as individuals are ordinarily most comfortable with are no doubt related to the professional or formal roles we may choose to assume as conflict resolvers, but these formal roles are not identical to the roles that conflict may demand of us. It is helpful for all individuals involved in a dispute to be aware of which role they are most comfortable with and under what circumstances. Although people play many roles in conflict, the following five seem the most prevalent.

Advocate (Negotiator)

Advocates press for a particular set of interests or needs to be met. If they are parties to the decision, they are in the negotiator role. Like all these roles, the advocate role can encompass a wide set of behaviors, from combatant at one extreme to problem solver at another, but the common thread is that the advocate tries to ensure that certain needs are adequately addressed.

Decision Maker (Arbitrator)

When individuals have the authority to make a decision (or a recommendation that carries weight), they are in the decision maker role. When they are making a decision among competing advocates, they are in the arbitrator role. Sometimes decision makers are in a formally neutral role (judge or formal arbitrator), but others are neither neutral nor unbiased (like parents making decisions in a conflict among children and bosses doing so among subordinates). Often a decision maker is also an advocate.

Facilitator (Mediator)

A person in the facilitator role is focused on the process of an interaction rather than the substance. Facilitators help others make a decision or engage in a productive interaction. A mediator is essentially a facilitator who is intervening as a neutral in a situation that has been defined as a conflict and for which resolution of some kind is desired.

Information Provider (Expert)

An important role in conflict is to provide relevant information to the others involved. When individuals have information to provide because of their particular training, education, or long-term experience, they are in the expert role.

Observer (Witness, Audience)

Observers fill a relatively passive role that is nevertheless key to many conflicts. Sometimes, like United Nations observers or election observers, they play a mitigating role. Sometimes, like those who engage in sensationalist reporting, they can contribute to the escalation of a conflict. Many conflicts cannot be understood without examining the role of observers.

There are certainly other roles people play in conflict (for example, coach, recorder, record keeper, cheerleader, publicizer, convener, gatekeeper). But these five are the key roles in the structure of most conflicts. Each can be played in many different ways, and each can contribute to conflict escalation or deescalation. Furthermore they are not usually encapsulated. Elements of several different roles are often present in people's participation in any given conflict, and no matter what a person's role is, he or she always has some of his or her own needs in play, even when occupying a formally neutral role.

Often individuals enter a conflict primarily in one role but then change roles, sometimes repeatedly and rapidly. Individuals frequently escalate a conflict when they pretend to play one role (for example, facilitator or information provider) but really occupy a different role (arbitrator or advocate). Clarifying or simplifying roles can be key to the resolution of conflict, as in the case of JoAnne and Morton.

> JoAnne was the director of human resources for a medium-sized corporation, and she was in a fix. Morton, one of the company's managers, was embroiled in a number of conflicts with other managers and many of his staff. His performance in many respects was outstanding, but he seemed to be a lightning rod for conflict. JoAnne had tried to facilitate some conversations between Morton and others, and she felt some of these sessions had gone well, but the problem persisted. JoAnne had also tried to coach Morton through several difficult interactions and felt that he had been receptive to learning. But then a formal grievance was lodged against Morton by one of his employees, who also requested to be transferred to a different department. JoAnne's role was to advise the grievant about company policies and to ensure that the grievance procedure was implemented in a timely way. She also had to make sure that the company's interests were represented in any final decision. In the end she decided that the employee's request for a transfer should be honored, despite Morton's objections. This led to a dispute between JoAnne and Morton. I was asked to come in and "make things better."
>
> One immediate step I took was to take JoAnne out of her role conflict. Once I took over the facilitation and coaching roles, it proved much easier to work through many of the conflicts in which Morton was engaged, because my role was less convoluted than JoAnne's had been. I had no power over his job and no role in representing the interests of the organization. JoAnne could then more clearly play the role of advocate for the company. This was her most essential role. When her role was simplified, the whole conflict deescalated.

As conflict resolvers, we are called on at times to play each of the five roles. For example, as a mediator, my overall role is that of the facilitator. But at different times during the course of my work,

I will be an advocate for certain things (such as good listening procedures or a realistic time frame), an arbitrator (for instance, by deciding who gets to speak next), an information provider (explaining, for example, whether I can be subpoenaed), and an observer. My effectiveness as a mediator requires that I know when and how to fulfill each of these functions.

People and Conflict

As in so many other efforts to understand human behavior, in conflict we face the structural versus individual dilemma: to what extent is behavior in conflict primarily a result of the structure within which the conflict takes place and to what extent does it reflect what individuals bring to that structure? Does the situation call forth the behavior or do individuals' values, styles, and role preferences determine their behavior. Obviously, both the nature of the conflict and the nature of the individuals involved are important. We err if we think we can understand a conflict without examining the values, styles, and preferences of the individuals. But we also make a mistake if we fail to pay adequate attention to the structural elements of the conflict. Understanding conflict requires paying simultaneous attention to both the individuals in conflict and the structure of the interaction.

Chapter Three

Power and Conflict

Power is the currency of conflict. Whether its exercise is intentional or not, when people are engaged in conflict, their power is in play. The choice in conflict is not whether to use power but how to use it. Power can be used intentionally or unconsciously, collaboratively or coercively, obviously or implicitly. When people try to meet their needs in the face of resistance or opposition, they are exercising power. Whether they will succeed or not depends in part on how much power they are able to muster and how wise they are in using it. The exercise of power is not necessarily coercive, antagonistic, escalatory, or combative, although it certainly can be any of these. All of us exercise power continually, and we often do so in a way that promotes rapport or reconciliation. If we do not understand the nature of power and how power affects conflict, we cannot understand conflict itself.

Realities and Myths About Power

People have many different images about what power is, some of which are quite misleading. Power is variously defined as the ability to act, to influence an outcome, to get something to happen, or to overcome resistance. For the purpose of understanding the dynamics of conflict, power may be defined as the ability to get one's needs met and to further one's goals. Power of this type (as opposed to the power of an engine or the power of the sun, for example) can be understood only in context. Even when we are

---

Parts of this chapter are adapted from B. Mayer, "The Dynamics of Power in Mediation and Conflict Resolution," *Mediation Quarterly,* Summer 1987, *16,* pp. 75–86.

talking about will power or the power of concentration, for example, we must understand the environment in which people are exerting this power and the forces with which they are interacting. Therefore, when we discuss power in conflict, we are speaking of power within an interaction. With one group of friends I may have great influence on what movie we will choose to see or on how we will settle a disagreement about where to go skiing, but with another group (or the same group under different circumstances), I may have very little influence. One key circumstance that defines our power is our intention and focus. If there is something I want very badly, and if I focus all my energy on getting it, for that moment my power will be greater than it will when I care only mildly about the issue or decision.

We can again look at parent-child interactions to get a quick idea of how complicated power dynamics can be. Imagine yourself as the parent of a four-year-old child who is accompanying you on what you hope will be a quick trip to the grocery store. Your child wants you to buy a candy bar, but for a variety of reasons you do not want to give in to this request. Now think about the different ways this interaction can play out and how likely it is that on some occasions the child will prevail and on others you will. If under all circumstances one or the other person gets his or her way, it is very likely that there are some serious problems in this relationship.

For a conflict to develop, all involved must have some power, even if it is slight, to bring to bear. In situations where one group completely dominates another, conflict is unlikely to exist, at least along the behavioral dimension. Instead, there is a *potential* for conflict, which may be realized as the dominated group develops power.

We have many misleading images of power. Perhaps the most prevalent is the idea that power can be balanced. This is a derivation of the view many have that power is a measurable quantity. I believe that *balance of power* is a confusing and possibly meaningless concept. We can look at differences in power, at whether someone has the power to make something happen, at sources of power, and at vulnerabilities to other people's power. But the idea that power can be balanced so as to produce some equality or even equivalence of power is very misleading. Such a way of viewing power fails to account for the dynamics of power and the interactional context in which power must be understood. Instead of thinking that people need an equivalence or equality of power, we might more usefully think that people need an adequate basis of power to participate effectively in conflict. They require enough power that others must at least consider their concerns and enough power to resist any solution that fundamentally violates their interests. This does not mean that disputants with an adequate base of power can always "win" or even always get a particularly desirable outcome, but they can at least engage in conflict with some hope of being influential and effective. Without this power, their participation in a resolution process may end up being the means for their needs to be ignored, their interests overrun.

A related problematic image is that of power as a fixed quantity in a relationship. That is, people often think of power as being in limited supply. If I don't develop and use my power in a relationship or conflict, according to this view, I will lose it. And the more power others have, the less I have. In human relations, power is more complex than that. Depending on how we use our power and the type of strength we draw from, our power can increase as our adversaries' power also increases.

Often the potential power that individuals or groups have can be realized only when it is joined to the power of the others in the conflict. Sometimes the best way for a group to enhance its own power is to use it to empower a potential adversary with which the group has some mutual and some conflicting interests. Similarly, the attempt to exercise power separately from or in opposition to others often leads to a loss of power. This dynamic may often be observed in negotiations between unions and management.

One of the most poisonous labor relations atmospheres I have seen existed between the union and management of a state hospital. There were as many outstanding grievances as there were represented employees, and these grievances were not getting resolved. The overall adversarial atmosphere was mirrored in many acrimonious interchanges between individual managers and union representatives. Despite numerous efforts by the parent union and the overall agency leadership to intervene, the situation was deteriorating and morale was sinking. A colleague and I were asked to work with the union and the management to help improve their relationship. There were many thrusts to our effort. We provided training, mediated interpersonal disputes, assisted in designing new grievance mechanisms, and facilitated discussions between the union and management teams where they could talk about their relationship.

A key step in the process occurred when we decided the time was ripe to mediate about sixty of the grievances collectively. All related to how overtime was assigned and calculated, and we felt it would be just as easy to negotiate them as a class as one at a time, and far more meaningful. It was a bold move on the part of management, the union, and us to try to do this. We were taking a big bite. Success would remove one major obstacle to improved relations and would allow people to look at some of the more fundamental issues of communication, trust, and decision making. Failure could discourage everyone and set the whole effort back (or maybe scuttle the whole process). We felt, however, that everyone would become suspicious of all the nice words the process was generating if no significant and tangible progress were made on important issues.

Once the negotiations got under way, a potential solution was not that difficult to figure out, but each side was terribly worried about giving in to the other and appearing to weaken its own position while enhancing the other's. However, everyone was also tired of the conflict and knew that some risks had to be taken to change things. With great trepidation the two sides reached an agreement, despite each fearing that it had been manipulated. But the upshot was that relations did start to improve significantly. After this, the union was able to talk over its particular concerns more openly and effectively with management, and managers were able to deal with some difficult personnel issues that they had been avoiding.

Later, when the state criticized some decisions the hospital management and union had made on other issues, they were able to work as a team to protect the hospital's interests. They were also invited to share their new approach to handling grievances with other facilities, which increased the prestige of both the union and the facility leadership. The decision to use their power jointly rather than in opposition to each other was very difficult. By taking a chance that might empower the other side to the risk-taker's own disadvantage, the management and the union increased their individual and collective power.

Types and Sources of Power

Power is an elusive concept because it has so many manifestations. Everyone has many potential sources of power, most of which he or she is often unaware of. Some of these sources are fairly independent from the conflict, but others can be enhanced or diminished by the conflict process. In fact, increasing power is often one of the goals people have in conflict. Some sources are best used sparingly, if at all; some are negative or escalatory. However, others are more constructive and amenable to repeated direct application.

Structural and Personal Power

We can identify two general categories of power: structural and personal. Structural power is lodged in the situation, the objective resources people bring to a conflict, the legal and political realities within which the conflict occurs, the formal authority they have, and the real choices that exist. Personal power has to do with individual characteristics, such as determination, knowledge, wits, courage, and communication skills.

Going back to the supermarket example, we can ask why the parent does not always get his or her way. The parent has the formal authority, financial resources, physical strength, and ability to reward or punish the child. But we know how often a child may prevail in this situation. Why? The child has energy, focus, desire, the willingness to use whatever power he or she may have (including embarrassing the parent), and usually a great deal of creativity. Often it is the variations in personal power that explain the widely different outcomes to conflicts that appear structurally similar.

A more serious example is one I have encountered in many divorce situations. One party seems to have the financial resources and the legal rights to successfully pursue his or her interests, but because that person does not have the determination, emotional resilience, or clarity of purpose of the other party, he or she ends up in a weaker position. This is one reason that victims of domestic violence are often so vulnerable in divorce negotiations.

As a general rule, conflict resolution systems and practitioners are more likely to be able to affect differentials rooted in personal power rather than in structure. For example, mediators can set up procedures to discourage intimidation, browbeating, unequal access to information, and so forth, but they can do little to change the fundamental resources available to each side or the legal framework that

defines the alternatives that the different parties have should negotiations fail. Changes in structural power usually require systemic
change and are often an outcome of a conflict resolution process.

Specific Types of Power

People can be enormously creative in finding power to bring to
bear in conflict, and there are several key sources of power that disputants repeatedly mobilize in conflict. Although some of these
sources of power overlap and although there are certainly others,
these are the ones I believe to be most useful for understanding
the kinds and sources of power individuals or organizations have
the potential to bring to conflict.

Formal Authority

Formal authority is the authority given by an institution, by a set of
laws or policies, or by virtue of one's position in a formal structure.
Principals, judges, police officers, executives, elected officials, parents, and military officers all have some degree of formal authority. Most people in leadership positions have some power based on
their formal authority and some based on their personal influence.
Formal authority is a form of structural power. How effective people are in using it is often related to their personal power.

Legal Prerogative

Everyone has rights and choices defined by law or policy. Disputants' legal rights and obligations often define their alternatives
to consensual agreements. An important related source of power
is the resources (financial and emotional) a person has to pursue
a legal case.

Information

Data and knowledge are important sources of power. In many situations the actions people take to share, discover, or conceal information are the key to how a conflict develops. A variation on the
power of information is expert power. This is the power that
derives from having expertise relevant to a conflict or access to
such expertise.

Association

Power also stems from an individual's connection with other powerful people or organizations. Political power is an interesting variant of this. Most political power stems from people's ability to bring the power of others to bear in a political context. The power of neutrals partly derives from their ability to maintain an association with all conflicting parties, thus making themselves valuable to each of them.

Resources

Control over or access to resources such as money, time, or labor is a major source of power. A related source is the ability to provide or deny resources to others. Resources may be either tangible or intangible. Tangible resources, such as money, personnel, or property, are extremely important, but it is sometimes the intangible resources, such as reputation, ability to handle stress, and physical endurance, that are more critical to people in conflict.

Rewards and Sanctions

The ability to provide or withhold meaningful rewards and the ability to impose negative consequences on others or to prevent those consequences are twin sources of power. All power can be defined to some extent in terms of the ability to reward or sanction. Generally, people think of rewards as more constructive than sanctions, but as sources of power there is sometimes very little difference between the two. Withholding a reward is essentially a sanction, and withdrawing a sanction is a reward. The power of a reward or sanction is often less defined by the action's severity than by its immediacy. The long-term threat of a lawsuit, for example, although serious, may be less influential on a corporate decision maker than the immediate prospect of increased sales revenues.

Nuisance

Related to sanctions as a source of power, this is the ability to irritate, bother, interfere, or harass, but it falls short of the ability to impose significant consequences or penalties. It is sometimes referred to as the "power of the flea over the dog." This may be the major power of the child in the supermarket.

Procedural Power

Procedural power arises from the ability to control or influence a decision-making process. This is separate from control over the outcome. The power of a judge in a criminal trial or a mediator in a negotiation is in large part procedural but certainly not insignificant.

Habitual Power

Habitual power derives from being in the position of trying to prevent change as opposed to fomenting it. Sometimes this is referred to as the power of inertia. It is usually easier to keep things the way they are than to change things. This power partially explains why community groups opposed to development have often been able to cause large corporations with considerable resources and political connections to stand down.

Moral Power

Power can flow from an appeal to the values, beliefs, and ethical systems of others or from an attack on the values of those with whom someone is in conflict. Also, people's belief that they are acting in accordance with important values is an important source of personal power. Mahatma Gandhi referred to this as the force of truth. When individuals are advocating what they believe to be a worthy cause, such as the rights of an oppressed group, that belief helps them be steadfast and energetic in their advocacy. Also, people are more likely to be swayed by a person perceived as doing good work than by a person viewed as interested mainly in personal gain. Of course an assertion of worthiness may also lead to a perception of self-righteousness, or it may bring into conflict people who do not share the same evaluation of the worthiness of the cause. When people portray themselves as the victim or the underdog, they are usually trying to invoke this type of power.

Personal Characteristics

People may derive power from a broad set of personal characteristics that they bring to bear in conflict. Their intelligence, communication skills, physical stamina and strength, concentration, wit, perceptiveness, determination, empathy, and courage are key factors in determining how well their needs will be met in any conflict.

Another factor is endurance. How long individuals can tolerate being in a conflict and how well they are able to withstand others' power is a key aspect of their own power.

Perception of Power

The beliefs people have about their power and that of others are often as important as the power itself. For example, if disputants believe that a court is likely to rule favorably or that they have the resources to go to court if necessary, the belief itself, regardless of its accuracy, can be a source of power, especially if others share it. Similarly, if others believe that a person has considerable resources or significant connections with powerful people, that belief alone can enhance the person's power. People's ability to modify the perceptions that others have about power is therefore itself a source of power.

Definitional Power

The ability to define the issues and the potential outcomes in a conflict is a crucial source of power. It makes a big difference whether workers see themselves negotiating for better wages, for their jobs, or for ownership of a plant. The framing of a conflict is often the key to how it is resolved.

Some of these types of power are more naturally constructive than others, but any of them can be used to escalate or deescalate a conflict. Some are more amenable to change during the course of a conflict. For example, disputants can often increase their power by improving their access to information and by developing effective associations with others. However, changing one's authority, legal position, or ability to impose sanctions may be more difficult.

Some types of power are compatible with others, some are not, and often conflict develops when a person tries to use incompatible types of power. If I try to get someone to do what I want by using moral authority and by threatening sanctions, I am very likely to be working at cross purposes with myself. The reaction of those who are threatened is likely to be defensive and hostile, diminishing their openness to an appeal to principle and fairness. However, there are also times when one type of power can be employed effectively only when it is supplemented by another. For example, legal power is often ineffective if a person does not have the resources to use it. Sometimes a person with formal authority in an organization has very little personal, moral, or association power. This can lead to serious organizational conflict. I have worked with a number of conflicted teams that were experiencing significant struggles between an individual with formal authority and an individual who had become the natural leader of the group.

These types of power mix together in complex ways, and seldom can they be neatly separated. Also, people's ability to use power effectively is mixed. Often powerful people end up in a weak position because they have not been wise in handling their power. This was clearly the situation in a dispute I observed several years ago in a social agency.

It did not take Louis long to dig a big hole for himself after being hired as director of a human services agency. Sid, one of his team leaders, had been the acting director while the search process for a new director was being conducted, and he had announced his intention to retire from the organization several months after the new director arrived. Sid now felt slighted and unappreciated for his contribution as acting director. Louis felt that Sid was undercutting him in many subtle ways, and thought that Sid needed to be put in his place. Both found plenty of ways to irritate each other and complicate their jobs. Sid made his views about the new director known to his colleagues but never attacked Louis directly. Louis openly criticized decisions Sid had made as acting director. Whenever Louis had an opportunity to use his formal authority over Sid, he did.

All this came to a head several weeks before Sid's departure, when Louis ordered Sid to place one of his staff on probation under very stringent terms. Sid refused, and Louis threatened to fire him. Sid replied to this threat by saying, in effect, "Go ahead, make my day." Of course Louis could not carry this threat out effectively in the time that remained before Sid's scheduled departure. As a result of this conflict, Louis's authority, leadership, and influence declined considerably, and this continued to be the case long after Sid had departed.

Louis had a considerable amount of power. He squandered it by relying almost exclusively on his formal authority and his ability to sanction. In the end he retained little real power to affect the climate in the organization. He had publicly taken on a popular employee in a relatively meaningless conflict that he could not win, and he never developed his personal power with his staff. Furthermore, instead of using their respective power together, Louis and Sid turned it against each other, doing considerable damage to the agency's program and to their personal standing.

Often the essential question in a conflict is not how much power the different individuals have, but how they choose to use it. As the example of Louis and Sid illustrated, power can be used effectively or ineffectively. The type of power people choose to apply, their timing, and their sense of how they can use their power to meet their needs are all critical to their effectiveness. The more disputants use their power intelligently, the more power they tend to have. Power that is expended ineffectively tends to diminish.

Implied and Applied Power

One of the greatest challenges in using power is how direct one should be in its application. Frequently, implied power is far more effective than power brought directly to bear on a situation. Developing the capacity to sue and building a strong legal case are often much more effective than actually suing or threatening to sue. Arming oneself with relevant information is usually more empowering than demonstrating how well informed one is. Developing alternatives to a collaborative solution is generally more important than threatening to use those alternatives. Understanding how to develop power quietly and to use it sparingly is one of the arts of effective conflict engagement.

Of course, this does not mean that disputants should never bring their power directly and overtly to bear. Sometimes it is important to use power to change a situation, and sometimes it is necessary to show a willingness to use power. But this is a very tricky proposition, and the mistakes people make in using power often lock them into nonproductive conflict. Unions, for example, in order to be effective negotiators, often need to develop a creditable threat of engaging in job actions or strikes. Sometimes, however, the ability to strike cannot be developed or projected without creating a momentum that makes a job action inevitable or at least difficult to avoid. It is tempting to believe that strikes are generally a sign of the shortcomings of either the negotiation process or the negotiators. But if a union never strikes or a company never shows its willingness to endure a strike, then the possibility of a strike or a lockout becomes a much less potent force in negotiations. Yet we have all witnessed strikes or other job actions that were clearly harmful to all involved and that occurred because a momentum was created by the overly direct application of this type of power. The sports world has provided us with several graphic examples of this. The 1998 lockout in the National Basketball Association caused the cancellation of a significant part of the season and led to considerable disenchantment on the part of fans. Both players and owners lost out, and in the end an agreement was reached that could probably have been concluded much earlier had the leaderships not locked themselves into rigid negotiating stances.

This raises the question whether we can prepare for war and peace at the same time. There are contradictions between putting our energy into collaborative conflict resolution efforts and at the same time preparing for an adversarial contest. For example, the more reticent negotiators are to share information, the more difficult it is for them to find creative solutions to contentious problems. But if negotiators readily share too much information, they can compromise their ability to prevail later in a legal forum. (I return to this issue when I discuss negotiation in Chapter Seven.) Nevertheless, people in conflict can and often must prepare to cooperate and to contest at the same time. If disputants do not develop their ability to be effective in an adversarial context, they often fail to give others a reason to work collaboratively with them. But if they focus too much on preparing for an adversarial contest, they will create a momentum that is hard to escape, and they will complicate the process of developing the rapport and establishing the communication necessary to work collaboratively. The art of conflict resolution depends in part on knowing how to balance these two needs. Although the idea that we cannot prepare for war and peace at the same time carries an important sentiment and value, it is a flawed concept if we are trying to understand how to engage in conflict effectively.

How Power Is Applied

Our sources of power are not the same as our uses of power. Wherever people's power derives from, there are three primary ways in which they can use it to try to influence others' behavior. First, they can appeal to other people's values and beliefs. By framing their persuasive efforts in terms of values and by making use of normative symbols, disputants attempt to get others to comply with their wishes by convincing them that it is the right thing to do. This is often called the *normative* approach to the application of power. A second approach is to appeal to people's self-interests or to indicate that they will obtain certain tangible benefits if they do what one wishes. This is sometimes referred to as the *utilitarian* approach. A third method is to try to force people to agree to something by threatening significant sanctions or by manipulating the external environment to take away their freedom of choice. This may be thought of as the *coercive* approach. Sometimes these three approaches are categorized as persuasion, reward, and punishment. Regardless of the terminology these are the key ways power is applied in conflict. (In this section, I draw on the work of Amitai Etzioni, 1975, particularly his discussion of organizational compliance theory. For other somewhat similar descriptions of the ways people exercise power, see Deutsch, 1973; Gamson, 1968; Kriesberg, 1982.)

I want my son to mow the lawn, but he keeps putting it off. First, I talk about how he agreed to do this, how little he really has to do around the house, and how important it is for the health of the lawn. Next, I say that I will pay him an extra five dollars if he will get it done within twenty-four hours. Finally, I say that if he does not get it done by the end of the weekend, I will hire someone else to do the mowing, and the fee will come out of his allowance. In this everyday example, we see the quick and to some extent consciously sequenced use of these different applications of power. We can see these same approaches in almost any conflict. Anytime we talk about the "carrot and stick," we are referring to two of these approaches. If we add the option of personal affirmation or some other social reinforcement (sort of a scratch behind the ear, a carrot, and a stick), then we have all three applications of power.

How do environmentalists try to influence policymakers? First, they argue that what they advocate is the right thing to do for the environment and thus they appeal to people's desire to do what is right. Second, they offer their political support and contributions. Third, they threaten lawsuits, direct action campaigns, or political retribution. We can look at almost any significant conflict, and we will see the use of these three different types of power.

Sometimes it is possible to use these different approaches together effectively, saying, in effect, "Let's work together on this; otherwise we will end up wasting all sorts of resources suing each other." Often, however, these approaches contradict or undercut each other. Should the United States try to promote democracy in China by offering the Chinese greater acceptance into the international community and a higher level of trade, or by threatening sanctions? This has been a policy debate for years. To try to take both approaches at once is unlikely to succeed. Containment and constructive engagement are simply not compatible. If a divorcing parent wants to discuss how to share parenting in the interest of the children, she or he is more likely to succeed using a normative, or persuasive, approach, emphasizing what is best for the children. To try to influence the other parent with financial incentives or threats of court action is likely to undercut the impact of the normative focus on the children's best interests. One of the most frequent dilemmas divorce mediators face arises when one parent tries to force the other to enter into a cooperative parenting agreement. Using coercion to set up a decision-making process that requires the use of normative forms of influence is seldom appropriate. I was once caught squarely in the middle of such a contradictory approach when I was trying, of all things, to provide training in collaborative decision making.

The intention of the new school superintendent seemed admirable, even visionary. He wanted to introduce a more cooperative management style to his district, so he asked me and a colleague of mine to provide all his administrators and principals with training in conflict resolution and collaborative decision making. But he did not practice what he preached. When we arrived, we found that the administrators had been ordered by the superintendent to attend and that he had further directed each one to develop a plan for initiating a team management approach in his or her division or school. All this occurred without any discussion among the managers, the principals, and the superintendent. Furthermore, the seminar had been scheduled for the week before school began, a terrible time for principals to be away from their buildings.

Needless to say, we found ourselves in the middle of a significant contradiction, which we should have discovered before we arrived. Somehow we had to find a way to provide people an opportunity to consider the team management philosophy for themselves, independently of the pressure placed on them by their boss. We did this by using real issues that concerned the whole district as case studies and as material for simulations. Using the procedures and skills we presented, the administrators discussed how to allocate financial resources to different programs, how to come up with unified disciplinary policies, and how to take a coordinated approach to responding to parent complaints and staff grievances.

By conducting these problem-solving discussions around topics that engaged the administrators, we created a situation in which they were able to begin to think about the collaborative process on their own terms. This also required the superintendent, rather reluctantly, to reconsider his own management style, now obviously at odds with what he was promoting for his administrators. Despite trying to make the best of the situation, neither my colleague nor I felt confident that there was much immediate chance for real change in the district's approach to management.

I have never seen a coercive approach to instituting a cooperative management process work. In fact I have never seen a utilitarian approach succeed as a primary means of inducing collaborative decision making and teamwork. Unless the primary motivation of most employees for engaging in new types of team structures is a commitment to these structures' underlying values and philosophy, these initiatives almost always fail.

Coercive approaches are sometimes necessary. People in positions of privilege seldom give away their advantages unless they are to some extent forced to do so. There are also times when normative or utilitarian approaches are inappropriate and disempowering. Stopping domestic violence, for example, usually requires, at least initially, some form of coercive intervention. The attempt to stop violence through rewarding people for changing their ways or through appealing to their values about human relations is not only ineffective but can in fact play into the cycle of violence.

Integrative and Distributive Power

When a sales tax was set to expire in Boulder, Colorado, at the end of 1992, two groups saw a golden opportunity to fund important programs, and each one organized a petition campaign to extend the sales tax. One group wanted the money designated for park and recreational facilities, the other for human services programs. At first, each group tried very hard to organize support for its particular proposal, both with elected officials and the public. But the more the groups organized, the more obvious it became that they were well on the way to defeating both initiatives. They therefore decided to work on a joint initiative, but each group was still focused on capturing as much of the potential revenues for its own purposes as possible, and the meetings were not going well. They asked me to mediate a joint proposal, and we succeeded in working out the terms of a joint initiative, and it did get on the ballot.

Now, however, other groups, including the city council felt that they were being left out; they organized against the measure, and it went down to a narrow defeat. This led to a wider dialogue that included business leaders, city officials, open space advocates, and others. For this dialogue to succeed, each group had to work hard to get beyond its tendency to advocate for just its own cause, and to look at the wider picture—to "wear a very broad hat," as one participant put it. As they did this, the whole power dynamic was completely changed. Instead of applying power against each other, they were now applying power to assist each other. In the end, as an outcome of further mediation, this expanded group agreed on a joint proposal that was overwhelmingly passed in an election at a time when many other tax proposals were being soundly defeated.

These one-time disputants made an important transition in how they viewed and used their power. They started to apply power with each other rather than against each other, and they focused on using their power to augment each other's influence rather than to get their way at the others' expense. When people use their power to increase the overall influence of all the parties involved in a dispute or negotiation, they are applying their power in an *integrative* way. When they try to get their way by directing enough power at others to force a compromise or concession of some kind, then power is being applied in a *distributive* way.

There are times when distributive applications of power are necessary. Sometimes the only way to attain a satisfactory outcome is at someone else's expense. There may be no more joint gains realistically available, and therefore, in order for one party to achieve greater benefits, another party needs to be induced to sacrifice something. But people in conflict tend to assume this is the situation; they do not fully explore the possibility of an integrative outcome. As a result, disputants are often quick to apply distributive power, and this tends to escalate conflict. The challenge in many situations is to find ways to redirect disputants from thinking about distributive power and to focus them on their potential integrative power. (For an interesting debate about the relevance of these types of power to the bargaining process, see Fisher, 1983, 1985; McCarthy, 1985.)

To describe this redirection, conflict resolvers often use the metaphor of Aikido. Practitioners of this form of martial art use the energy of the attacker to deflect an assault and avoid violence. They respect the attacker, take the attacker's perspective, and join their energy with the attacker's energy rather than resisting that energy (see Crum, 1987).

The Power of Alternatives

To a large extent people's choices in conflict are determined by their power. The more resources, information, authority, or endurance an individual has, the more choices he or she has. But it is also true that power is defined by choices. Often the best way to enhance one's power is to develop better choices. It is generally useful to develop both alternatives to negotiated agreements and alternatives for negotiated agreements. That is, it is important for people to maximize the choices they have should the negotiation not result in a satisfactory agreement, and it is also important for people to create alternatives that can be brought to bear within the negotiation itself. Developing alternatives is not simply about having a way to opt out of a collaborative process; it is about making it more likely that collaboration can be successful.

Like the exercise of power, the development of choices can occur in a distributive or integrative manner. I can develop alternatives that give me leverage over others, or I can develop alternatives that make it more appealing for other people to work with me. Similarly, I can develop my alternatives independently of others or in concert with them.

Sometimes, by spending the time to both identify alternatives and put out the effort necessary to make them feasible, disputants can completely change the power relationship. That notion is what is behind this very practical advice from a consumer service organization ("New Cars," 1999): "If you know how much markup is in a car's asking price, you're in a better position to ask for a discount. And if you know what you want, you needn't depend on advice from a salesperson who may be trying to push a high-profit or slow-selling model. . . . The surest way to get the best price is to shop for the same model at several dealerships. If you're armed with the invoice price, you should command more respect from the sales staff" (pp. 16–17).

Power and Social Justice

Collaborative problem solving and promoting social justice are not the same thing. One of the major criticisms of mediation and related cooperative approaches to the resolution of conflict is that they do not necessarily promote social justice or protect the unempowered. Unless all the players in a problem-solving process have sufficient power to represent themselves effectively, a collaborative process can easily result in an unjust conclusion. This concern has been raised in many different contexts. Advocates for victims of domestic violence have been concerned that mediation may lead to further victimization. Community activists have worried that negotiation with developers may become a means of co-optation. Environmentalists have been afraid that policy dialogues may ease the pressure on industry to improve its performance and undercut the rigor of regulatory enforcement.

There is no doubt that all these problems are real and that cooperative efforts can lead to unfair results, just like any other decision-making process. Certain circumstances call more for organizing than for conflict resolution. One version of a mediator's nightmare, I have long thought, would be getting plunked down in Montgomery, Alabama, in 1956, to resolve the dispute between Rosa Parks and the Montgomery bus company. What was important about the Montgomery bus boycott was that it became a rallying point for the nascent civil rights movement. Only after the advocates of integration had organized themselves, obtained widespread demonstrations of public support, and raised the issue to the national stage, did it make sense to try seriously to resolve the dispute. After a year of successfully boycotting the bus services, obtaining massive publicity and public support, and demonstrating that African Americans could challenge the white power structure, the power dynamics had gone through a monumental change. When the leaders of the boycott had developed enough support and power to obtain the kind of outcome they wanted, they, the bus company officials, and the city leaders did participate in discussions, which were organized by the churches of Montgomery. A negotiated agreement was then reached that ended the discriminatory policies of the bus system. This was a crucial step in building the civil rights movement and furthering the cause of social justice.

Collaborative conflict resolution efforts are not the enemy of struggles for social justice, but neither are they, in themselves, movements for social change. The important question is whether such efforts are in some way impeding unempowered individuals' or groups' access to sources of power that they might otherwise have. There are two ways in which they may do this. First, they may deter people from choosing avenues of conflict resolution or decision making that might give them access to more power. For example, if a victim of domestic violence chooses to negotiate an agreement rather than seek the protection of a court order, she or he might end up in a less powerful and more dangerous position. Second, they may lead people to seek a solution before they have developed their own power to a fuller level, as could have occurred in Montgomery.

It is important to view these possibilities in context however. Movements for social justice and individual empowerment progress in many different ways. Progress is intermittent and characterized by frequent setbacks. Unions have often had to settle for minor gains after hard struggles in order to maintain support from members or simply to survive. Environmentalists have sometimes decided to participate in lopsided processes because the alternative was to have no voice at all. Victims of domestic violence have often chosen to sacrifice many things to which they might have a legal right because what they needed most was a quick and relatively safe way out of the relationship. There are times when movements grow by collaborating in the short run in order to consolidate some gains and encourage people to continue a longer-term struggle. There were many criticisms, for example, of the negotiated agreement that ended the grape boycott in the 1970s because important goals had not yet been achieved. But the judgment of the United Farm Workers leadership was that it was time to produce tangible results for union members and to move on with the struggle in other ways.

These decisions may have been far from ideal, but they may also have been the best that could be achieved given the political, personal, and financial resources of the less powerful party. This is not to justify the social situation that created this choice. But sometimes a collaborative process is the best way for individuals or groups to choose among the limited options they realistically have, even if all of these options are poor. Furthermore, there are also times when it is better to accept defeat in the name of a longer-term organizing effort than to cooperate prematurely for token gains.

It is important to be aware of the different implications for social justice inherent in different approaches to engaging and resolving conflict. On one hand, pushing for the resolution of a conflict before those involved have realized their potential for enhancing their personal power or achieving social justice raises major ethical questions. Providing a seemingly benign collaborative process that interferes with the access people would otherwise have to more empowering conflict resolution approaches also raises questions. On the other hand a less than ideal resolution may be a necessary intermediate step along a complicated and unpredictable road toward social justice.

None of this means that the field of conflict resolution is ethically neutral about social change. Built into the underlying philosophy and approach of most practitioners is the notion that people who are empowered to assert their interests in a collaborative yet forceful manner are able to advocate for themselves effectively and to make good decisions about complex problems. From the empowerment of individuals, socially constructive outcomes will ensue. This implies a belief and a commitment to *deep democracy* as a foundation for social and personal change. Building this deep democratic foundation means providing not only a format for democratic decision making but also the tools and skills to make such decision making a vital part of people's everyday life. It means giving people access to a significant voice in all the major decisions that affect their lives. For this kind of democracy to be a reality, people need to be protected from oppression, coercion, and violence from those in more powerful positions. Conflict resolution as a field is thus implicitly and usually explicitly committed to empowering people as individuals and to extending democracy and freedom from oppression to everyone.

Power is a complex phenomenon that operates in many often contradictory ways. The use of power can escalate or deescalate a conflict. It can create resistance or overcome it. People can employ their power to create momentum for constructive dialogue and collaborative negotiations, or they can use it to beat others down and to prevent cooperation. Everyone in a conflict has choices about how to use power and how to respond to power. But there is one choice none of us has, whether we are disputants, mediators, or decision makers—we cannot choose to have no power.

Everyone brings power to a conflict. Everyone also brings a set of values, beliefs, and approaches that are rooted in his or her culture. To complete an understanding of the nature of conflict it is necessary to consider the impact of culture on the individuals involved in a dispute and on the conflict process itself.

Chapter Four

Culture and Conflict

Sometimes we are blind to the impact of culture on the conflicts we are dealing with, and sometimes we are overwhelmed by it. Even though culture is the medium within which conflict plays out, to most of us it is as invisible as the air we breathe. As a result it is often easy for us to overlook the critical role cultural norms and practices play in creating conflict, affecting its course, and influencing the way people approach resolution. Conversely, when we do focus on culture, it is easy to view it as the overwhelming determinant of what will occur. Furthermore, as conflict resolvers we often feel hopeless about altering the ways disputants from different cultures approach conflict. When we view a particularly destructive approach to conflict as rooted in cultural practices, we often feel powerless to intervene. We also often have a difficult time distinguishing the impact of culture from the dynamics of dominance.

When we consider the interactions of cultures in conflict, I think we often focus on the wrong question. It is not the differences among cultures that are the most intriguing but the continuities or similarities. And it is not just the difficulties that different cultural practices put in the way of conflict resolution that are instructive but the ways in which people transcend those difficulties as they work across cultural boundaries. The truly amazing thing is not that cultural differences exacerbate conflict but that people often manage fairly well in communicating and relating to individuals from different cultures.

Although conflict theorists have given a great deal of thought to the interplay of conflict and culture and although much has been written about how conflict plays out in different cultural settings, our understanding of how to deal with cross-cultural conflict is still underdeveloped. The challenge we face is to take the enormous impact of culture on conflict into account without becoming either overly deterministic (culture determines conflict behavior) or relativistic (everything—values, behavior, communication, and needs—varies by culture). Cultural norms and practices are critical forces in conflict, but culture does not tell the whole tale. Furthermore, each culture contains many subcultures, and each subculture many groups. Each has a different set of approaches to conflict, just as each of us as individuals do. Culture is also not static. Just as culture affects the course of conflict, conflict affects culture.

What Is Culture?

What do we really mean when we refer to culture? We speak of organizational culture, gender culture, the culture of a community or town, generational culture, and of course ethnic culture, among others. For our purposes, culture may be considered as the enduring norms, values, customs, and behavioral patterns common to a particular group of people. In this sense everyone belongs to multiple different and overlapping cultures, a situation that creates internal conflict at times. The overlapping pattern formed by all these cultures, people's cultural matrix, affects individuals' behavior in conflict and their ability to handle conflict. However, people's own cultural patterns are often invisible to them, because they experience them as a natural part of their environment. As a result, people act within the confines of their cultural matrix often without an awareness that this matrix strongly affects their perceptions of themselves and of others and therefore their behavior in conflict.

Cultural Variables and Continuities

What are the variables in the ways different cultures handle conflict? What are the continuities, or commonalities? The second question is probably the harder one. There are many clear and poignant variables in cultural approaches to conflict, but the continuities are much harder to discern. Some might argue that there is no consistency across all cultures, that culture determines everything about people's approach to conflict (the relativist view). However, I find it a reasonable working hypothesis that there are continuities in the ways people handle conflict and that these continuities go across the bulk of the cultural, ethnic, class, and social divisions in which most of the conflicts that we deal with take place. To what extent this stems from human nature, the common characteristics of the economic, social, and physical environment of most cultures, the increasing impact of a global culture, the high degree of intercultural interaction, or the structure of conflict itself is impossible to determine.

No culture is characterized by one specific conflict style that all its members exhibit. Because individuals differ, each culture will contain a range of behaviors and approaches to conflict. But different cultures do have different norms about conflict behavior, and acceptable behavior in one culture may be deviant in another. For example, in a typical middle-class American community one is likely to encounter a conflict style that tends to be direct, rational, and linear. In contrast, many other cultures have a style that tends to be indirect, emotional, and intuitive. This does not mean that everyone in these cultures has these typical characteristics, or that these characteristics are operative at all times and under all circumstances. Rather I think it means three things: first, although the same *range* of individual styles might be found in all cultures, the *distribution* of these styles varies, so that compared to some other cultures, the middle-class American community tends to have a greater percentage of people whose approach to conflict tends to be direct, rational, and linear; second, the norms of each culture *reinforce* one conflict style over other styles; and third, the behavior that predominates in a conflict *usually* exhibits certain characteristics. Some cultures may suppress individual differences more than others or provide harsher sanctions for exhibiting behaviors different from those allowed by the social norms or the enforced approach of a dominant group. Even so, there is still a range of approaches to conflict, even if sometimes more circumscribed or undercover, in all societies. This is therefore one important continuity across cultures—the multiplicity of ways in which conflict is handled.

The existence of such a range of styles across cultures is what helps individuals from different cultures interact and deal with each other in conflicts. There are individuals in each cultural group whose conflict and communication style is different from that group's normative style and closer to the standard approach of other groups. These people can therefore act as natural *translators* or as *bridges* to other cultures. Furthermore, because of this range of approaches, every culture has some experience in dealing with different styles, even those it labels deviant. The more rigid a culture is and the less it allows different approaches to be employed or different values to be articulated, the less experience and the fewer translators it will have to assist in resolving conflict with individuals or groups operating with different cultural norms and the more difficulty it will have in dealing with cross-cultural conflict. This is true whether the culture is the dominant one in the conflict setting or not. The most enduring empires have been those that allowed different cultures to flourish under their jurisdiction.

Also, I believe all cultures may be described in terms of predominant approaches to avoidance and engagement in conflict. These approaches are universal tendencies that exist by virtue of people's participation in social structures. There are characteristic ways in which each culture avoids and engages in conflict, but the competing tendencies, or pulls, are always present.

How can we get a more specific handle on cultural variables and continuities? The wheel of conflict presented in Figure 1.1 offers one way of understanding the impact of culture on conflict. Roughly speaking, the closer to the center of the wheel we look, the more cross-cultural continuities we will find, and the more we focus on the perimeter, the more cultures will vary. The more we focus on the genuine human needs at the core of conflict, the more we will see patterns that are constant across cultures. As we shift our view toward the surrounding dynamics and move further away from a focus on human needs, the more dramatic the differences among cultures. Cultural gaps are best bridged when people find a mechanism to focus on the fundamental needs at the heart of a conflict. The more people's focus is on the surrounding forces independent of their connection to the underlying needs, the more difficult it is to bridge cultural differences. Let's look at each element of the wheel from this perspective.

Needs

Needs are the key area of continuity across cultures. All humans have survival needs. In all conflicts, disputants have interests. Everyone has identity needs. People understand their needs very differently, they express them in many ways, and they try to meet them in many ways. How people experience the identity-based needs of community, autonomy, intimacy, and meaning changes dramatically, and the relative weight each need has under different circumstances is also variable. But the needs themselves are not that different. One key to reaching out across cultures is to understand how people experience and satisfy these needs in their cultural context. The types of human interests are relevant across cultural contexts as well. Everyone has psychological interests (the need to maintain face seems pretty universal), procedural interests (some may care more about democratic process, others more about decorum and tradition), and of course substantive interests. Everyone has survival needs—although these may be more variable than we might at first assume. All cultures provide some mechanisms for people to experience autonomy, intimacy, community and meaning, and when those identity-based needs are significantly threatened, no matter the culture, conflict is almost sure to ensue.

Emotions

It is a common belief that people from other cultures lead emotional lives that are entirely different from one's own. Many people seem to think that someone who comes from a very different background is unlikely to respond to conflict or loss with the same range of emotions as they do. In fact, human beings across a wide range of cultures exhibit similar emotional responses. If people are insulted or attacked, they respond with anger or fear. If they experience a major loss, they grieve. If they accomplish something very important to them, they rejoice. For all practical purposes, people from different cultures experience the same range of emotions in conflict, and for conflict to be dealt with, mechanisms for the release and validation of feelings are necessary.

But which emotions are considered acceptable and how they may be expressed vary tremendously. In some cultures any overt display of strong feelings violates important norms, and therefore feelings are either suppressed or are expressed only subtly and indirectly. In others the ability to express emotions strongly and dramatically is valued. Which emotions are acceptable and which are not can also vary. Expressing anger or an upset may be more or less acceptable than expressing excitement or love. In some contexts it is accepted that emotions can change rapidly and that there is no loss of face in expressing a feeling and then letting it go. In other settings the expression of strong emotions is more likely to lead to a serious loss of face or a permanent change in a relationship. This is related to how acceptable it is to acknowledge the existence of a conflict at all.

In the United States, expressing a disagreement or acknowledging a conflict does not in itself usually threaten the relationship. In fact, naming a conflict and acknowledging its existence often calms an interaction and circumscribes the degree to which a dispute might affect a relationship. Here, there are norms that promote the expression of feelings. Actually, in much of white middle-class America, the norm seems to be that it is OK to describe and discuss strong feelings but not to display them too dramatically—at least not in social or business settings. White Americans are more likely to lose face if they "lose" an important conflict or if they lose control over their behavior. In other cultural contexts, however, the expression of disagreement or the admission of a conflict is a severe and often permanent challenge to a relationship. This can lead to some interesting conflict dynamics.

Three cultures intersected when a Caucasian colleague of mine mediated a dispute between a Native American and a Hispanic living in a housing project. Their ethnicity was different, but all three were single mothers. Anna, the Native American, had called the project manager to complain about the misbehavior of the adolescent sons of Maria, the Hispanic woman, which had included "appropriating" some lawn furniture and spraying Anna's five- and seven-year-old daughters with a garden hose. The police were called and paid a visit to Maria and her sons. Maria was furious at being "ratted on" and proceeded to confront Anna in no uncertain terms about going to the project manager rather than to Maria. Anna, uncomfortable with being confronted and with the level of emotionality that was being displayed, said almost nothing but complained again to the project manager. The situation seemed to be escalating so the mediator was brought in.

In the mediation, Maria again started to escalate the conflict and Anna again withdrew, in keeping with the ways both were accustomed to handling emotions in conflict. The mediator suggested that they each had strong feelings about what happened and what they wanted, but what they first needed to do was to understand each other's concerns more fully. That was almost all she had to do. Maria and Anna began talking about what it was like to be single parents in this project, how little support there was for children of any age and how few facilities, and how much each of them felt under duress. They walked out, almost arm in arm, leaving the mediator to wonder why she had been needed in the first place.

The emotions these single mothers experienced were similar, and the needs motivating them could easily be understood across their cultures. But their different norms about expressing emotions and dealing with conflict directly were major barriers to their communication. When the interaction centered on their cultural continuities, as opposed to their differences, they could quickly find common ground. Interestingly, the mediator, operating from her cultural context, had to struggle with a desire to have a more substantive agreement, but the two in dispute both came from a background where the establishment (or reestablishment) of the relationship was far more important than any of the specifics of the dispute.

Different cultures exhibit variations in acceptable and effective ways of acknowledging and validating feelings. Many conflict resolvers seem to think that articulating a nonjudgmental understanding of another person's expressed emotion is the best way to validate that emotion. This is not always the case, not even in middle-class America. Some people need their emotion to be reflected, acted upon, or overtly recognized in some way in order to feel heard. However, many others do not want an expression of emotions to be named, focused on, or directly addressed. For many, another person's quiet physical and emotional presence or nonverbal acceptance is more validating and less embarrassing.

Communication

Given the extreme variations in the ways people communicate, depending on age, gender, ethnicity, and other factors, it is amazing that we ever understand each other at all. People from different cultures vary in how directly they communicate, how they use verbal and nonverbal cues, how they develop rapport, and how long they take to establish a personal connection before moving to substantive discussions. Their communication may vary in pace, in loudness, in whether it tends to be linear and sequential or circular and parallel, and so forth.

We are aware of many of these differences. They fuel much of our humor and literature. From Mark Twain to Garrison Keillor, American humorists have used stereotypes about the ways people from different cultural backgrounds communicate and interact to create vivid characters and to poke fun at human foibles. Outlandish though these depictions may be, they demonstrate the wide variation in communication styles, the stereotyping that occurs as a result, and the difficulty that this causes in handling issues that arise across cultures.

One way of understanding cultural differences in communication is to look at the themes that underlie people's communications styles. We find these in people's metaphors and in the underlying worldview their communication implies. This method of understanding provided a colleague and me with the key to overcoming an impasse when we were asked to mediate a dispute between a Native American group and a large corporation.

> The disputants could have been speaking two different languages (and maybe in a sense they were), given how little each seemed to understand of what the other was saying. The Native Americans, who were representatives of the tribal government, and the corporation, which had a large facility located on tribal land, had many common interests. They had a lot to offer each other, but every time they communicated the conflict seemed to escalate. The members of the Native American group employed a normative or value-based style of communication; they focused on their identity-based needs, particularly on the importance of preserving the tribe's sense of autonomy and community. Their language was full of references to the tribe's sovereignty, its dignity, and its efforts to preserve the Native American heritage in the face of continuous

pressure to conform to the business and legal practices of white middle-class America. The corporation used a more utilitarian, or interest-based, style of communication. Its representatives were outcome focused, concentrating on what made "business sense" for both groups. Their language was replete with references to "sound business practices," "mutual economic advantage," "costs and benefits," and so forth.

Each group, in its own way, was trying to understand and address the other's concerns, but this was not working. When the business representatives discussed their interests, the Native Americans felt that their culture and values were being dismissed and that they were being told money was more important than identity. When the Native Americans discussed their identity concerns, the corporate representatives felt that they would never "get real" and focus on the issues that had to be resolved. They felt that they could spend forever listening to and validating the cultural issues of the Native Americans, but that they would never get around to working on the business questions that were important to them.

The key to our getting a handle on this case was to listen to the language and terminology that each group kept using. The differences were dramatic. So after listening to both sides long enough to get a feel for the communication obstacles, we shared our observations with both groups. We expressed our sense that the members of one group were communicating about their values and the members of the other about their business concerns, and we suggested that both were important. We also very explicitly discussed the different types of language they were using. This seemed to strike home for both groups. Their challenge, we said, was to understand and acknowledge both issues in language that made sense to each other. Then we coached each group briefly (it was important not to patronize the groups through overcoaching) about how they might do this. I am sure that these communication styles continue to this day to interfere with their relationship from time to time. But during this particular interaction each was able to understand to some extent the two groups' different approaches to communication and to translate from one communication style to another well enough to draft a set of proposals to take back to its respective leadership.

Different cultures communicate their thinking in very different ways during conflict. Some cultures convey meaning through stories, anecdotes, metaphors, and comparisons. Others use logic and analysis. In some cultures, so-called objective presentations, heavily loaded with facts, charts, supporting documentation, and the

symbols of professionalism are highly valued. But there are many cultures in which such an approach appears cold, manipulative, and unreal. In these cultures, the personality, values, life experience, and commitment of the speaker is the key to establishing credibility.

The meaning of gestures, eye contact, and even particular words varies from culture to culture as does their potential for generating conflict. In some cultures direct eye contact is a sign of attention and respect. In others it can convey insolence and challenge. I still get confused about when *bad* means bad and when it means good. In some cultures, people can use many angry and hostile words, but as long as no one touches anyone else, there is no direct challenge to fight. When someone touches someone else in anger (for example by jabbing a finger), however, a fight becomes almost inevitable. In other groups such touching is not seen as a "call down" to fight, but the use of certain key words (*mother, faggot,* or *liar,* for example) is. The culturally based misinterpretation of the meaning of certain words or gestures can thus lead to a quick and dramatic conflict escalation (see, for example, Kochman, 1981).

Different cultures have different behavioral norms about communication. For example most Americans and Western Europeans value taking turns, speaking one person at a time, and taking subjects one at a time. Interrupting is considered rude (although when the person doing it comes from a dominant group or power position, it is expected rudeness). If I say, "Pardon me, but you are interrupting," I am delivering a very clear message that the person is behaving inappropriately. However, in many cultures, overlapping conversation is natural and acceptable, and most conversations are characterized by several people talking at once, often about different subjects. When someone from one background, accuses someone from a different background of interrupting, we may be seeing cross-cultural conflict in action.

These dynamics can be present when people are talking in the same language, but when their languages are different, there is an added dimension. The structure of language varies greatly. For example, Americans tend to use the conditional tense much more than is usual among people in parts of Eastern Europe. To certain Europeans, therefore, Americans often sound as if they are beating around the bush, whereas to Americans Europeans sometimes seem rude and blunt. This is to some extent a result of their languages. Words that have similar meaning in different languages often have very different emotional impacts. When people must communicate through translators, the richness, nuance, and emotional complexity of a message can easily be lost, and the intent of the speaker can easily be misinterpreted.

With all these differences in how people communicate, it is easy to overlook the commonalities. The most basic constant is that everyone fundamentally wants to be understood and will usually respond well to others who are making genuine, respectful efforts to grasp what is being said. In fact, even in conflict, people will usually try to help each other understand what they are saying. If they sense that others are sincerely trying to communicate and to understand, people will usually try to find ways to clarify, explain, or simplify in order to facilitate communication. In the middle of a conflict, the need for this can be exasperating, and it is easy for people to doubt each other's sincerity of purpose, but the natural desire to understand and be understood often comes through even under very difficult circumstances.

Another commonality is that all human communication is multidimensional. All individuals convey meaning through what they say, how they say it, and what they don't say, through both verbal and nonverbal messages, and through both the emotional and rational components of their messages. People everywhere interpret communication, usually unconsciously, on all these levels. When one type of communication is not working, people instinctively resort to another. Certain types of nonverbal communication are fairly universal. For example, how someone looks, sounds, and behaves when angry, sad, happy, or confused has important similarities across cultures.

Values

Basic value differences can cause conflict among different cultures, and so can values about conflict itself. Three types of values about conflict are important to consider: values about content, process, and outcome. Content values concern the subject of the conflict itself. What kinds of issues is it appropriate or inappropriate to engage in conflict about? For example, in some cultures it is fine to argue openly about religion and politics, but in others it is considered inappropriate. Process values concern how conflict is conducted. How should issues be raised and to whom? Is it all right to raise a conflict directly with an elder or a superior? Should one negotiate with one's subordinates? How transparent should disputants be about their thoughts and plans? When should they suggest solutions? How freely should they share their emotions? Outcome values suggest what kinds of results are acceptable. Do people value compromise, collaboration, winning, or self-sacrifice?

Despite the many differences in values, disputants almost always share values as well. These concurrences of values can be links that help people get beyond their differences. Some values are almost universal, but any two cultures are likely to share many less widely held values as well. As the following example illustrates, it was their common values that led the Smiths and Nelsons to overcome their very fundamental differences about who should rear Jonah.

> Jonah, a half Asian American, half African American boy, was four years old when his parents' rights were terminated as the result of a history of severe abuse and neglect. He had been placed for two years with the Smiths, Caucasian foster parents who now wanted to adopt him. Shortly before the adoption process entered its final stages, the Nelsons, a maternal aunt and her husband, who had previously been unknown to the adoption agency, were located. They said that they were interested in adopting Jonah. A study of the Nelsons by the adoption agency indicated that this African American couple was also quite capable of providing Jonah with a good home. The Nelsons felt very strongly that they should be given preference because they were relatives and because of the racial issues involved. The Smiths were equally adamant about the importance of keeping Jonah in the only stable home he had ever had. The differences between the families were reflected in similar discussions among the staff of the agency. This had the makings of a very destructive and potentially protracted court battle. The conflict was therefore referred to me for mediation. Due to the ethnic issues involved, I co-mediated it with an African American colleague of mine.
>
> Whenever the Nelsons and the Smiths discussed the relative importance of biological family, race, and continuity of care, they found themselves in deep conflict. They simply did not agree, and their different values about this were a source of great contention. But there were two very important unifying

factors. One was that both couples cared deeply about Jonah. The other was that they shared many more values than they disputed. Both were very committed to children, marriage, and family. Both took a hard line against the use of drugs and alcohol. Both were very religious. In mediation they were each able to see that their value differences were more about priorities than about fundamental disagreements. That is, all felt that Jonah needed continuity, stability, and connection with his biological family. All felt that racial identity was an important issue. When they were able to find a way of talking about and sharing their common values, they were able to begin to relate to each other more effectively. Eventually, an interim agreement was reached. During the time this agreement was active, the Nelsons visited with Jonah, with the participation of the Smiths. As time went on the Nelsons adopted the role of aunt and uncle, and an ongoing agreement about contact was worked out. In the end the Smiths adopted Jonah, but the Nelsons assumed an active role in his life.

Structure

All cultures establish structures for handling conflict, but these structures can be very dissimilar. People accustomed to one structure may feel alienated or exploited when they are forced to use a very different one. Some cultures promote a democratic and rights-based approach to conflict resolution, whereas others use a more hierarchical and power-based approach. Cultures vary in the degree to which they rely on systems rooted in formal authority and position or systems focused on personal prestige and influence. They also differ in whether they have mechanisms for counteracting differences in power and prestige or whether they believe that such differentials form a legitimate basis for determining outcomes. Some societies have very well established legal systems that can be relatively easily accessed to settle many conflicts. Other societies have few such formal structures, and those that exist are viewed with suspicion. Even in societies like the United States, however, that have highly developed formal structures for resolving conflicts, most disputes are still handled on an informal basis. Without the natural mechanisms for conflict resolution that are embedded in families, communities, and other small-group structures, any formal system would be quickly overwhelmed. This is true of every culture and society.

Another structural variable is the role of family and community in conflict resolution. In some cultures the extended family is the prevailing social structure and geographical mobility is relatively low, whereas in others there is great mobility and less powerful extended family systems. This has a great impact on how conflict and decisions are handled in these societies. In Australian Aboriginal communities (and in many other traditional cultures), conflict resolution is the purview of the elders of the community. For anyone else to take on the role of mediator or arbitrator is unthinkable. It is also a violation to go to outside structures, such as a court system, to resolve an internal conflict.

Despite these structural differences there are important and sometimes surprising cultural continuities as well. Almost all cultures have rights-based approaches and a rights framework within which certain types of conflict can be conducted. They also always have informal mechanisms for handling conflict. When investigating how conflict is handled in different cultures, one can usually start by asking two significant questions. What are the formal and informal mechanisms for addressing conflict? (Cultures always have both.) And what are the structural inducements and obstacles for different groups or individuals to using those mechanisms? (Cultures always have these inducements and obstacles too.)

History

Cultures are not bound by their historical patterns, but each culture's approach to conflict cannot be understood without an appreciation of its people's key historical experiences with conflict. In the countries and satellite states of the former Soviet Union, even as people try to learn a more democratic and participatory approach, it is easy to see the impact of a long history of centralized, hierarchical, and often repressive means for handling conflict. The impact of the Holocaust on Jewish cultural attitudes toward conflict is profound. It affects attitudes toward conflict engagement, avoidance, compromise, and social justice, among other things. All cultures carry with them historical experiences about what works in conflict and what does not and what the likely outcomes to conflict might be. In the history of most cultures, there are key events that have come to symbolize cultural values and beliefs about conflict. In understanding cultural approaches to conflict, it is important to understand both the general historical context in which conflict has been handled and the key events that form the common cultural memory or experience of conflict.

When U.S. or Western European conflict resolvers share their ideas and experiences with people from different backgrounds, they often encounter historically based attitudes about conflict that are very different from their own. Unless these experiences can be understood and the services or training altered accordingly, the value of a Western approach to conflict resolution for other cultures may be very limited, as a colleague and I found in Bulgaria.

> Conflict in the Balkans has a much more ominous meaning than in the United States. Over the last several years, a partner and I have worked closely with colleagues in Bulgaria to establish a project to promote cooperation among different ethnic groups. When we began the project, we envisioned it as a program for ethnic conflict resolution. Our Bulgarian colleagues very politely but firmly let us know that it would not work to think of it in that way. In Bulgaria, which borders on Yugoslavia, Macedonia, Greece, Turkey, and Romania, conflict means ethnic cleansing, civil war, and high levels of violence. Furthermore, Bulgaria's history is the story of domination by one or another foreign empire. Bulgaria has a history of coming out on the bottom in conflicts, unless rescued by other powerful players. Conflict is associated with loss, destruction, social chaos, and outside domination. It is definitely not seen as an opportunity to work out differences and search for collaborative solutions. Faced with this cultural history, we decided to think about the project as a program to build multicultural cooperation. This was a critical first step in bringing different ethnic groups together to discuss issues that were of concern to them and also in helping us understand how we might work productively with our Bulgarian colleagues. [For more information about the Multi-Cultural Cooperation Project in Bulgaria, see Mayer, Wildau, and Valchev, 1995.]

History also sometimes provides the bridge by which different cultures can begin to understand each other better. Often different cultures share certain historical experiences. When I worked in Poland a number of years ago, I was very grateful when some of my colleagues there took me on a tour of the Warsaw ghetto. My Polish associates and I were all children or grandchildren of people who had suffered very much at the hands of the Nazis. This element of shared history was an important bond, despite the fact that they and I had grown up in completely different circumstances. Even when individuals from different cultural groups have very little shared history, the process of learning about each other's past and the ways this history has influenced each party's approach to communication and conflict resolution can be an important tool for building increased understanding among them.

Handling Culture in Conflict

Given all the different ways that culture influences people's interactions in conflict, how does it happen that most of us normally succeed in overcoming these differences? Although cultural differences breed conflict under many circumstances, most of the time people bridge these gaps fairly well. Despite the publicity and focus that is so often placed on ethnic conflict, in most parts of the world different ethnic groups are able to work through their differences well enough to live, work, and play side by side.

There are several, sometimes paradoxical approaches that help people handle cultural differences successfully.

Cultural Sensitivity and Cultural Obliviousness

Being attuned and open to ethnic, class, gender, and other cultural differences is often key to handling conflict. Conflict engagement is a continuous learning process that in part involves becoming familiar with other people's cultural approach toward conflict and communication. The more open and respectful disputants are about the different approaches others have to conflict, the more successful they will be in dealing with conflict across cultures. Increasing one's cross-cultural awareness and competence is a lifelong challenge, and engaging in conflicts across culture is a powerful learning tool, when people are open to that learning. It may not be easy, but it is rewarding.

However, sometimes people handle cultural differences best by ignoring them and reaching out on a simple person-to-person basis, focusing on the individual rather than the culture. Sometimes, being too focused on cultural issues or differences can undercut a person's basic ability to interact with others. The fundamental desire to connect with others is a core continuity across cultures. An overemphasis on cultural differences, particularly on the part of someone from a dominant culture, can be patronizing and controlling. Of course the ideal is for conflict participants to synthesize these two approaches, to be sensitive and respectful of cultural differences and to relate to each other as individuals, not as simple carriers of particular cultural patterns.

Focusing on One's Own Culture to Learn About Another

I did not really understand English grammar until I studied a foreign language. Similarly, I do not think people can really understand their own culture until they spend time in a different one. Unless someone has something with which to contrast his or her patterns of behavior and beliefs, it is hard to recognize what they are and to understand how culturally relativistic they may be. In learning to deal with conflict in other cultures, the first key is to recognize the conflict patterns that characterize one's own. Once people articulate the many different cultural norms about conflict from which they operate, it is easier for them to become aware of the ways their norms might differ from those of others. Of course, as with language, it is very hard to do this until one has experienced other cultures in some depth.

Beyond Sensitivity: Enjoying Cultural Differences

When I think of what has helped me bridge cultural gaps, it is more than just sensitivity; it is enjoyment of the differences, even when they arise in conflicts. For the most part people are curious about each other's background and culture. When someone is upset or angry, this curiosity may not be what is in the forefront of his or her consciousness, but it is still there. Differences in the ways people in conflict approach a situation, although potential sources of frustration and complication, are also stimulating, engaging, and fun. Furthermore, they provide an interesting and valuable mirror to one's natural tendencies. If people can have a sense of humor and fascination about this, they can approach cultural differences as a source of strength and creativity as well as recognizing the obstacles they can also impose.

Recognizing Realistic Limits—And Pushing Them

People can learn a great deal about how to interact across cultural boundaries and about the various approaches of other cultures to conflict. Individuals from vastly different backgrounds can work through issues effectively and in doing so can become much more cross-culturally competent. This is a key to promoting a more peaceful world and to achieving many of our personal goals as well. Although it can be a daunting task at times, it is rewarding and often fun to do this. But there are limits as well. No one can know what another culture is really like unless he or she has lived inside it for a long time (and maybe not even then). People can peel the outer layers of cultural practices, but there is a limit to how deep they can go in understanding other cultures, just as there is a limit to how far anyone can go in understanding another person.

The more people understand their own culture, the deeper their understanding of others can be. The more they work with other cultures, the greater their sensitivity and understanding can become. In the end, however, everyone must recognize the limits on their understanding and plan accordingly—especially when conflict is high and much is at stake. By respecting the limits on their ability to grasp the depth of other cultural realities, people show respect for other cultures. Disputants cannot totally abandon their own culture in order to adapt to another, neither should they demand that others abandon their cultures. Instead, when dealing with other cultures, people must find a way of respecting other approaches and opening themselves up to different ways of communicating, without abandoning themselves in the process. How can they do this?

They can recognize limits and push them at the same time. If an individual comes from a culture in which communication is generally linear and one person speaks at a time, but is now dealing with a culture in which *polychronic*, that is, multiple and simultaneous, conversations are the norm, that person may well want to develop tolerance for this new communication style. But he or she will also find it necessary at times to express a need for more linear communication as well, in order to be effective and genuinely present in an interaction. People must often negotiate behavior that allows individuals from different cultural backgrounds to participate fully and with power. This was a lesson driven home to me by my own inability to ignore a television.

> When I was a youth worker in New York and Colorado, I would frequently visit people in their homes. Many of these people had a norm that allowed polite and focused discussion while the television was playing in the background. I found that I could not communicate effectively under these circumstances. Either because of my own cognitive limitations or because of the culture I came from, I found the TV extremely distracting. Initially, I thought people were being rude or dismissive of me, and maybe some were, but I also experienced genuine warmth and interest from many others.
>
> At first, I did not feel right asking people to turn their TV sets off so I could focus. I tried ignoring the television, sitting so I could not see it, and increasing my powers of concentration. Sometimes this worked; usually it did not. Finally, I found myself, somewhat apologetically, explaining that I was having a hard time focusing and asking whether the TV could be turned off or down or whether we could talk in a different room. Mostly, people were fine with my request, but I am sure that several of them felt I was being bossy. It was a dilemma I struggled with repeatedly, and if I were in the same situation today, I am sure it would still be a challenge. But if I had not taken care of my own needs, stemming at least in part from my upbringing, I would have been less able to bridge other more important gaps.

Respecting and Seeking Diversity

Those who work across cultural boundaries, and that essentially is everyone, should be aware of the need for diversity within their own groups, teams, or organizations. A commitment to diversity in organizations and education is not simply about being politically correct; rather it is about increasing everyone's ability to be effective in a multicultural world. It is also important to recognize when it is time to enlist the aid of people from different backgrounds in order to work successfully across cultural boundaries. Of course sometimes cultural, class, ethnic, gender, or other barriers are exactly the reason it is necessary to bring in third parties to help disputants resolve conflicts.

Separating Culture from Exploitation

Are some cultures racist, sexist, violent, abusive, rigid, or immoral? All cultures probably are at times. Or more precisely, all dynamic cultures have to deal with issues of power, exploitation, violence, prejudice, and the like. Different cultures have different ways of handling these tendencies, but to see them as embedded in individual cultures rather than as possible products of human interaction within most social structures is not accurate, helpful, or fair. It is not German culture that produced the Holocaust, American culture that produced My Lai, or Native American culture that produces high rates of alcoholism. It is important to understand the social forces that have led to these developments and to understand how they interact with culture. But is also important to understand culture separately from this. Otherwise, when in conflict across cultural lines, it is easy to condemn the opposing culture itself or to see oneself as in conflict with a culture. It is more helpful to view culture as a positive if complicated and sometimes paradoxical force.

As I write this, NATO planes are bombing Serbia in an attempt to deter aggression against Kosovar Albanians. How can the horrific ethnic cleansing carried out by Serbian troops and militias against the Kosovars be explained? Did this happen because the Yugoslavian president, Slobodan Milosevic, is evil or crazy? Was it rooted in the destructive nationalism that runs rampant in that region? Was it a natural outcome of a harsh and violent culture? I do not think an explanation that relies on assertions about evil, insanity, or cultural dysfunctions is either helpful or accurate. There is no doubt that there was evil and craziness aplenty in the Nazi leadership, for example, but that does not explain the Holocaust. It is too easy, too comforting to resort to such simplistic analyses. The truth is much more complicated, significant, and scary.

To begin to understand how such horror could happen, we have to look at the historical factors, the structure out of which these developments arose, the values that were in play, how people interacted and communicated, and above all the fundamental needs that people were asserting or defending. We have to look at the forces promoting a genocidal response and the reason that restraining forces were not adequate. Looking at things in this way is scary because we are forced to face the possibility, even likelihood, that such behavior will occur again. Such an approach makes us give up the distancing from these events that we achieve when we label other people or cultures as crazy or evil. When we can understand these horrors without resorting to such easy explanations, we begin to see how maybe they could happen in our world as well. But only by having the courage to do this can we begin to develop the understanding that can aid in preventing such atrocities in the future.

Culture and Power

Much of what appears to be cultural conflict is really an attempt at cultural domination or forced acculturation. When one culture is in a more powerful social position and can impose many of its norms and structures on other cultures, then the dynamics of dominance and submission must be considered. Under these circumstances, the dominated culture is likely to learn a great deal about how to operate within the more powerful culture. It is less likely however that the dominating culture will learn as much about how to work with the less advantaged group. But dominance and influence are different phenomena. The less powerful culture may in fact intrude many of its norms into the more dominant group, despite its weaker position.

A clash of cultures is usually about conflicting norms and values. Past conflicts in the United States between the view of the majority and the view of the Mormons about polygamy or between the majority and Hmong views about child marriage rituals may be viewed as examples of a genuine clash of cultural values (not that other factors were not involved) in a context of cultural dominance. Many other so-called cultural wars, however, are probably less about values and more about dominance. For example, it can be argued that the history of U.S. drug laws is less about culture than it is about efforts to provide a social control mechanism for dealing with immigrant groups (for example, the passage of opium laws is related to Chinese immigration and of marijuana laws to Mexican immigration). In understanding cross-cultural conflict, it is important to distinguish between issues of values and dominance. Mixing them together makes it harder to focus on the issue of power and can unnecessarily entrench people in a values dispute. But separating them can also be very difficult.

Dominant cultures often try to strip less powerful groups of many of their cultural practices and symbols. In its simpler form, this action involves enforcing a certain style of communicating, dressing, or interacting. At other times it involves a much more deeply rooted effort to prevent people from practicing their religion, speaking their language, or continuing to live in their own communities. Such efforts strike at core identity-based needs of the dominated cultural group—their needs for autonomy, meaning, and community. Occasionally, it is cultural differences that genuinely fuel such a conflict, but more often it is the threat that a privileged group or elite feels from a subservient one that is the driving force. Thus such conflicts are more often about power and social justice than about the clash of cultural values.

How Cultural Differences Help

It is easy to focus on the ways that cultural differences complicate and confuse a conflict. But perhaps the more profound impact of diversity on conflict is positive. So much about effective conflict engagement involves a learning process. Conflict provides an opportunity for disputants to learn more about themselves, the people with whom they have a conflict, and the issues involved. If they can make use of this opportunity, they will be more effective as conflict participants. This is true whether we are talking of family, communal, organizational, or international conflict. When disputants are operating on familiar territory, it is often hard for them to take on this learning, to reflect on themselves and to take a broader view of their situation. All too often they are far too sure of themselves. But when there is conflict across cultural boundaries, disputants cannot rely on the easy explanations or set responses that they may use in other circumstances and are often forced to be more self-reflective. Furthermore, the interplay of different cultures can increase disputants' creativity, allowing them to increase the options that they bring to bear on a particular conflict.

This discussion is not meant to dismiss the difficulty and often the tragedy that cultural conflict can entail. The most serious conflicts in our world, with the gravest consequences, involve cross-cultural issues. They cannot be ended by easy solutions that simply involve goodwill, sensitivity, and open-mindedness (although these qualities always help). But even in these dreadfully serious situations (in Bosnia, Kosovo, Northern Ireland, the West Bank of Palestine, Rwanda, and so forth), the ultimate resolution must involve something other than the simple separation of the cultures. Resolution must involve a new approach to interaction, in which the diversity of people becomes a source of strength and not a cause of tragedy.

Part Two

Resolution

Chapter Five

The Nature of Resolution

With conflict, comes resolution, or at least that is normally our goal. But what do we mean by resolution, and how do we achieve it? We use the word in very different ways, and we have many ideas about what it implies. In the field of conflict resolution the usual assumption is that resolution is equivalent to agreement about particular issues underlying a dispute. If the parties to a dispute can agree on an outcome that is mutually acceptable, then the conflict has been resolved. When a divorcing couple agree upon a parenting plan or the division of assets, then a resolution has been attained. When environmentalists, government officials, and industrialists agree on regulations for emission controls, then a resolution has been achieved. When a manufacturer and a plaintiff in a product liability case agree on a settlement, the issue has been resolved. When Bosnian Muslims, Croatians, and Serbs agree on boundaries and governmental structures within Bosnia, there is resolution to a conflict.

But in each of these situations resolution is limited at best. Are the divorcing couple still in conflict? Do disagreements remain among environmentalists, regulators, and industry? Do product liability issues remain? Does conflict continue to characterize the relationships in Bosnia? Of course. Even when agreements are reached on very narrow issues, it is likely that not all the parties experience genuine resolution. The image of disputants coming together to consider a major conflict, arriving at an agreement that adequately satisfies their essential concerns, and thereby fully resolving the conflict suggests a very misleading goal for conflict resolvers. Most serious conflicts do not have such neat resolutions. Often the disputants cannot even imagine a solution that would

97

constitute such a complete and liberating resolution. That is because resolution and agreement are not the same.

Resolution has many aspects, and serious conflicts are seldom resolved in simple ways. Resolution occurs through a series of different activities, over time, and usually with many setbacks along the way. It is a process of letting go of conflict, of moving past it, and of gaining the energy, lessons, and growth that a conflict has to offer. This process can be somewhat liberating because it frees up the energy that has been tied up in the conflict, but it can also result in a feeling of loss when the conflict has provided meaning and focus for people. In the resolution process each party usually becomes increasingly clear about his or her essential needs and secure in the belief that these needs are being met. Achieving a resolution involves work and movement along several dimensions.

Dimensions of Resolution

The dimensions of resolution parallel the dimensions of conflict. The process of resolution occurs along cognitive, emotional, and behavioral dimensions. We can think of each dimension in terms of the individuals embroiled in conflict or in terms of the conflict system as a whole.

Cognitive Resolution

Whether disputants have reached resolution in a conflict depends to a large extent on how they view the situation. If they believe that the conflict is resolved, perceive that their key issues have been addressed, think that they have reached closure on the situation, and view the conflict as part of their past as opposed to their future, then an important aspect of resolution has been reached. Sometimes people make a deliberate decision that it is time to move beyond their conflict. They are resolved to be done with it, and if they can hold to that resolve, they have to some extent willed themselves to resolution. Resolution at this level can precede or result from resolution of the emotional or behavioral components. Mostly, however, the cognitive dimension of resolution develops in tandem with the other dimensions.

In considering the conflict system as a whole, we need to look at the beliefs and perceptions that seem to dominate the interactions among the different parts of the system. For example, there often comes a time after a divorce has been finalized when former family members no longer define themselves as being in conflict. Sometimes gradually, sometimes suddenly, a change occurs and the situation is redefined in the family system from one in which conflict is the predominant theme and defining characteristic to one in which cooperation or minimal involvement is the model. Individuals may arrive at this at different times and to different extents, but when this change becomes the dominant ideology within the new family system, then the redefined family as a whole will begin to operate in accordance with this new belief.

Resolution on the cognitive dimension is often the most difficult to attain because people tenaciously hang onto their perceptions and beliefs about a conflict. Disputants may be locked into a set of behaviors and anchored in an emotional response as well, but people can decide to change behavior, and emotional responses often vary quickly and repeatedly. Beliefs and perceptions are usually more rigid. They are often the cornerstone of a person's sense of stability and order, particularly in the midst of confusing and threatening situations. People cling to their beliefs and perceptions because to question them threatens to upset their sense of themselves and their world, and this sense is an essential guide through difficult times. Also, many people equate changing their views of a situation with admitting that they were wrong, something most people do not readily do.

Although difficult to reach, this is also the dimension in which some of the most profound change can occur during the process of conflict. When disputants change their essential view of the people with whom they are in conflict, the nature of the conflict, or the issues themselves, a long lasting and important type of resolution can occur. This possible result underlies some very interesting and important conflict resolution activities, such as victim offender mediation, ethnic reconciliation programs, South Africa's Truth Commissions, and citizen diplomacy initiatives. These efforts are all founded on the recognition that if people do not change their view of each other, if they do not learn to see each other as human beings, and if their basic beliefs about a conflict remain locked in an adversarial frame, genuine resolution is unlikely.

Often it is not possible to work directly or exclusively on this type of resolution. If the perceptions of a person in conflict are to change, they are most likely to do so through progress on the other dimensions of resolution, through a variety of healing and confidence-building activities, through events that force the person to reevaluate his or her views, and through time and maturation.

Two ways conflict resolvers try to help disputants move toward cognitive resolution are the creation of cognitive dissonance and the successive reframing of the conflict. Cognitive dissonance occurs when two values or beliefs held by an individual come into conflict with each other, forcing some level of change in that person's belief system (Festinger, 1957). When mediators say to divorcing parents, "You have to decide whether you love your children more than you hate your ex-spouse," they are attempting to invoke cognitive dissonance that will move people away from their embattled stance. The hope is that a new cognitive framework will result that will be more amenable to a resolution process.

Reframing (which I discuss more fully in the next two chapters) is an attempt to recast the way in which the conflict is presented to provide a greater likelihood that resolution can be achieved. When a mediator helps two business partners redefine the issue of how to divide up work responsibilities as the question of how to work together to keep the business from going under, a significant reframing of the conflict has occurred. Invoking cognitive dissonance and reframing the conflict are both efforts to help disputants alter their perceptions about the nature of the conflict, the issues, the choices, and the other participants. These approaches are not effective unless they are part of a larger resolution strategy, and they lose their power when used in a manipulative or overly facile manner. But they are often part of an effective resolution effort because they do address the cognitive aspects of the conflict.

Emotional Resolution

The emotional dimension of resolution involves both the way disputants feel about a conflict and the amount of emotional energy they put into it. When people no longer experience the feelings associated with a conflict, or at least not as often or at as high a level of intensity as when they were fully engaged, then an important aspect of resolution has been reached. This may be the most volatile dimension of resolution because emotions change rapidly and repeatedly. Disputants may reach a great deal of emotional closure on a conflict, but then an event or interaction occurs that reawakens their feelings, and suddenly they feel right back in the middle of it.

People experience emotional resolution in very different ways. Some disputants process conflict primarily through this dimension. If they feel better, the conflict must be resolved; if they do not, then no matter what else has occurred, the conflict is still as bad as ever. Others, however, tend to minimize or suppress this aspect of conflict and are often unaware whether they feel emotional closure. In any multiparty conflict a variety of different approaches to this dimension are likely.

> A sure way to experience the emotional dimension of conflict is to find that one's water supply has been poisoned. Several years ago, through the actions of several industrial plants, the water supply of an unincorporated community in the midst of a midsize city was contaminated. An agreement was worked out under which the city would build sewer and water facilities for the neighborhood, at no charge to the residents, and be reimbursed for its costs by the industries that had caused the contamination. However, in accordance with the city's long-standing policy, the water could be provided only if the neighborhood were incorporated into the city. This led to a complex mediation about the terms of the annexation.
>
> Although the neighborhood residents recognized that they were receiving valuable services, which would significantly increase their property values, they were not pleased with many of the regulations they would be subject to once they were incorporated. Residents felt that they were being forced to incorporate in order to receive clean water and should therefore be afforded flexibility about zoning, planning, transportation, and related regulations. The city staff felt the neighborhood was already getting a very sweet deal and much greater financial and planning flexibility than any other newly incorporated area.
>
> In order to reach the complex and comprehensive resolution finally attained, a great deal of time was spent by residents, city officials, and me in working through the emotional, procedural, and substantive issues. We

had neighborhood meetings, conferences with city officials, a variety of negotiating procedures, and many problem-solving meetings. The final agreement
was approved by virtually the entire neighborhood and the city council. The
neighborhood is now incorporated, receiving water and other services, and
there appear to be no outstanding issues related to this conflict.

Despite what appeared to be complete agreement on all the issues, however, there was great variation in how much resolution different participants
felt. Representatives of both the neighborhood and the city were unhappy that
they had had to spend so much energy coming to an agreement. People on
all sides felt disrespected, nit-picked, and misunderstood. There were also significant disputes within each negotiating team. In the end virtually everyone
agreed that the outcome was a positive one that met everyone's essential interests. However, the degree to which people felt they had reached resolution was
incredibly varied. Some felt that the outcome justified the effort and that the
conflict was over. Others continued to see themselves in conflict. They alluded
to how exhausted they were and said that they never should have had to work
that hard to receive a reasonable response from the other side.

For those who continue to feel in conflict, perhaps time and the distance
it brings will help them achieve more complete resolution. But it is also possible that other events will keep the conflict alive and that it will take some people a long time to reach a feeling of resolution. This variety of reactions to a
multifaceted conflict is the norm rather than the exception, even when almost
all the substantive issues have been settled.

One of the best clues to a person's degree of emotional resolution
is the amount of emotional energy he or she continues to put into
the conflict. If a person continues to spend a great deal of time
thinking about a conflict, cannot discuss it without lots of emotional intensity, or needs a great deal of ongoing support to cope
with the emotional aftermath, he or she has clearly not reached
resolution along this dimension.

To some extent emotional closure is a natural result of time
and distance, but it also occurs as disputants become more convinced that their essential needs have been addressed. Sometimes
people cannot arrive at an agreement until they experience
progress on this dimension, but at other times it is only through a
settlement that they can gain the perspective and distance from
a conflict that allow an emotional resolution.

Although it may be easier to think of emotional resolution in terms of the experience of individuals, the concept applies to systems as well. Conflict systems are containers and transmitters of emotional energy. If a system is characterized by a high degree of emotionality, this may overwhelm the individuals involved, regardless of their personal feelings. Similarly, as a conflict system moves toward resolution, individuals who are still very emotionally involved may be carried along toward closure or their emotionality may be marginalized.

This is not an abstract concept. We see it all the time. In a conflict between union and management, the level of emotional energy may be so high that individuals with an emotionally neutral stance are distrusted or pressured to join the emotional mainstream. But when the union and management are ready to move to a less intense emotional relationship, those individuals who continue to be wrapped up in the emotional drama of the conflict become less influential and are often pressured to "relax."

How do people attain emotional resolution? This is usually a complicated process, and we do a disservice to our understanding of resolution by oversimplifying it. Disputants do not often reach resolution simply by "working through their feelings." Having an opportunity to express feelings and having them acknowledged by others is frequently an important part of reaching emotional closure, but it is seldom enough. People can occasionally succeed in suppressing their feelings until those feelings eventually go away, but this is normally not possible if the feelings are strong or the conflict intense.

Often emotional resolution requires a period of escalation during which people experience a conflict more intensely. Sometimes disputants also need a cathartic release of some kind, but this can also escalate a conflict to the point where resolution becomes more difficult. Everyone has his or her own way of working on the emotional dimension of conflict, however people seem to experience several common elements in emotional resolution.

- Feeling they are accepted as individuals and their personalities and values are not under attack (or no longer under attack)
- Feeling they can maintain their dignity, or "face," as they move to resolution

- Feeling their core needs are respected and addressed
- Having enough time to gain perspective and experience healing
- Having others accept their feelings as valid and values as legitimate
- Feeling genuinely and nonjudgmentally heard

The role of forgiveness and apology in reaching emotional resolution can also be critical. I have noticed that delivering an apology is usually more important to reaching closure than receiving one, and forgiving is often more important than being forgiven. Both apologizing and forgiving, when genuinely offered, are acts of emotional resolution. In effect each is a way for people to put some part of the emotional aspect of a conflict behind them. By offering an apology or forgiveness, disputants move themselves toward emotional resolution, even if their action does not have that effect on others. In fact the most powerful apologies or acts of forgiveness are those offered without any expectation of reciprocation.

To be genuine and effective apologies must be unconditional. Someone who is genuinely sorry about something is remorseful regardless of whether someone else forgives him or her or has an apology to make as a response. It is more effective to offer a narrow but genuine and unconditional apology than a broadly framed but conditional statement. Becoming clear about what one is really sorry for is therefore essential for an apology to be effective. However, this is not to say that one person's feelings of remorse cannot be triggered or released by another person's apology.

Forgiveness is also potentially very powerful, but it can be seen as patronizing or self-righteous. In terms of emotional resolution, genuine forgiveness is important not primarily because of what it does for others but because of what it does for the forgiver. Although it can be very healing to be forgiven, a person has to see himself or herself as having done something that requires being forgiven in order to accept it. Forgiveness is essentially an act of letting go and of accepting the essential humanity of people with whom one is in conflict.

Some of the post powerful experiences I have had as a conflict resolver have occurred when genuine acts of apology and forgiveness have occurred. For example, I considered my time with Jim and Ray to be a real gift.

Jim and Ray worked in a manufacturing facility. Jim had been Ray's supervisor for several years, and the two had also been friends, Ray looking at Jim as somewhat of a father figure. Ray was seen as a difficult employee by the management of the facility, and Jim often acted as a peacemaker between Ray and others. Their relationship took a dramatic turn during a tense labor dispute when Ray openly criticized management and needled Jim about being a manager. Jim, under a great deal of pressure during this period, lost his temper and called Ray a "loser, troublemaker, and an asshole to boot."

Ray filed a grievance, and Jim asked for a medical leave of absence. The grievance was never acted on because Jim was gone, Ray's requests were somewhat vague, and neither the union nor the management was sure how to proceed. Jim's leave lasted more than a year, but then he had to return or lose his job. For a variety of reasons, he had to be placed in the same position, returning as Ray's supervisor. I had been working with this facility on designing a new grievance process, and as Jim's return approached, both the union and management asked if I would be willing to mediate this dispute. Both felt it was a no-win situation, but one with which they were stuck.

I met with each of these men, listened to their stories, and discussed the possibility of mediating their dispute. Jim was ready to do anything to put this behind him, but Ray was very reluctant. He told me how painful the incident had been and was not sure there was anything Jim could do or say that would really help. I asked whether he wanted an apology, and he said that might help—if he believed it.

Clearly, putting pressure on or simply encouraging Ray to mediate would have been counterproductive. Instead, I just asked him to think about it and to let me know if he had other thoughts or questions. I also told him that I did not feel mediating was necessarily the "right" thing for him to do, but it was an option to at least consider. That is where things stood for over a month. Finally, the afternoon before the last day of my final trip on the grievance project, I got a call from Ray saying he had decided he did want to meet with Jim. Hastily, I scheduled individual meetings with each of them and then a joint meeting for the following morning.

First, I met with Ray. He wanted an apology, and we discussed what would make it feel genuine to him. All he could say was that he would have to see how he felt—he did not know whether anything Jim could say would make a difference. He also wanted to tell Jim how he felt. I asked Ray if there was anything he was sorry that he had done. His first response was that he was the victim in this interchange. I said that might be, but it did not mean there was nothing he regretted. He acknowledged that he could be pretty provocative and that he could tell he was getting to Jim. At this point I delivered a little homily about apologies, explaining my view that they could not be bargained for and that the only meaningful apology was one freely given. I said that if there was something Ray was sorry for, it would be valuable for him to say it, even if he felt that Jim's apology was incomplete or insincere. I asked Ray to think about how he could express the effect that Jim's statement had had on him in a way that Jim might understand. I had a similar discussion with Jim, encouraging him to think about what he was really sorry about and also to think about what he needed to say about Ray's behavior.

The joint meeting resulted in one of the most amazing interchanges I have seen. At first, Jim and Ray were both extremely tense and nervous. There was some small talk, and then I asked Jim to say what was on his mind. Jim talked about how horrible this whole experience had been for him, how much he had enjoyed having Ray as a friend, and how bad he felt about losing their relationship. He then looked at Ray and said how sorry he was about what he said and how hurtful he knew it had been to Ray. At this point I suggested that Jim give Ray a chance to respond. Ray accepted the apology and said he knew that he could be a "pain in the ass" and that he understood that this had been hard for Jim as well.

Ray then talked about how hard it was for him to trust an older man and especially one in a position of authority, and how bad it felt when this trust had been violated. Jim listened carefully to this and reiterated how sorry he was. He then went on to say how hard it had been for him to have Ray as a friend one minute and to be needled by Ray in front of his unit the next, especially because he felt he was always defending Ray to other managers. Then they went on to talk about what they had each gotten out of their friendship and how much they missed this.

In the end they agreed they wanted to try to work together, and they even set up a time to go out for a cup of coffee. Almost as an afterthought Ray agreed to drop the grievance. Both of these rather tough looking working-class men had tears in their eyes—as did I—and they both looked as if some enormous burden had been lifted from their shoulders.

Behavioral Resolution

When we think of resolution, it is the behavioral dimension we usually have in mind. We think of resolution as being about what people will do (or not do) or what agreements they will make about what they will do. There are two aspects to behavioral resolution.

One has to do with discontinuing the conflict behavior and the other with instituting actions to promote resolution. Stopping fighting is one part of behavioral resolution. Taking steps to meet each other's needs and to implement a new mode of interaction is another.

Sometimes there is a specific act that symbolizes or actualizes the cessation of conflict behavior and the initiation of resolution behavior. Formal agreements, peace treaties, contracts, and consent decrees are examples of this. Sometimes less formal or institutionalized acts function in the same way—a shake of the hands, a drink together, a hug, the initiation of a joint activity, giving flowers, and so forth. At other times the conflict behavior simply ceases, sometimes gradually and sometimes abruptly, and the resolution behavior begins, without any obvious demarcation between the two. There are conflicts in which all that needs to occur is the cessation of conflict behavior. This is particularly true when the disputants will not have any relationship after the end of the conflict.

Agreements and solutions operate primarily in the behavioral dimension. Although a solution can affect people's emotions and perceptions, they cannot really agree to feel differently or to have different perceptions about the situation. Feelings and perceptions change but not simply through agreeing to change them. However, an agreement to behave in a certain way does have meaning.

The bulk of the 1995 agreements made in Dayton about ending conflict in Bosnia had to do with disengaging from conflict behavior and achieving certain guarantees that this behavior would not restart. To this extent behavioral, if not cognitive and emotional, resolution was reached. But the conflict is clearly not over on the behavioral dimension either, because efforts to promote resolution behavior have not been highly successful. Attempts to create an effective joint government, resettle refugees in their former communities, deal with severe economic dislocation, and bring the perpetrators of some of the worst atrocities to trial have been largely ineffective. So the agreement dealt with one aspect of behavioral resolution but not the other. This is often the case in conflicts, whether they occur in societies, in communities, or in families. Unless we are dealing with a conflict in which there will be no future interdependence or interaction among the disputants—no "shadow of the future" (Axelrod, 1984)—and in which nothing more than the cessation of certain behaviors is necessary to end the conflict, then it is important to address both elements of the behavioral dimension to reach full resolution.

Full resolution of conflict occurs only when there is resolution along all three dimensions: cognitive, emotional, and behavioral. But such closure does not often happen in a neat, orderly, synchronized manner. Sometimes disputants are happy to call a conflict resolved when they have achieved significant resolution on one or two dimensions. Not that people think of it in this way, but this is how they often experience it. Although resolution along one dimension encourages resolution along the other dimensions, the reverse is also true. People in conflict may experience a significant setback in their progress toward resolution on one dimension when they do not experience progress along another. Furthermore, different disputants in a conflict often experience differing degrees of resolution along the various dimensions. Sometimes this difference becomes the basis of a trade-off that allows an agreement to be reached. People will often make a psychological concession, for example, in exchange for a behavioral agreement. Enduring resolution of deep conflicts, however, generally requires some significant progress toward resolution along all three dimensions.

Outcomes, Transformation, and Social Change: The Purpose of Conflict Resolution

There is a rich and ongoing debate about the appropriate goals for conflict resolution practitioners. Should conflict resolvers have a purpose beyond helping disputants attain an agreement? What is the resolver's responsibility for protecting the weak or unrepresented? Is conflict resolution about ending disputes, building peace, achieving social justice, or transforming relationships? I believe this is a very important and needed discussion that can help clarify the fundamental work of the conflict resolution field. Unfortunately, like everyone else, conflict resolvers do not always practice what they preach. A tendency exists for advocates of one approach to oversimplify the views of other approaches. Although the following discussion runs the risk of falling into the same trap, it summarizes some of the primary points of view, or beliefs, and some of the (more reasonable) criticisms that have been leveled against them.

Belief: dispute resolution is about helping people reach agreements to end their conflicts. Conflict resolution is neither therapy nor political organizing. Although solid agreements that genuinely meet the interests of the parties to a conflict can lead to both personal and social change, that is a by-product of effective dispute resolution activities, not a direct goal. Were this the primary purpose of conflict resolution practitioners, they would become just one more advocacy group trying to impose its own agenda on a problem-solving process. The power of collaborative approaches to conflict resolution is that they empower participants to advocate effectively for their own interests in a safe and constructive environment where they do not have to deal with externally imposed agendas. People come to dispute resolution practitioners for help in arriving at a settlement to a conflict. They want this help to be powerful and effective. They do not come to experience personal growth or transformation or to clarify their feelings. Any agenda beyond those that the parties have explicitly bought into the process is manipulative and disempowering.

Critique: focusing on agreements, outcomes, or solutions is also an agenda. At the extreme we see the all too frequent practice of dispute resolution through arm-twisting, in which people are pressured to agree through relatively coercive means. Practitioners of this approach are often more focused on getting an agreement than on finding a way to meet disputants' essential needs. Even those who practice a gentler approach within this framework often fail to understand that each conflict is often a symptom of an underlying concern that the parties are either unwilling or unable to articulate. Furthermore this approach often overlooks the cognitive and emotional dimensions of resolution. Even though disputants often want a fuller resolution of their conflict than can be achieved through a simple outcome-based negotiation, they find it easiest to focus on the more tangible aspects of the resolution process. Unless conflict resolution practitioners offer people the opportunity to work on the deeper and broader issues they are facing, it is likely that they will focus on a shallow resolution that will not genuinely address their needs. This approach can be as upsetting and alienating as traditional legal processes but without the procedural safeguards.

Belief: dispute resolution has a great potential to encourage personal transformation, and such transformation is often essential if conflicts are to be effectively addressed. Mediation in particular has the power to transform the way people relate to each other and to a conflict. This point of view is forcefully presented in the work of Robert Bush and Joseph Folger (1994). Transformation happens primarily through the process of empowerment and recognition that is a potential part of every conflict resolution process. A significant obstacle to achieving this potential is the narrow focus on outcomes that is typical of many mediations. Opportunities for empowerment and recognition are lost when the process is so focused on achieving an outcome that more profound communication is not encouraged and at times is actively suppressed. There is no such thing as a neutral party because everyone has an agenda. If the goal of conflict resolution professionals is to arrive at an agreement no matter what, they are imposing that agenda on the process even as they claim to be neutrals. Ignoring the transformational potential of mediation not only denies participants and society an important opportunity for growth but often fails to address the real, underlying needs that people have in conflict. (For another, more broadly conceived—and profoundly moving—take on transformation, see Lederach, 1995, 1997. He focuses more on the transformation of relationships and systems of interaction than on personal change.)

Critique: transformation often does occur as a result of experiences people have with conflict and its resolution, but usually not through a direct effort to make transformation happen. One paradox of the mediation process may be that people are more apt to have fundamentally transformative experiences during it because it does not have personal growth as its primary purpose. Many people are willing to engage in mediation (as opposed to therapy, for example) precisely because it is a focused and limited intervention. Furthermore, most skillful mediators look for opportunities to empower people and help them recognize each other's concerns and humanity. This is simply good mediation practice. But when changing people becomes part of an ulterior purpose, then the potential of dispute resolution practices to give people power over decisions in the midst of conflict can get lost. The experience of reaching a settlement in a complex dispute is in itself empowering and opens the door to deeper levels of recognition among the parties far more than would a direct and independent effort to achieve empowerment and recognition.

Belief: dispute resolution cannot be conducted fairly without addressing power imbalances and issues of social justice. In the absence of a commitment to deal with power inequities, dispute resolution procedures become just one more way in which victims of social injustice are further disempowered. Neutrality in the face of social injustice contributes to the furtherance of injustice. Conflict resolution as a goal makes sense only when coupled to an active commitment to ensuring that power inequities are corrected. Again, there is no such thing as genuine neutrality, either structurally or personally.

Critique: if dispute resolvers are expected to take on the task of eliminating structural inequalities in society, not only will they be ineffective in dealing with conflicts but they also will be unable to add much to movements for social justice.   This approach is patronizing to disputants in assuming that they need the assistance of a third party to make sure they do not make inappropriate choices. A credible process conducted in an impartial manner is often extremely valuable to disempowered people. Although there certainly should be screening procedures to make sure that only appropriate resolution processes are used, the choice of processes also has to be made in light of the realistic alternatives. Sometimes collaborative decision-making procedures give people the best opportunity to play a relatively weak hand. Advocates of the social justice approach often deliver fewer real accomplishments than do well-constructed conflict resolution forums. These forums are designed to provide procedural justice, which in the end is the foundation of social justice. (For a spirited exchange about this approach, see McCrory, 1981; Susskind, 1981; Stulberg, 1981.)

Belief: the goal of conflict resolvers ought to be deeper analysis and understanding rather than negotiated agreements. Similar to the transformative belief but focused more on the resolution of international issues and ethnic disputes, this approach critiques many international peacemaking efforts because they fail to address the root causes of conflicts. The most renowned advocates for this approach are John Burton and his colleagues at the Institute for Conflict Analysis and Resolution at George Mason University (Burton and Dukes, 1990). Proponents argue that mechanisms are needed for helping people analyze the deeper levels of human needs, particularly identity-based needs, that are at the root of most profound conflicts. Unless disputants are helped to fully understand both their needs and those of others, a genuine resolution of conflict is not possible. When a process places its major focus on solving a particular conflict, the underlying issues are often ignored, and instead of genuinely solving the conflict, the process allows issues to continue to fester and often escalate. Advocates of the analytic approach sometimes refer to events in the Middle East, Northern Ireland, and Bosnia as examples of this dynamic.

Critique: this approach embodies an unrealistic view of the way progress occurs in resolving serious conflicts. There is a time for analysis and reflection and a time to seize the opportunity to make progress by arriving at agreements on divisive issues. As tangible progress is made on specific issues, people become better able to address the deeper and more complicated needs that drive their conflict. If people in Bosnia, Kosovo, Croatia, and the Middle East had to wait for the identity-based needs of the disputants to be thoroughly discussed and addressed, many opportunities for progress toward resolution would be lost and probably many lives as well.

Belief: disputes are resolved when key interests are addressed. The goal of dispute resolution according to Fisher and Ury (1981) is to obtain a solution that addresses the most important interests of the different parties. This can be done through an interest-based approach to negotiation, in which disputants' interests and principles are explored, as opposed to a power-based struggle over whose position will prevail. The goal of dispute resolution is to arrive at a solution to the conflict, but one that addresses the key interests of the different parties. Resolution does not need to distinguish between needs and interests because one is just a deeper expression of the other. Negotiated agreements are the major outcomes that should be sought in most conflicts.

Critique: most serious conflicts are based on a deeper level of needs than is captured through an exploration of interests. Furthermore, interests are not static but change as people interact. This approach is too rationalistic. It does not recognize the role of power and identity in the conflict process. Focusing on interests should be viewed as a tactic, not as an overall philosophy of conflict resolution. As a tactic it can be very valuable, but it is not always appropriate. Disputants can often arrive at effective agreements without dwelling on their interests, and sometimes doing so can become an academic exercise divorced from what is really important to people.

Although skillful conflict resolvers probably instinctively use the best insights from all these approaches, adherents of each point of view handle conflicts in somewhat different ways. Let's consider how each might approach a typical community conflict. (The example is based on an unmediated dispute that took place several years ago.)

> The Beechwood County Department of Human Services plans on establishing a group home for teenagers in a middle-class residential neighborhood in the town of Holmes. A group of neighborhood residents have circulated a petition opposing this plan and threatening court action. The petition raises concerns about traffic, the impact of the teenagers on the local school, and the effect on property values. One of the supporters of the group home, an advocacy group for youth, has countered with a statement that suggests the real problem is racism; Holmes is a predominantly white community, and many of the teenagers will be minorities. The Beechwood County Board of Supervisors has asked for help from a conflict resolution professional in resolving this dispute. This professional might pursue one of the following approaches.
>
> *Get an agreement.* The neighbors, teen advocates, and the Department of Human Services (DHS) need to come up with an agreement that everyone will accept. In this way the neighbors' concerns can be met, a plan for the group home can be formulated, and a negative court battle can be avoided. To saddle this process with an attempt to work through everyone's feelings about community, race, and the needs of teenagers would overwhelm it and throw a considerable obstacle in the path of finding a solution.
>
> *Encourage personal transformation.* These people need to hear each other, to understand and recognize the underlying concerns that everyone has. This presents a wonderful opportunity to break through some serious stereotypes and misunderstandings. There are at least three major reasons why this

should be done. First, if the group home is to move into the neighborhood, these folks will have to live with each other. If they do not recognize the legitimacy of each other's concerns, the stage will be set for a long-term problem. Second, no workable agreement is likely to emerge unless efforts are made to encourage empowerment and recognition. Third, the neighborhood residents and group home staff and clients can do much for each other if each group can change its perceptions of the other side.

Address social justice issues. Unless the disparity in power between these wealthy residents and the potential group home clients are addressed, the likely victims in a negotiated solution will be the teens. Compromises may be agreed to that will negatively affect the youths and perhaps the workers staffing the home, and these are the people likely to be underrepresented in a conflict resolution process. The intervener should ensure that the outcome does not exploit the unempowered.

Provide conflict analysis before attempting conflict resolution. The disputants should concentrate on understanding their deeper needs and how these are in play in this conflict. An appropriate analytical process will get to the deeper issues that people have concerning the group home proposal and the neighborhood reaction to it. If the parties try to arrive at a negotiated agreement instead, either there will be no resolution at all, or if there is one, the conflict will continue to emerge in various forms, to the detriment of the teenagers, the neighborhood, and everyone else involved.

Address everyone's procedural, psychological, and substantive interests. Rather than focus on the various positions people have taken, it is important to help people express their interests, consider the principles that should govern an agreement, and evaluate their alternatives. If this is done, a creative problem-solving process that genuinely addresses the interests of those involved can lead to a solution that will maximize joint gains. The question should therefore be, How can the neighborhood residents' concerns about safety, property values, and traffic be addressed while the DHS's need for a suitable group home in an appropriate neighborhood is also met?

Probably any of these approaches, if skillfully applied, could help the group home and the neighborhood residents reach a mutually beneficial resolution. In the end the best guidance about which approach to take in such a conflict and how deep or extensive an effort to make will come from the parties themselves: the neighborhood residents, youth advocates, group home staff, and the Department of Human Services.

There are of course other approaches to conflict resolution, and there are variations on each of the ones I have described. Also, many other critiques have been made. There is truth in each of these points of view and each of the critiques. But I believe there is also a great deal of confusion generated when proponents of one approach mischaracterize others or attack an extreme version of an approach as though it were representative. On the one hand, for example, critics of the transformative approach have argued that transformative mediators have pushed disputants to achieve empowerment and recognition even when those individuals are clearly eager to arrive at a settlement of their particular dispute and do not want to delve into deeper issues. However, the advocates of transformative mediation have gone to great lengths to address this concern through how they contract with people at the beginning of the mediation process. On the other hand, transformative mediation proponents have criticized other mediators, suggesting that they are generally so focused on achieving outcomes that they will not allow the parties to communicate genuinely with each other, even when they want to do so. Presenting the worst practices of representatives from a particular viewpoint and using these to critique the whole approach is neither helpful nor fair.

Pursuing Resolution at the Appropriate Level of Depth

I have suggested that the genuine resolution of complex conflicts requires emotional, cognitive, and behavioral resolution. It also requires that people's essential needs be addressed at an appropriate level of depth: that is, deep enough to address the real concerns people have that are motivating their engagement in a particular conflict, but not so deep as to require them to work through fundamental life issues that are beyond their practical motivation. Thus one major challenge for conflict resolvers is to find a way to address people's needs at the appropriate level of depth. Another is to handle the different dimensions wisely, so that each is approached when possible and as appropriate.

These challenges may be met in many ways, and to suggest that one outcome or one approach is superior to all others is to erect a barrier to understanding the nature of conflict and of resolution. Resolution occurs in stages, with setbacks, and in many unpredictable ways. Sometimes the quickest way to get specific agreements is to help disputants put agreement aside as an immediate goal and to concentrate on analyzing the conflict and communicating with each other. At other times the quickest road to empowerment and transformation is to help the parties succeed in resolving smaller or more immediate issues. The art of conflict resolution requires an analysis of each situation, and the most powerful practitioner is the one who can apply differential approaches based on this analysis.

In most circumstances, resolution is not a fixed end but a process. Those of us interested in resolution need to learn to listen very hard to the people involved in each conflict and to understand the level at which they are experiencing the issues. We then need to search for the right level of depth at which to intervene or to engage disputants. Because an appropriate level of intervention for one person or one stage of a resolution may be wrong for another, we can never be sure whether we have found the optimal level, and we have to keep attuned to this search throughout the resolution process.

If we look at Bosnia, the Middle East, Northern Ireland, or Guatemala, we can see the dynamics of this issue demonstrated in very interesting ways. In each of these places, agreements were made that settled some aspect of a deeply rooted dispute but that fell short of resolving all the fundamental issues or satisfying the identity-based needs of the people involved. Yet each of these agreements allowed the parties, at least temporarily, to disengage from an extremely destructive pattern of conflict behavior. Will this lead to longer-term, more deeply rooted peace and to a more just society, or has the situation been patched over in a way that will cause greater conflict later?

Fundamental resolution of deeply rooted conflicts and the achievement of social justice must be viewed as long-term efforts and goals that are ongoing and complex. Conflict resolution activities can be part of this process, but only a part. They are one element in a much larger picture, and unless they are seen in that context, it is impossible to have a reasonable and flexible approach to choosing how and where to apply them.

Collaborative Problem Solving and Alternative Dispute Resolution, or, Why Put the "A" in ADR?

As the conflict resolution field has developed, it has been referred to in a number of revealing ways. It has been called *alternative dispute resolution, collaborative problem solving,* and sometimes simply *mediation and arbitration.* Each of these terms conveys a certain value base. Collaborative problem solving implies that conflict resolvers are in the business of helping people work out their disagreements together and on a voluntary basis. Alternative dispute resolution raises the question of alternative to what? Conflict resolvers will answer this in different ways, but what most people seem to mean is that ADR is alternative to court-based decision making. Equating the field with mediation and arbitration essentially ties it to the work of third-party neutrals. Moreover, there are contradictions between these different concepts. For example, arbitration is seldom about collaboration, and court systems are increasingly incorporating mediation into their work.

As the conflict resolution field grows and becomes more institutionalized, it is going to become less alternative. Some have suggested that the word *appropriate* be substituted for alternative. Others have suggested that *conflict management* is a more appropriate term than conflict resolution for describing what we do. These differences are not just linguistic quibbling; they reflect the field's basic identity issues.

I believe that the field needs to be viewed in a broader way. A healthy approach to dealing with conflict requires a spectrum of conflict resolution approaches. What I believe is important is to deepen our understanding of the range of processes and skills necessary to handle conflict effectively and of the ways to choose among them and also link them together. This issue is addressed further in Chapter Ten.

Two particular roles, I believe, are at the core of much of what occurs in conflict resolution. Everyone is a negotiator every day, and this is the first and primary role people bring to most conflicts. Similarly, the mediation role is both a professional approach to conflict and a basic life skill. People's effectiveness in these two core roles is key to how effectively they can operate across a broad range of conflict resolution activities. But it is important to remember that conflict resolution as a field goes beyond negotiation and mediation. And underlying all effective approaches is the ability to communicate.

Chapter Six

Communication

At the heart of both conflict and resolution is communication. We engage in conflict and in its resolution through communication processes that are direct and indirect, purposeful and accidental, verbal and nonverbal, symbolic and concrete, interactive and one way. In conflict, there is no more important area to understand or skill to develop than effective communication. The good news about this is that communication skills can be learned, applied, and enhanced. The bad news is that good communication is harder than most people realize. Most of us who work as conflict resolvers believe we are effective communicators (at least when we want to be), and most of us are able to articulate the essentials of good communication. But like everyone else, we are only sporadically effective as communicators, particularly in the midst of highly charged situations. The communication process poses the largest challenge to our effectiveness as conflict resolvers but also the greatest opportunity to enhance that effectiveness. Communication is a very broad topic, but for the purposes of understanding conflict resolution, we can concentrate on answering four critical questions:

- What is the basis of good communication?
- How do people connect so that each person feels genuinely heard?
- How can disputants communicate what they have to say in a constructive and effective way?
- How can a conflict resolver help turn ineffective, destructive, or nonproductive communication into more constructive interchanges?

These are fundamental questions for people interested in conflict resolution, and they are relevant across cultural boundaries and at all stages of a conflict. This does not imply that complicated issues, deeply bitter feelings, or long-lasting antagonisms can be made to go away simply by communicating effectively. Communication is only one part of the resolution process, but it is a critical part. Without effective communication, it is hard to do much about conflict. In this chapter, each of these questions is considered.

The Basis of Good Communication

Good communication stems from intention not technique. If people put their full and focused energy into communicating, they can make lots of mistakes and still be effective. Conversely, no communication technique will substitute for a lack of commitment and a desire to hear or to be understood. Too often communication is viewed as a set of behaviors or procedures. If a person learns the right mechanisms for communication, he or she will be effective. But most of us have had the experience of communicating with someone who is consciously using a specific communication approach, such as an "I" message or active listening, and have come away feeling patronized or not genuinely heard. Most of us can also think of times when we have employed good communication practices but have not been focused, or *present*. This can be frustrating to the persons on both ends of a communication.

If we watch people genuinely connecting, we will observe lots of behaviors that are supposedly poor communication techniques. People will interrupt, ask closed questions, make self-referential statements, try to problem solve too quickly, and inject humor when someone else is trying to make a serious point. Yet they will still genuinely connect with one another, and each will feel heard. Why? The key is their intention and focus. If one person genuinely wants to understand what another person is saying, and is willing to work at it, that intention will come through, despite behaviors that might not seem desirable. Similarly, if people want to express themselves so that they are understood clearly and if they are willing to work at it, the chances are that a successful interchange will occur. But all the good techniques in the world will not make up for a lack of genuine interest in what someone else has to say.

This does not mean that behaviors and techniques are not important; they are. People can learn to be better listeners, to deliver difficult messages more effectively, to reframe toxic language, and to be attuned to nonverbal communication. But these techniques are not at the heart of effective communication. When a person's attitudes are not conducive to communicating, his or her behaviors cannot help but convey this.

Good communication starts with an understanding that no one is always effective at listening to others or conveying his or her ideas clearly. Although effective communication may come more naturally to some than to others, it is never to be taken for granted. Being attuned to the possibility, even the likelihood, that one has not communicated effectively may sometimes feel unnatural, but it may also be the most important thing that can be done to improve communication.

I believe that the following attitudinal principles are the basis of successful communication for everyone, particularly when dealing with conflict.

Caring about what others are saying is the key to good communication. If people genuinely care about what others have to say, their desire to understand will get communicated. If they do not genuinely care, that too will be communicated.

There is always new information to learn from a communication. When people listen with one ear while composing a response to what they think others are about to say, real communication has not occurred, even when their conjecture is correct.

Good communication requires focused energy. When people focus their attention, their energy, and their best listening and articulation skills on an exchange, others generally feel respected, even in the midst of conflict. Communicating clearly in the midst of an intense interaction is tiring for a very good reason—it takes a lot of work.

Effective communication requires a joint effort between speaker and listener. Effective communication is interactive and iterative. People have to work together to make a complex interchange successful, particularly in the midst of stress. Directly or indirectly, people have to verify whether they have really understood each other.

Communicating is different from persuading, evaluating, and problem solving. When people are focused on communicating, they are trying to understand what others are saying, and are helping others to understand what they are trying to convey. When people focus instead on convincing others that they are "right" or on evaluating the merits of what the others have said, effective communication is less likely.

Tolerance of people's difficulty in communicating (including your own) is essential. These principles are all ideals and goals to strive for. People do not become better communicators by setting up a new orthodoxy about human interaction and then judging each other in accordance with it. No one can always be focused and completely attentive. Everyone mixes up communicating, persuading, and problem solving at times. It is important to be respectful of others who are trying to communicate effectively and to avoid becoming so conscious about the rights and wrongs of good communication that one can not interact in a natural and unselfconscious way. Thus the final principle:

The best communication occurs when people are genuine and natural. Communicating is about interacting as human beings. This means being real, being oneself, speaking from the heart, and connecting with others on the basis of human personalities, which by definition are flawed.

Listening and Connecting

Although those of us who work as conflict resolvers mostly recognize the importance of good listening to dispute resolution, we often fail to understand the heart of what listening is about. Often our idea of being a good listener involves an image of listening as a one-directional communication process. Effective interpersonal communication is always interactive and requires those involved to form what is in essence a partnership in communication. People have to help each other communicate, especially when they are in conflict. Also, people can listen in a way that promotes a connection or that inhibits one. Let's look at each of these issues further.

The Communication Loop

What changes a conflict dynamic from an adversarial contest to a joint search for resolution? It is not necessarily that people come to feel differently about their adversaries or to view the conflict differently. What seems to be central is that people start to feel a connection with their adversaries, almost a partnership, based on a different kind of communication than they have had before and an understanding that they need each other to find their way through the conflict. Mandela and de Klerk, Sadat and Begin, Rabin and Arafat, and Trimble and Hume did not necessarily change their views of each other and learn to like each other or even to respect each other. But they did connect, and they did come to view each other as necessary partners in the peacemaking process. Of course good communication alone can not resolve deeply rooted problems if other conditions are not favorable. Communication is a necessary but not a sufficient condition for the resolution of complex conflicts.

These connections did not happen through the simple process of good listening. They occurred through a complicated process of individuals' learning to communicate with each other. All these political leaders had to learn how to decode the messages they were receiving, how to deliver their own ideas so that they would be understood, and how to develop a suitable atmosphere for communication. Beyond that they all needed to find a way to cue each other when they were grasping what was being said and when they felt they were being heard. This is no easy task to accomplish against a background of long and intense conflict and personal antagonism. As these leaders worked to reach their agreements, third parties played a critical role in most cases in encouraging this communication. This process is not relevant just to huge international conflicts. It happens every day in workplaces, families, schools, and as in this example, communities.

My plan for breaking an impasse came very close to blowing up in my face. In the middle of a very difficult policy dialogue about the use of wildlife control measures on agricultural lands, I asked two key participants representing opposing interest groups to try to arrive at a set of proposals to present to the whole group. As one of the facilitators of this dialogue, I had noticed that these two seemed to be genuinely struggling with how to accommodate each other's concerns. I thought that if they could develop some principles of agreement, the whole group might be able to use these principles as a template for a broader discussion. They too were aware of this and were willing to give it a try. The problem was that they disliked each other a lot.

Jonathan, an architect, represented a local environmental group. Charles had been a rancher and was currently a lobbyist for farmers and ranchers. He was also well known as an auctioneer. Jonathan was terse, blunt, suspicious, persistent, and very creative. Charles was easygoing, friendly, funny, and sure of himself, but he also had quite a temper. Jonathan would make a suggestion, lay out its merits, anticipate criticism, and suggest why the criticism was misdirected—all in one statement. To Charles this sounded arrogant and rigid, even when he thought there was merit in Jonathan's proposal.

As Charles listened to Jonathan, his body language would become more tense, his brow more furrowed, and the few statements he made more clipped. When he responded, he tended to tell an anecdote or make an analogy; sometimes he would tell a joke. This was his way of stating his concerns about Jonathan's proposals; mostly he was concerned about how hard it would be to sell these ideas to his constituents rather than about the ideas themselves. To Jonathan, Charles's responses seemed evasive, illogical, or irrelevant. Jonathan would react by leaning forward, speaking a little louder and more intensely, and occasionally pointing his finger (behaviors that almost always escalated the conflict). Even though the two were making progress on some joint proposals, their communication was breaking down, and they were both on the verge of losing it with each other.

During this time they each discussed with me their frustration about what was happening. Each interpreted what the other was saying as manipulative and unreasonable. Neither was picking up cues from the other about what kind of communication worked and what kind did not. Yet both were really trying to communicate. I asked Jonathan what he had noticed about how Charles reacted to his proposals—what kind of communication seemed to get through to Charles and what did not. It almost did not matter what Jonathan's answers to these questions were, because just being asked them was a bit of a revelation to him. They implied to him that he should pay attention not only to what he was saying but how he was saying it. He had been so focused on the substance of his ideas that he had not appeared to pay any attention at all to how he was conveying them. I also asked him to interpret the messages behind a couple of Charles's anecdotes. I suggested that he think about spending more time drawing Charles out and that he convey his ideas more slowly and in smaller segments. Jonathan was quite open to such coaching.

Charles was less interested in suggestions about how to communicate. I asked him what he wanted Jonathan to understand about what he was saying. He told me a couple of stories, the gist of which was that he felt environmentalists did not understand the marginal economic situation of small farmers and ranchers. I expressed the hope that Charles would lay this concern out in no uncertain terms, and I suggested that Jonathan seemed to like bluntness. Neither of these two representatives fundamentally changed how they communicated, or what they thought of each other for that matter. But they did become slightly more attuned to each other's cues, and they were able to work out several proposals to take to the group that were crucial to the dialogue.

Communication needs to be interactive to be effective. As listeners, we have to help speakers deliver their messages so that we can understand them and so that we can remain present in relation to these messages. As speakers, we have to help others listen so we feel heard. This means that we have to listen as we deliver a message and deliver feedback as we listen. This communication loop is a necessary part of effective interchanges. People's ability to connect with each other, particularly in the course of an intense and significant interaction, is dependent on their ability to tune into the often subtle messages that reveal how a communication is being received. These *meta-communications* (communications about communication) are delivered in many ways. People change their body language or tone of voice in ways that indicate whether they are comprehending a communication or feeling heard. They also convey their energy level, frustration, appreciation, or confusion in various ways. Sometimes a speaker will tell others directly that he or she is not feeling heard or understood. Sometimes a listener will say that he or she understands something or, conversely, that he or she is confused. But more often meta-communications are less direct or overt. Speakers have to learn to "read" their audiences. Students acquire very effective ways of letting teachers know when they are bored. Children are always training their parents how to speak to them. All such methods are critical to the success of human relations, which require such complex but powerful interactions to make communication work. Jonathan's and Charles's respective inabilities to pick up on each other's meta-communications were in large part responsible for their difficulties.

No one is always effective at delivering or decoding meta-communications. Frequently, one party to an interchange feels that she or he has successfully connected with another, but this sense is not reciprocated. One complicated aspect of cross-cultural communication is the variation in how individuals from different backgrounds engage in the communication loop. Some groups need very active and clear messages of connection during a communication, with head nodding, verbal assents, and intense eye contact. Others prefer much lower-key and more subtle feedback. When cultures with different engagement patterns interact, interesting disconnects can happen.

> Several years ago one of my colleagues was conducting a training program in Warsaw during which a lively discussion occurred as people expressed very different viewpoints. He was listening attentively to the discussion and nodding his head as different arguments were put forward. In the United States this gesture normally signifies that we are being attentive and comprehending what is being said. It does not necessarily mean that we agree. But in Poland the participants interpreted it as a sign of agreement with the speaker. So when my associate responded to people with opposing points of view by nodding his head, he appeared hypocritical to the group. Fortunately, enough rapport existed that people were open about their perception, and an interesting discussion about cross-cultural communication ensued.

The failure to develop a successful communication loop is one of the main sources of communication breakdown and building this loop is one of the primary ways in which dispute resolution procedures can make a major difference. In the Middle East, Yugoslavia, and Northern Ireland, for example, the role of third parties has been crucial. In these situations trust was so low and animosity so high that it was first necessary to establish an effective communication with a third party who could then help the primary antagonists to establish a more effective communication process. Effective communication loops between the intermediaries and each of the parties can often become the basis of a workable system of communication among the disputants.

Successful communication in conflict is usually iterative. Disputants need to try and try again to complete the communication loop. Unless they have the opportunity to do this, they cannot correct or refine their communications, they cannot work together to clarify messages, and they cannot achieve the richness of communication necessary to engage in a serious resolution process. Therefore one common goal of conflict resolvers is to keep communication flexible and ongoing. If I state an absolute position or belief firmly and publicly, then it becomes very hard for me to modify it in accordance with others' reactions to it. One of the problems with interacting primarily through formal written communication is that this medium of interchange introduces a major source of inflexibility into the interaction. Written communication tends to be more explicit than oral communication and certainly more committing because it so readily becomes part of a formal record. These features can make interactive and iterative communication much more difficult to encourage.

Listening to Connect, Listening to Debate

Not all listening promotes effective communication. The type of listening that breeds connection is almost always related to a genuine desire to understand what others are trying to communicate. Listening, even if focused and energetic, that is mostly motivated by a desire to debate, argue, convince, or discount, is likely to lead to further conflict and distance. We may think of the former as *integrative listening* and the latter as *distributive listening*. That is, one kind of listening attempts to connect the listener with the speaker to see whether both persons' concerns, ideas, and perceptions can be integrated to promote understanding and to see whether both have needs and ideas that can be jointly pursued. The other seeks to parcel out the rights and wrongs or to learn what someone is thinking in order to use that information for gain at the other person's expense, that is, to pursue a distributive goal. Like other elements of conflict behavior, these types of listening are usually mixed together, and which one is dominant can change rapidly and frequently.

Speaking with Power

Communicating clearly in conflict takes courage. Delivering difficult messages powerfully, clearly, and at the same time respectfully is often a daunting challenge. Because people are not usually eager to engage in conflict and are often insecure about how well they can handle a conflict, they often raise conflict ineptly or unproductively. Probably the most common tendency is to not raise a conflict at all, to hope that the issue will go away, or to allude to the conflict indirectly, even surreptitiously. People are often more comfortable taking "shots" at each other, making snide or cutting remarks, or finding safer surrogate issues to squabble about than they are raising their real issues in a serious manner that demands a response. In addition, many disputants raise issues in a way that is dramatic, forceful, and clear but brooks no response, no dialogue, and no engaged interaction (as discussed in Chapter Two). But a powerful stance is not one that attempts to forestall a reaction or disagreement but one that is offered with confidence that one has a right to one's feelings, with an assurance that the needs expressed are legitimate, and with a belief that conflict can be carried out with dignity. Even when someone is in a seemingly powerless position, an effectively delivered message can have a strong impact.

> In many parts of the world Roma people ("Gypsies") continue to be the targets of racism and discrimination. Unemployment is rampant, death rates are high, and many continue to live in horrible shanty towns. Common attitudes among officials of social welfare, education, and labor agencies reflect this racism. Roma culture and the Roma people are blamed for their own situation, and overt expressions of racism are everywhere. Roman C. is a respected Roma leader in a small city in Bulgaria. I have worked with him for several years as part of a multicultural cooperation project. On the outskirts of his town is an extremely poor Roma village that receives almost no services. There are no sewers, water lines, or paved streets. Unemployment exceeds 90 percent. But the neighborhood has recently received electricity.
>
> When several families failed to pay their bills, however, electricity to the whole village was turned off, even though most households had paid. The people in the village approached Roman for his assistance. He had grown up in this neighborhood and still had relatives living in the area. Roman, together with several colleagues from our project, went to the town hall to complain to municipal officials. First, he had to listen to hostile and racist remarks about the people in the village—about how untrustworthy they were and how turning off electrical service was the only way to ensure payment. Roman was used to this. He had heard it all his life. After listening respectfully he made this statement, with a quiet voice but a great deal of fervor.
>
> "Our people have problems, and we should take responsibility for them. It was not right that certain families did not pay their bills. But you too must take responsibility for your mistakes. It is not fair to punish the whole commu-

nity for what a few families have done. You would never do that to your own community, but because we are Roma you think you can do it to us. We will not accept this, and you must find another way of handling this situation. We will work with you to find a fair way of dealing with this problem, but our community has so little, and this you must not take away from us."

Roman did not immediately get the response he wanted, but he persisted. After a number of meetings, during which he persistently delivered versions of this message, the municipality relented and installed mechanisms so that in the future just the electricity of those who did not pay their bills would be turned off.

Like listening effectively, raising difficult issues productively is often more a matter of attitude than technique. For example, it is usually better to use *"I" messages*—that is, to speak in terms of one's own concerns, needs, and feelings—than to use "you' messages— to offer judgmental or prescriptive statements about what others have done or ought to do. But having the attitude that underlies an "I" message is more important than using the linguistic formula. If the underlying attitude is prescriptive or judgmental, then all the "I" messages in the world will not ultimately prevent others from reacting aggressively or defensively. Conversely, if speakers genuinely believe that more than one point of view is possible and that their concerns are not the whole story, this will come through even when they make an occasional prescriptive or judgmental statement. Roman delivered quite a few "you" messages in his statement, and he certainly did not frame his comments entirely in terms of how he felt. But he still managed to convey both power and respect, because he felt them. Here are some of the attitudes and beliefs that can help people speak with constructive power.

All of us have a right to our opinions, needs, concerns, and wishes, and we have a right to have them heard. Individuals who need others to give them permission to express their views will find it harder to speak with constructive power. When people believe that they do not have to justify their concerns or their desire to be heard, they will find it easier to give voice to those concerns in a calm but forceful manner.

Others also have the right to their opinions and concerns, and they too have a right to be heard. Asserting one's own needs and views is not about shutting people up. In a conflict, no one has to justify his or her feelings or defend his or her right to have an opinion. Disputants may, however, have to explain and clarify their needs and beliefs, and they have the right to ask others to do this as well.

Other points of view are possible, and new information will always have the potential to cast a situation in a different light. In other words, it helps if people are open to the possibility that they might be wrong or at least that they might change their minds about some aspect of a conflict once they hear other perspectives.

Expressing concerns or raising issues is different from convincing people that one is right. One of the surest ways to evoke a defensive or hostile reaction is to raise an issue as an argument (the speaker's counterpart to distributive listening). Expressing a concern and stating a point of view is very different from delivering the opening statement in a debate. If I say that I am upset with you for always being late and that this has caused me a lot of problems, that is in itself a powerful statement. If I then go on to list all the reasons why it is not fair for you to be late, and to counter all your potential excuses even before you have raised them, then I am trying to shut off your reaction, and you are likely to find it hard to hear my real concerns.

Timing is important, and it is also important to take the time necessary to deal with important issues. People do not have to unload all their concerns and ideas in one statement or interchange, nor will they find it wise to squeeze important communications into inappropriate time frames. Sometimes there is no ideal time to raise a difficult or painful issue, but there are often very bad times. When I am rushing out the door to pick up a young child who is waiting for me outside her school is probably not the best time for you to tell me how furious you are with me.

Presenting one's concerns is different from solving a problem. One of the biggest mistakes a person can make is to raise an important problem and then try to solve it in the same statement. Although it may at first appear to be a constructive approach, it has the effect of focusing others on whether the solution is acceptable rather than on understanding the speaker's issues or needs. It may also be an attempt to impede people from expressing their reactions to the issues or concerns that have been raised.

The fact that I have a conflict with you does not mean that there is something wrong with you or with me. There is a difference between being angry about what someone is doing and viewing her or him as a bad person. When disputants can hold onto this distinction, it is easier for them to raise their issues forcefully without attacking others personally. Maintaining a sense of the essential humanity of the person with whom one is in deep conflict can be very difficult, but it is one of the keys to productive communication in disputes.

Initial reactions are not necessarily final reactions. Everyone has the right to an initial emotional reaction to a communication. My right to my feelings does not mean that you have no right to get angry with me when I express these feelings. If I feel you have been cheating me out of my fair share of a joint business, I have a right to express my opinion. That does not mean that you do not have the right to be furious at me for jumping to this conclusion. My raising an issue in a constructive way does not mean you have no right to be angry, upset, or sad in response.

Raising issues effectively does not automatically mean they can be solved. Just because a person is careful to communicate respectfully that does not mean an issue will go away. It just means that that person has done his or her best to set the stage for an effective conflict resolution process.

It is important to communicate in a way that gives others the best chance of understanding what one has to say. Attentiveness to someone else's communication style is important, especially in conflict. Disputants should be aware of their language, the complexity of their presentation, the metaphors they use, and the buttons they might push. One of the arts of communicating is adapting one's language to others' communication style without being patronizing or phony. I cannot effectively adopt hip-hop lingo to relate to adolescents, but neither do I have to employ professional jargon.

Stating something clearly does not mean that others have understood it. Conflicts escalate when people become convinced that the way they meant to express something is the only honest way in which someone else could have heard it. No matter how clear or careful a person has been in expressing an idea or feeling, others can honestly misunderstand it or interpret it in different ways.

These attitudes are not concepts that most people can simply adopt or will upon themselves, but they are often the keys to effective communication. An important part of the work that we do as conflict resolvers is helping people raise their concerns in a powerful and respectful way. We do this in part by helping people to adopt these attitudes in their communications.

Framing a Conflict for Resolution

All of us make sense out of our world through language. How we describe an event not only influences our understanding of it but also often affects how the event unfolds. Conflicts are both exacerbated and alleviated by the language disputants use to characterize them and by the way in which disputants frame the issue, their concerns, or their views. One of the most powerful tools for resolving conflict is the process of *successive reframing*. Framing refers to the way a conflict is described or a proposal is worded; reframing is the process of changing the way a thought is presented so that it maintains its fundamental meaning but is more likely to support resolution efforts. Successive reframing comes into play because complex conflicts or issues cannot easily be effectively reframed in one clever effort. Instead the process requires multiple efforts, refining and deepening each reframing until disputants begin to see a greater potential for resolution. (For another interesting take on reframing see Bandler and Grinder, 1982.)

For example, reframing commonly occurs in divorces when legal custody of children is an issue. Disputes over custody often seem intractable, partially because of the framing of the parenting issue. Custody tends to call forth a distributive, all or nothing, either-or presentation of important parenting questions. Furthermore the concept of custody promotes images of control and possession as opposed to responsibility. What mediators and others working with divorcing parents often try to do is to reframe the issue to a question of parenting rights and responsibilities. This promotes a more integrative and flexible response to the issue, and it emphasizes obligation not just control. In many natural resource disputes the issues are presented as protecting the environment versus encouraging economic development or as government regulation versus the rights of property owners. Both of these formulations set up a value conflict that is difficult to resolve as well as an either-or choice. Often it is more productive to consider how economic strength can be enhanced through wise environmental practices or how promoting a sound economy can help preserve the environment.

Principles for Effective Reframing

None of these changes in framing comes easily when positions are polarized, people are angry, and issues are complicated. Reframing has to occur through an interactive and iterative communication process. It has to reflect the basic needs that are being expressed, and it has to be done with the parties, not to them. Adhering to the following principles helps promote a successful reframing effort.

The framing of issues and ideas is important. Perhaps this is obvious, but if we think of reframing as simply word games or manipulation and not as an important key to unlocking disputants' thinking and enhancing their ability to communicate with each other, then word games are probably what we will engage in.

In all presentations of important issues there is truth and there are challenges. Even in the most hostile, negative presentation of an issue, there is information about a person's concerns and attitudes that can be useful in moving a resolution process forward. Similarly, even in the most collaborative-sounding presentations, there are challenges to be faced in clarifying and addressing key concerns.

Constructive framing is about clarity and honesty, not about smoothing difficult issues over. Often a successful reframing will make a conflict seem more severe. Frequently, the hardest conflicts to resolve are those that people present in vague, indecisive, and confusing ways in order to avoid confronting serious disagreements. Sometimes a reframing process starts by highlighting the disagreements and the importance of the issue. If reframing attempts to minimize the seriousness of a dispute, it will not in the end be constructive.

Reframing has to be reflective of the most important needs of the parties. One of the keys to an effectively framed conflict is that the essential interests or needs of the key participants are reflected in the framing. Reframing that does not include people's primary needs is not genuine and will not work. Another key is that the framing must capture not just the content of those needs but the intensity with which they are felt.

Successful reframing is interactive and iterative. Disputants will not change their way of thinking unless they are personally engaged in the reframing process. An important reframing seldom happens in one brilliant instant. It requires work, successive trials and refinements, and a gradual reorientation of both attitudes and perceptions. Although there will be times when one statement or intervention catalyzes or symbolizes change, such moments almost always rest upon previous extensive effort.

Levels of Reframing

Reframing works in different ways at different levels. As conflict resolvers, we have to gradually work our way to deeper levels if we are to be truly effective. Often we start by trying to remove the toxicity and provocation from the presentation of an issue or proposal, but in the end we are trying to help people tell a different story, one that is more constructive, hopeful, and flexible. I have observed four essential levels at which reframing occurs. They are related and intertwined with each other, but they operate at different levels of understanding. All have an emotional and a cognitive component to them. Each description is accompanied by an example of a client's framing and a mediator's reframing. These examples simply show how the content of a framing might change. They are not meant to suggest that simple restatement, without an iterative and interactive process, will get people to look at things differently.

Detoxification Reframing

At the detoxification level, reframing is essentially about changing the verbal presentation of an idea, concern, proposal, or question so that the party's essential interest is still expressed but unproductive language, emotion, position taking, and accusations are removed. This is the simplest level and mainly deals with helping people get past their emotional response to the way someone's thoughts have been presented. The hardest part of this type of reframing is to make sure that neither the underlying concerns nor the intensity with which they are felt get minimized or discounted in the reframing process. The most common tactic is to replace value-laden language and positional demands with interest-based formulations.

Framing: He could care less about our child. All he is worried about is how much of his precious money he is going to have to pay in support.

Reframing: You don't think that he is really motivated by your child's well-being, but you are clear that he wants to minimize how much money he has to pay.

Framing: Hell will freeze over before I agree to work with that jerk again. It was torture last time we were on the same team, and I won't subject myself to his arrogance and sadism again.

Reframing: You had a very bad experience working together, and you do not want to repeat it. In particular you felt exposed to certain behaviors and attitudes that you do not feel you should have to deal with in the workplace (or elsewhere).

Definitional Reframing

In definitional reframing the focus is on redefining the issue or conflict so that the resolution process can be more integrative. This involves a conceptual reframing and often takes the form of presenting an issue as a mutual problem to be mutually solved. At this level the cognitive aspect of the conflict is usually the most significant target of the reframing effort. The key is to incorporate the essential needs or concerns of all the parties in a common problem statement or suggestion. Often definitional reframing involves changing the level of generality or specificity at which an issue or idea is presented and also altering the time frame in which it is being considered. When parents argue about where the children will spend Christmas Day, a mediator may suggest that they consider what principles they believe should govern decisions about where children will spend important holidays and birthdays over time. If this reframing reflects the key concerns of the parents, a successful redefinition may have occurred. If not, more work needs to be done. The challenge is to avoid defining the issue so generally or broadly that the immediate interests are lost and so narrowly or specifically that underlying concerns are not addressed.

Framing: We have to decide who has custody, where the children will live, and how much time they will spend visiting the other parent.

Reframing: We have to decide how we are going to share our responsibilities as parents and what kind of time the children will spend in each of our homes.

Framing: Are we going to protect the unique quality of our community, or are we going to give in to the city's demands that we conform to the regulations that will in the end turn us into just one more yuppie neighborhood?

Reframing: How can we preserve the uniqueness of our community within the city's regulatory framework? [Both detoxification and redefinition are involved in this example.]

Metaphoric Reframing

Metaphoric reframing attempts to find a new or altered metaphor for describing a situation or concept, thus changing the way in which it is viewed. Sometimes this means finding a metaphor that all parties can use or translating one party's metaphor into a metaphor recognized by the other party. We often explain our circumstances, our feelings, and our ideas through metaphors, analogies, aphorisms, and proverbs. These images and stories often take on a life of their own, and they sometimes constrict people's thinking or define situations in ways that make resolution difficult. Also, what is a very clear and cogent metaphor for one person may be confusing or irrelevant to another or it may have a very different meaning. I may think "bluffing is part of the game," and you may value being "a straight shooter," but in the end we may all have to "face the music" and "step up to the plate."

A while back, when working on an organizational dispute in Canada, I was initially thrown by the participants' colorful and constant use of metaphors drawn from hockey. It took me a while to realize just what it meant when one person turned to another and said, "I think you just entered the crease, and I'm calling a foul." Once I got the idea, however, a whole new means of communication was opened.

Metaphoric reframing is subtle and requires a great deal of sensitivity to the underlying meaning a metaphor or adage has for people. It also requires considerable perceptiveness about the ways metaphors can shut down or open up communication. Nevertheless, it can be a very powerful way of bringing about a new understanding of a conflict and of its resolution possibilities. A changed metaphor cannot be imposed upon people, however, and third parties need to monitor the metaphors that they use as well.

Framing: He just wants to be a Disneyland Daddy while I continue to slave away like Cinderella, doing all the unpleasant grunt work of being a parent.

Reframing: Being a parent is like climbing a mountain. It can be an exhilarating experience, but it involves a lot of hard work. The more work you put in, the more the exhilaration. We both need to participate in both aspects of the experience.

Framing: You want to turn this into a hunter's paradise at the expense of a lot of defenseless animals who can't hire lobbyists or lawyers.

Reframing: Humans and animals need to live in balance with each other in this ecosystem.

Shifting the Conflict Paradigm Through Reframing

At the level of the conflict paradigm, reframing addresses the fundamental way in which disputants view or analyze the conflict. Normally, it means changing the way in which an individual sees herself or himself in the conflict system. It involves looking at the relevant world in a new way and changing how people make sense of the conflict.

Often it requires changing the *story line,* the dramatic view people have of their conflict. A number of writers (Hale, 1998) have analyzed people's ways of understanding a conflict in terms of the dramatic framework they use. For example, a tragic frame implies powerlessness to influence a conflict and a sense of fatalism or inevitability about how the conflict will turn out. A comic frame, however, implies a multiplicity of options over which disputants have considerable influence. By changing how the action is described, how different participants are characterized, and how the setting is presented, the dramatic frame can be altered.

However it is accomplished, the process of helping people tell a different story, one that is less hopeless, less polarized, and less populated by good guys and bad guys is often key to helping them view a conflict differently. Sometimes using a different theory to explain why certain events have taken place is a key aspect of this level of reframing. Obviously, this kind of reframing is not simple or facile. It requires that people listen to each other in new ways. Often it requires establishing processes that allow disputants to tell their stories to each other in a rich and powerful manner and then work to create a new story that incorporates the main elements of each disputant's story line. Unless Palestinians and Israelis, for example, can alter their existing stories to include the essential elements of each other's stories, it is hard to imagine how a full resolution process can occur. But through a variety of dialogue groups, peace camps, citizen diplomacy efforts, and similar activities, this process is occurring, and it is probably fundamental to the success of peacemaking efforts taking place on the diplomatic level.

One framing: I have worked hard to make a good education available to my children. They are good students and have the test scores to prove it. But because of affirmative action, some minorities can get into law school, and get scholarships to boot, just because of how their ancestors were treated in the past. That has nothing to do with my children, and it is unfair.

Another framing: Our children have had to endure inferior schools, racially biased testing, and an ongoing pattern of discrimination. Yet when given a chance to receive a decent education, they have done very well, have become community leaders, and have begun to break the cycle of racism in education and employment. Affirmative action is merely a means of preventing an ongoing pattern of institutional racism.

Reframing: Everyone has been hurt by the history of racism and discrimination in American education and employment. Minorities have been subjected to inferior education, and now the students of today are being forced to face the consequences of a long-term problem. However, it is also true that educational institutions need to prepare the professionals and leaders who can confront the major problems of our world. These leaders need to be able to work with all elements of our society and need to be armed with the wisdom of the many different cultural groups in America. Furthermore, the diversity of a student body is one of the greatest assets an educational institution has to offer. It is critical that this diversity not be achieved at the expense of any particular group.

Our educational institutions need to develop the capacity to educate qualified students from all backgrounds and the evaluative tools to recognize these students despite the very different educational backgrounds they might have had.

This last example shows how hard it can be to attain a genuine reframing of the conflict paradigm. But such reframing may also be the most profound change that conflict resolvers can help disputants bring to their approach to serious conflicts.

Reframing is an essential part of the communication process that leads to resolution. It occurs naturally, but it is also an area in which intentional efforts can often be very effective. However, reframing can also be manipulative. It can be used to talk people out of their concerns or feelings or to water down a conflict or an issue. Although this may occasionally work in the short run to bring about agreements, it is almost never effective in achieving a significant level of resolution on important issues. In fact, manipulative reframing leads to disputants' mistrust of the process of resolution and of the third parties who are involved. The art of reframing is to maintain the conflict in all its richness but to help people look at it in a more open-minded and hopeful way.

Communication is a system of interaction. In some sense communication is always flawed, because it is impossible simply to put one's thoughts and understandings directly into someone else's head. In the struggle to communicate and to overcome the obstacles that get in the way of our truly understanding each other in tense situations, genuine creativity can emerge. When individuals in conflict view the truth as existing not inside them but among all the people involved in the dispute, then they are more likely to achieve a higher level of understanding and empathy. This view is the foundation of all profound resolution processes.

Chapter Seven

| **Negotiation and Advocacy**

Negotiation is a basic life skill that we use every day in many ways. We use it in making business arrangements, family decisions, plans with friends, and commercial transactions. When we work out special arrangements about bedtimes and chores with our children, we are negotiating. When we decide which movie or restaurant we will go to with our spouse, we are negotiating. When we agree on a division of work responsibilities with our colleagues, we are also negotiating. Why is it then that when people think of an interaction as a negotiation it suddenly seems more tense, challenging, or tricky? Labeling an interchange as a negotiation seems to take it out of the everyday kind of transaction that everyone is used to and at which we are mostly competent. Suddenly, people start thinking that there are going to be winners and losers, that a game is being played, and that people are out to take advantage of one another. People believe they will have to compromise on issues that are important to them, and they suddenly become concerned about how open to be about their needs and alternatives.

Popular Assumptions About Negotiation

Let's consider some of the more common assumptions that people make about negotiation.

Negotiation is a game. The metaphors we all use in discussing negotiation often come from sports, poker, or some other game. We talk about "putting our cards on the table," "raising the ante," "calling a bluff," "scoring a knockout," "reaching a stalemate," "playing hardball," and the like. Thinking of negotiation as a game has its useful side. It makes some of the dynamics clear. On the one hand games tend to involve a known process, standards of conduct, and a relatively clear goal. On the other hand games are normally about winners and losers, about fixed-sum outcomes, and about being more competent or clever than the other players (who are viewed as opponents).

Negotiation is about compromise. Many people resist negotiation because they think it implies having to compromise on important issues or values. Although negotiation may involve compromise, that is not its necessary result. In some negotiations people may have norms that promote compromising and considering the point of view of an adversary. But these norms about compromise may make people resistant to negotiating when they are very angry at another party or adamant about their position.

Negotiation is about giving up power. Parents are often resistant to the idea of negotiating with their children, managers with their employees, or police with suspects because this implies giving away power inappropriately. Ironically, these kinds of negotiations occur all the time but without the label. Negotiation often involves applying power, recognizing someone else's power, or discussing arrangements that may realign power, but it does not necessarily imply giving away power. In fact it is sometimes a way of exercising power more effectively.

Negotiation is about being nice. Do people have to be friendly or deny their anger toward others when they negotiate? Do they have to treat others as if they approve of them in some way? Of course not. They do have to be willing to communicate with the other parties. But they do not have to pretend that their feelings are anything other than what they are.

Negotiation is about being nasty. Sometimes people assume that to negotiate you have to be belligerent, hard-nosed, and tough—in other words the opposite of friendly. Many people resist negotiation because they do not want to behave in these ways, but they worry that the alternative to being nasty is being vulnerable.

Negotiation is a complex process. The consequence of thinking of negotiation as a complex interaction is that people feel intimidated by it—they do not feel they can master it and therefore feel very vulnerable. Although it has its complexities, its essence is fairly straightforward.

Negotiation is okay only when it is a win-win process. Maybe in a perfect world all negotiations would be win-win processes, but in our world that is not possible or even desirable. Sometimes compromise is necessary. Sometimes one side really ought to lose. People do not encourage collaborative approaches to negotiation by being naïve about its win-lose aspects or by labeling suggestions for distributive solutions as violations of the higher values in human interaction.

Although one or more of these assumptions may apply to some negotiations, none of them automatically apply to all negotiations, and they can cause people to take rigid approaches to dispute resolution, or to resist participating in a process that might be to their advantage. So, if these assumptions do not define negotiation, what does?

What Is Negotiation?

Negotiation is an interaction in which people try to meet their needs or accomplish their goals by reaching an agreement with others who are trying to get their own needs met. Whether we call it problem solving, bargaining, cooperative decision making, or communicating, when two or more people try to reach a voluntary agreement about something, they are negotiating. They may be communicating directly, in writing, or through a third party. They may be friendly, hostile, positional, or open-minded; they may have good alternatives to negotiation or no acceptable choices. One of them may have a great deal of power and may not have to negotiate to meet his or her needs, or each may genuinely need the other in order to accomplish his or her goals.

Does negotiation have to be voluntary? Participation in negotiation is not always voluntary. Labor and management are sometimes required to negotiate, as are people involved in grievances, civil suits, and divorces. However, if participants have no choice but to accept a particular outcome and no opportunity to advocate for their needs, then it is not negotiation. Sometimes a dictated or top-down decision is presented in the guise of negotiation, but this is not negotiation. Negotiation is also different from supplying information or a point of view to a decision maker. Unless people make some effort to reach a mutual agreement, they are not engaged in negotiation. However, when they do make such an effort, even if the pressure is great, the power skewed, and the alternatives few, then the process is some form of negotiation.

Negotiation implies advocacy. As negotiators, people advocate for their interests or for the interests of an individual or group that they represent. Advocates sometimes have no role in a decision-making process other than to promote their own or others' interests. Thus a negotiator is always an advocate, but an advocate is not always a negotiator. Rather than viewing problem solving as an effective means of advocacy, people often think that the advocate's job is to claim as much as possible of a limited pie. They often measure competence by the advocate's fervor and forcefulness. But often the most zealous advocate behaviors are not the most effective, even though they may allow advocates to point to how unwavering they are in pursuit of their goals.

Sometimes an advocate or a system of advocacy (for example, the legal system, a trade union, an employee relations department) cultivates adversarial skills. At other times more collaborative or flexible skills are encouraged. Some of the resistance to collaborative strategies is based on concerns about their effectiveness, but some of it stems from an absence of collaborative negotiation experience. When people or organizations are confident in their ability to advocate in an adversarial manner that is the approach they will naturally rely on when the going gets tough and negotiations become tense. The decisive moment in the following major labor management negotiation occurred when a few key people made a courageous decision to try a less familiar and comfortable approach.

> The wounds from the last strike had not yet healed, but new contract negotiations were about to begin. The leadership and the union of a very large corporation were determined to avoid a repetition of that last encounter, but their relationships remained very tense. Together, they hired two mediators from CDR (of whom I was one) and a third mediator from a local conflict resolution organization to work with them as they prepared for the negotiations. We were asked to train the two bargaining teams in collaborative negotiation

procedures and to facilitate a discussion about how they might implement these procedures in the upcoming talks.

We worked with about twenty people from each side at a four-day retreat, sometimes in their separate teams, sometimes together. The training component was fascinating because everyone used the exercises to act out their fears and stereotypes about each other. At one point in a role-play, a key management negotiator made an agreement with a key union negotiator and then reneged on it. The people on the simulated team of the union negotiator were furious. As it happened, however, one of the other members of the simulated management team was in actuality a union negotiator, and this person, with a lot of laughing and playfulness, had urged the management negotiator to renege. The debriefing for this simulation was an eye-opener for everyone. Despite the fact that it was just an exercise, in many ways it was the real beginning of the negotiations.

After this simulation, when the actual union and management teams began to discuss how to conduct the upcoming collective bargaining talks, some interesting parallels in the internal dynamics of the two groups became evident. Some people in each group wanted to use a more collaborative approach and to end the personal attacks that had characterized previous negotiations, but there were also those who feared that under the guise of collaboration they were going to be manipulated.

People struggled with this dilemma until a crisis point was reached. This occurred after one group had taken a chance and offered some important procedural and psychological concessions. The initial reaction of the other team was negative. Team members discounted the concessions and responded by once again venting their anger about the previous contract negotiations. The first team was very discouraged and was about to abandon the effort to design a new approach.

I met with the members of the second group at this point and said that they had reached "crunch" time. They had to decide whether to take a risk or to return to previous patterns of interacting. If they did not make a decisive conciliatory move now, it would be a while before they again had such an opportunity. A tense debate followed during which one of the most respected negotiators in the group said that it was time to start doing things differently. In a subsequent joint meeting, the second group expressed real appreciation for the concessions that the first group had made and reciprocated in a heartfelt and eloquent way. This really surprised the first group and went a long way toward alleviating the tension. During the final day of the retreat, both teams were productively engaged in setting up new procedures for negotiating and for union-management interactions in general.

Not everything went easily after this of course. Change is gradual and halting. But the negotiations did proceed much more smoothly, and in a relatively short amount of time a new contract was signed. Negotiators repeatedly referred to the discussions they had had during the retreat. Their willingness then to take some risks carried over to the actual negotiations.

Being an effective advocate is not equivalent to being either adversarial or collaborative. It means being competent at furthering the particular set of needs for which one is advocating. The strategic question that all advocates face is how to be credible as an adversary and at the same time be genuinely open to the potential that collaborative approaches offer. This dilemma is at the heart of most negotiations.

The Negotiator's Dilemma

How can negotiators protect their interests while developing cooperative relationships? This is the negotiator's dilemma. How do they enlarge the pie (create value, expand options, develop win-win outcomes) and also get as big a share of the pie as they want, deserve, or need (claim value, protect their interests)? This dilemma is one of the main problems that the field of conflict resolution has attempted to confront.

The problem negotiators face is that approaches that may maximize their effectiveness in one dimension often interfere with it in another. For example, to promote a cooperative negotiation, it is usually important to share information, to be candid about one's fundamental interests, and to be honest about one's alternatives. However, this can give valuable information to the other party should he or she decide to engage in hardball negotiations or to sue. Conversely, when people withhold this candor and proceed as if they are likely to end up in court, their chances of engaging in a collaborative negotiation process diminish. In this way disputants often create a self-fulfilling prophecy.

This dilemma is not hopeless. Negotiators do not have to choose one extreme or the other. But the dilemma is real and affects everyone's behavior in complex negotiations. The effectiveness of a negotiation is then largely determined by how well people handle its two major dimensions.

The Dimensions of Negotiation

There are two ways in which the parties to a negotiation can try to meet their needs. They can each try to claim as large a share of the available benefits for themselves (or the people they represent) as they need or want, or they can try to increase the total amount of benefits available to everyone. Each of these approaches can be found in almost all negotiations, and each tends to be associated with a particular set of strategies. (For other interesting descriptions of these dimensions, see Lax and Sebenius, 1986; Mnookin, 1993; Thomas, 1983; Walton and McKersie, 1965.)

To the extent that a negotiation is about gaining as much as possible of what is available, it is distributive. That is, as outlined in Chapter Two, the essence of this approach to negotiation involves an effort to come to an agreement about who gets how much of the benefits, values, goods, or services that are available. Unless relatively unlimited amounts of benefits are available to be distributed (in which case a substantive negotiation is probably not necessary), people operating along the distributive dimension are trying to get their needs met at someone else's expense. They are therefore in a structurally adversarial position (even if their behavior does not reflect this). When most people think about negotiation, this distributive dimension is what they have in mind.

Alternatively, people can try to meet their needs through increasing what is available for all and making sure everyone's needs are adequately addressed. To the degree that people are pursuing this integrative dimension, they have the common interest of increasing the pie and their needs are integrated. Addressing the distributive realities while achieving the integrative potential is often the major challenge that negotiators face and is another aspect of the negotiator's dilemma. This challenge was clearly demonstrated in a unique conflict resolution process that dealt with a highly contaminated site in an urban setting.

At one time, the Murray Smelter in Murray, Utah, was the largest lead ore smelter in the world. It was operated by the ASARCO Corporation until it closed in 1949. The site was then sold in parcels and used for a variety of purposes including concrete casting, asphalt production, warehouses, and trailer parks. It was eventually determined that this location contained some of the highest concentrations of arsenic and lead in the state. It was therefore designated for possible listing as a Superfund priority site for environmental clean up. The city of Murray viewed the site as having prime potential for commercial development. It was located near a major interstate highway, right on the route of a planned light rail system, and near the city's business district. City leaders wanted to avoid Superfund listing and to find a way to coordinate the clean up and redevelopment.

The cost of the clean up would be reduced significantly if the proposed roadway on the site could be a repository for low-level hazardous waste. The required levels of remediation would also be reduced if the site were covered with paving or other relatively impermeable barriers, and if it were not used for residences or for purposes that would require people to work outside. If a redevelopment plan could be worked out that would involve the sale of certain properties, a guarantee about future usage, ongoing monitoring of groundwater, and the construction of an appropriate roadway, considerable benefits could be achieved for everyone. The clean up would be cheaper, quicker, and more effective; the city could develop this site into a prime commercial (and taxable) location; and the frequently contentious process of allocating responsibilities and agreeing on clean-up levels and technologies could be shortcut. However, this was a very big if. Many pieces had to fall into place, each of which could have been subverted by any one of the many players involved. Much could be achieved for everyone, but only if no person or organization tried to claim too much of the benefit.

In order to work out the complex details of this plan, the Environmental Protection Agency (EPA) organized a roundtable process to discuss clean-up and redevelopment options. A CDR colleague and I served as facilitators. Participants included representatives from Murray, the EPA, the Utah Department of Environmental Quality, the state Attorney General's Office, the Utah Transportation Authority, ASARCO, all property owners and renters with long-term leases, the U.S. Department of Justice, and eventually the potential developer. The regulatory requirements and reconstruction plans for the nearby interstate, which related to preparations for the Salt Lake City Olympics, produced considerable time pressure.

Many aspects of the negotiation were distributive. How much land would each property owner allocate for the roadway? What contribution would be made by those whose property did not abut the road? How much would different parties contribute to the clean up? Many of these negotiations had to occur among people who had a history of conflict. If they had become too focused on meeting their needs at the expense of others, the whole process would have failed. A series of complicated distributive negotiations played out against the background of a powerful integrative potential. If these negotiations had focused solely on the integrative or win-win aspects, they would not have worked, because some distributive decisions had to be made. If any of these collateral negotiations had broken down or led to a court process, the whole opportunity could have collapsed. Naturally, some parties acted as if they were perfectly willing for that to happen and even threatened it from time to time.

In the end, however, the integrative opportunity prevailed. An overall agreement was reached, which led to a consent decree. Clean up began in the summer of 1998, the roadway was built and became the repository for the on-site storage of low-level waste, and the property is being developed for commercial purposes.

As in this example, all negotiations have distributive and integrative aspects, but at any given time, one of these dimensions tends to dominate the spirit of the discussions. It is important for conflict resolvers to understand the primary characteristics of each approach and the underlying attitudes that define them.

Distributive Negotiation

When negotiators are functioning primarily along the distributive dimension, they are focused on how to get the most of what is available for themselves or the people they represent. A distributive negotiator uses a variety of tactics to convince other parties to agree to the allocation of benefits that the negotiator wants. Some key characteristics of distributive negotiation involve specific ways of framing issues, applying power, using alternatives, sharing information, and reaching agreements.

Issues tend to be framed in terms of how to compromise among conflicting needs or how to choose among mutually exclusive alternatives. The distinguishing feature of distributive negotiation is not whether the issue is framed in harsh or gentle language. Distributive negotiation can be very friendly, and integrative negotiations can be very hostile. The key is that the issue is presented as a question about how to divide up a limited resource.

Power is applied to wrest concessions out of other parties. Rather than using power to develop creative options or to persuade others of the joint benefits to be accrued from a proposed solution, the parties apply power to convince others that they have no good alternative but to make concessions. In a distributive negotiation, people tend to be very focused on whether they are giving up or enhancing their power. People also tend to focus on their "rights," on whether they are getting "the best deal," or on how well they are doing relative to others rather than on whether they are arriving at a wise solution that meets their needs.

Alternatives are used as leverage to convince others to compromise or to give up potential benefits. Whereas in an integrative negotiation alternatives are used to enhance creativity and expand the options, in a distributive negotiation negotiators talk about how strong a court case they have and how willing they are to walk away from a negotiation. They argue that they do not really need an agreement but that the other negotiators surely do. In short, they play *alternative games,* attempting to manipulate each other's perceptions about the alternatives to a negotiated settlement in order to leverage each other into making concessions.

Distributive negotiators often refer to the "bottom line." They discuss this as if it were a definite location on the spectrum of possible outcomes: "Bottom line is I want the children to live with me during the school week"; "I am willing to sell this car for $7,500, but that is the bottom line." Generally, people use bottom line to mean the boundary between acceptable and unacceptable outcomes. But what determines this boundary and how porous is it? Typically, when people view their BATNA, their best alternative to a negotiated agreement (Fisher and Ury, 1981), as better than the potential agreement, they have reached their bottom line. If I think I am better off refusing to make a deal than to sell my car for less than $7,500, I have reached my bottom line. This is not, however, a simple cost-benefit consideration. People also think about whether they will lose face, about whether it is better to get nothing than to accept an unfair deal, about whether they would rather inflict pain on someone else than meet their own needs, and so forth. A bottom line is at best a moving target, always subject to changing circumstances, new information, and evolving emotional stances.

Furthermore, people arrive at their bottom line through an interactive process as they try to influence each other's perceptions of the alternatives. If I am in a distributive negotiation with you, I may want you to believe that I have many viable alternatives and that you have none. In addition, I may try to convince you that I am near my bottom line so that you will make concessions to obtain an agreement. In evaluating whether I have reached a good agreement, I will try to figure out whether I have gotten the most I can out of you, that is, whether you are close to your bottom line.

Information is a key item in the negotiation. Information is shared to the degree that it will convince others to compromise. Information that points out the weakness of others is helpful; information that points out the limits of one's own alternatives is not. The way information is shared also reflects the dimension of the negotiation. When information is presented as an argument for a particular outcome, that is usually a sign of a distributive approach. If it is presented as data to help everyone develop and evaluate alternatives, it is more likely that an integrative process is underway.

Agreement is reached when the parties accept a proposal they believe to be better than their realistic alternatives. This is normally a very subjective determination. People often evaluate their alternatives unconsciously or at best impressionistically. They rely on emotional information as well as logical cost-benefit analysis and factor in such things as loss of face and the emotional costs of continuing the process.

Distributive negotiations are not necessarily adversarial. People can work together in a friendly and open manner to decide how to apportion a limited resource among themselves. Most purchase and sales negotiations are friendly, collaborative, and distributive. However, when negotiations are about resolving a significant conflict where the stakes are high, relationships poor, and emotions raw, a distributive approach is likely to be contentious.

Integrative Negotiation

In integrative negotiation lies the solution to the negotiators' dilemma. The more the integrative dimension of a negotiation can be maximized, the more the dilemma will fade away. As described earlier, to the degree that this dimension is present in a negotiation, people are oriented to enlarging the pie, that is, to maximizing the benefits available for distribution among them or to meeting all parties' essential needs in some way.

Information is central to a successful integrative negotiation. There are two essential approaches to developing integrative, or win-win, outcomes, and both require an exchange of information. One is based on similarity of interests, the other on dissimilarity. Integrative solutions can be attained when people have a common interest that they can jointly pursue. Both parents usually are concerned about the well-being of their children. Environmentalists and industrialists often share a desire for predictability in governmental procedures for enforcing environmental regulations. These joint interests can form the underpinning of an integrative negotiation.

But having different interests is another basis for conflict resolution, as long as the interests are not in direct opposition to each other. If one parent wants to have particular influence over educational decisions for a child and the other wants to guide that child's religious upbringing, they have a basis for an integrative negotiation. Similarly, if one partner in a business dissolution cares about liquidity of assets and the other is concerned about long-term growth, they have an opportunity for an integrative solution.

Realizing the integrative potential, however, requires the parties to share enough information that they can discover their common or complementary needs. Much of what characterizes effective integrative negotiation is therefore related to enabling a free flow of information.

Integrative negotiations tend to be characterized by the following principles (which I originally developed for the CDR *Mediation Process Training Manual,* CDR Associates, 1986).

Integrative negotiation is about successful relationship building. Although most negotiations involve relationship-building activities, integrative negotiations are particularly dependent on them to be effective. This does not mean that people have to like, trust, admire, or enjoy each other. They do, however, have to be able to relate to each other well enough that they can work together to enhance the integrative aspect of the negotiations.

Integrative negotiation is about communication. Of course all negotiations involve communication, but specific attention to enhancing communication is usually necessary to maximize the integrative potential in bargaining. Negotiators create a communication system. It may be carried over from previous interchanges, or it may be freshly created, and its nature strongly affects how the negotiation proceeds. Negotiators are seldom aware of this, but the creation of a communication system is often the result of a negotiation within the primary negotiation. In an integrative negotiation, creating this system often becomes a conscious focus of attention.

Integrative negotiation is about education. The more intense an integrative negotiation effort is, the more it will involve a process of mutual education. It is important that key participants educate each other about their concerns, the constraints under which they are operating, the choices they feel they have, and the relevant information they are bringing to the table. Normally, this needs to occur before the parties focus on solutions or outcomes.

Integrative negotiation is about problem solving. Sometimes all that needs to occur in a negotiation is an exchange of information, a clearing of the air, or an assertion of beliefs and values. Normally, however, negotiation involves an attempt to reach an agreement about an issue or concern. To the extent that a negotiation is integrative, this process will take on the aspect of mutual problem solving. As negotiators start to view their task as pursuing a mutual solution to a mutual problem, it is natural for them to become more integrative in their approach.

Integrative negotiation is a principled process. There are three ways in which an integrative negotiation needs to be a principled process, and if it is not, the efforts to achieve joint benefits can easily be undercut. First, it is important that the negotiation be conducted in a way that meets the fundamental behavioral norms of the different participants. Although some people may feel that lying to people, misleading them, and intimidating them are acceptable behaviors in a negotiation, these behaviors do not promote mutual problem solving, effective communication, or rapport.

Second, integrative negotiations are often characterized by agreements in principle that define the mutual gains being sought. This allows the distributive elements present in almost all negotiations to be addressed without threatening the overall integrative thrust. If parents agree in principle that their children should have full access to both of them, that full access means at least 40 percent of the time, and that each parent has a right to be involved in essential decisions about the children's education, religion, and geographical location, then the distributive discussions of holidays, specific schedules, and transition arrangements are less likely to undercut the overall integrative effort.

Third, integrative negotiators try to distinguish between the basic principles or values they are promoting and the ways in which these can be realized. They can be very adamant about their essential concerns and values, and very insistent that these are addressed, but they remain open to a variety of ways in which this can occur.

Integrative negotiation is an interest-based process. Interest-based negotiation and integrative negotiation are not identical (as I discuss later in this chapter). A distributive negotiation may be conducted through a careful consideration of each party's interests. But an effective integrative negotiation usually requires negotiators to have a clear view of both their own interests and those of the others involved. Moreover, an integrative approach deals not only with people's substantive issues but with their procedural and psychological concerns as well. Usually the immediate focus of integrative negotiations is at the level of interests, but sometimes it is necessary to address more fundamental concerns relating to identity or even survival. A successful integrative negotiation finds the optimal level of depth at which to pursue meaningful joint benefits.

Integrative negotiation makes creativity the heart of problem solving. Developing mutually beneficial options takes considerable creativity. It is usually easier for negotiators to see how their needs can be met through others' concessions than to develop alternatives for joint gain. The challenge in integrative negotiations is to develop an atmosphere that promotes this creativity. One of the main reasons to work on establishing rapport, reducing tension, and building trust is to promote a negotiation culture in which it is safe and beneficial to be creative. Often people in negotiation processes have norms that stifle creativity. For example, it is often hard to brainstorm when negotiators believe that they cannot suggest an option for consideration unless they are willing to commit to it. How open or closed a process is also affects how creative people can be. Too closed a process is likely to shut out inputs that might enhance creativity, but too open a process makes individuals much more careful about what they say.

Integrative negotiation involves a genuine partnership among the participants. Unless negotiators become partners in the pursuit and execution of mutually beneficial solutions, it is hard for an integrative negotiation to take place. Partnership does not imply being friendly or ignoring conflict. It does mean that people must learn to work together to define issues; develop suitable negotiation procedures; educate each other; create a constructive negotiation culture; obtain important information; develop options for consideration; evaluate, modify, refine, and select options; and implement and monitor agreements. Practically speaking, it means more of this work is done jointly and less of it separately.

Integrative negotiation is not a panacea, nor is it always an appropriate goal for negotiators. However, it is often the key to solving otherwise intractable conflicts. All negotiations have both distributive and integrative dimensions. As important as it is to help people locked into a distributive process to see the integrative potential, it is also essential that integrative negotiators do not shy away from addressing the distributive elements of a problem.

The question often arises of what will occur when one negotiator is taking an integrative approach and the other is taking a distributive approach. However, the question itself betrays a misunderstanding of the interactive nature of negotiation. It may be that one party is being more aggressive, adversarial, or hostile than the other, but the degree to which a negotiation develops along the distributive or integrative dimension is a product of the interaction among the participants, not the individual behavior of any one negotiator. People behave in an integrative or distributive way because the situation calls for it or because in some way it meets their needs. The interaction of their approaches, which is itself a sort of negotiation, determines the nature of the overall process.

The task for conflict resolvers is to make sure that the integrative potential is maximized, to find a way of approaching the distributive elements without escalating a conflict, and to promote a negotiation culture that allows people to be effective advocates and effective partners at the same time. This is how we can help people resolve the negotiator's dilemma.

Positional and Interest-Based Negotiation

Since the publication of *Getting to Yes* (Fisher and Ury, 1981), the concepts of positional and interest-based negotiation have become central to many conflict resolvers' view of the negotiation process and the ways they try to intervene in it. Moreover, people tend to equate positional negotiation with a distributive approach and interest-based negotiation with an integrative approach. But the concepts are not the same, and we miss the underlying dynamics in negotiation when we confuse them. The distributive and integrative dimensions of a negotiation are defined by the degree to which the emphasis of the negotiation process is on dividing up benefits among the parties or on maximizing benefits for all. Positional negotiation is differentiated from interest-based negotiation by the degree to which the process focuses on a proposed solution or an analysis of interests and needs. In positional negotiation, people focus on a series of proposed solutions (positions), which they defend or alter depending on the circumstances. In interest-based negotiation, people discuss their needs and concerns and look for options to address them. One set of concepts is about the basic structure of negotiation—how people define their purpose and their fundamental orientation toward accomplishing it—and the other is about tactics and attitudes.

In addition, the distinction between positional and interest-based negotiation is often overemphasized and this may be misleading. A single-minded concentration on positions can quickly lead to adversarial and polarized interactions, for example. So, as a tactic, focusing people on a consideration of interests as opposed to a debate about proposed solutions is often very effective. As a conflict resolution trainer, I have found that the concepts of positions and interests are useful to people who want to learn new ways of approaching conflict. They provide a tangible way of distinguishing between cooperative and adversarial approaches and suggest some useful tactics. But there are several problems with placing these concepts at the center of an approach to collaborative negotiation.

All negotiations involve a focus on both interests and positions. Even the most adversarial bargainer will often express his or her interests and explore those of other parties. And even the most interest-based negotiator cannot and should not avoid presenting proposed solutions at various times during a negotiation. It is naïve to think that a simple focus on interests will change the fundamental nature of most negotiations or that an exchange of statements about positions is always a counterproductive activity. Often such an exchange is a useful and necessary step in an orderly and productive consideration of the nature of the conflict and the needs of the parties. Considering interests in the abstract is sometimes less effective than uncovering them through an analysis of the rationale behind the solutions that negotiators propose, as was the case in the following instance.

> In a negotiation about the location of a roadway through a community, early efforts to talk directly about stakeholders' interests elicited broad and somewhat bland statements about noise, accessibility, esthetics, and so forth. There was no new information here, and some people felt that they were going through an academic exercise. However, when particular proposals (positions) about roadway location were put forward, two things occurred. People became more engaged and creative, and a much richer discussion of interests ensued, as people sought to understand the rationale for each proposal.

Although a focus on interests may lead to a more effective communication style, it is the change in how people communicate that is really important, however that change occurs. As discussed in the previous chapter, what usually needs to occur for a negotiation to be successful is for people to learn to communicate effectively. If people really listen to each other and try to understand what is at stake for all participants in a negotiation, they will naturally focus on each other's needs.

Negotiators' basic attitude about what they are trying to accomplish is also more significant then whether they are focusing on positions or interests. Are people trying to win or to solve a problem? Do they see the other negotiators as enemies, adversaries, rivals, partners, or colleagues? Do they see the negotiation as a contest or a dialogue? Individuals' different attitudes may be reflected in how positional or interest-based their negotiation style is, but it is the attitudes that are usually the driving force.

Furthermore, positions and interests themselves are not as different as they might first appear. The difference between positions and interests is usually a difference in depth of analysis and style of presentation. If I ask for custody of my children, that is a position. If instead I say it is important to me to be the primary parent with sole decision-making authority, then I have presented my interests. But these interests can be presented as a new position. I can demand to be the primary parent with sole decision-making power. The interests behind this new position might be that I do not want to have to communicate on a regular basis with my ex-spouse and I want my children to attend my neighborhood school. But these interests too can be put forward as positions.

What is important is whether negotiators have understood each other's needs at the appropriate level of depth. If the parties stay too shallow in their exploration of each other's needs, they will find themselves bargaining without a clear picture of the real concerns motivating the negotiation. If they go too deep, they will be trying to solve problems that may be unsolvable or at least beyond what is currently at stake. The problem with positional bargaining is not really its focus on positions as opposed to interests but its adversarial manner of presenting ideas, its lack of depth in exploring the parties' needs, and its failure to establish effective communication among negotiators.

How Negotiators Reach Closure

The process by which people agree to solutions in negotiations is often complex. There are several interrelated processes that are usually in play.

The Closing of the Way

There is a Quaker saying that "progress occurs as the way closes behind." In a healthy negotiation, as more information is shared and more effective patterns of communication develop, options are identified and possible paths are opened. However, equally important is that potential approaches to resolution become narrower. Without such narrowing, closure is very difficult. People often agree to rule out options because they are unworkable or unacceptable to at least some of the participants. At other times, as more information is shared, it becomes clear that certain approaches will not work whereas others hold potential. There comes a point in many negotiations when the parameters within which a negotiated agreement is possible become very clear. At this point participants have to decide whether an agreement within these parameters is better than no agreement at all.

The Convergence of Integrative and Distributive Negotiation

In most negotiations there are limits to the integrative potential of a resolution process, and there are also boundaries outside of which distributive agreements are not possible. An optimal solution to a negotiation may sometimes be thought of as one in which no party can achieve any additional benefits except at the expense of another party. In other words the full integrative potential of the situation has been achieved. Social scientists sometimes refer to this outcome as *Pareto optimality*, because it was discussed by Italian social theorist Vilfredo Pareto (Lax and Sebenius, 1986).

The nearer negotiators get to this point in a problem-solving process, the more difficult it becomes to find ways of achieving further mutual gains. As this happens, it is natural for negotiations to begin thinking more distributively, for everyone to look for ways to claim a greater share of the pie. That is why, even in the most collaborative negotiations, there is often a lot of horse trading and increased tension at the end. Similarly, negotiations that have been primarily distributive tend to reach a point where there is little left on the table to be divided up. At this point, people's attention may well turn to whether there is a way to expand the pie. In these ways, integrative and distributive negotiations tend to converge. The way in which people bounce between these dimensions can sometimes look like this elaborate dance.

Brenner Enterprises, a small exercise equipment manufacturer, had been renting space in a building owned by the Warren family. Brenner had three years left on its lease, but the Warrens wanted to terminate the lease early in order to take advantage of a lucrative offer by the XYZ supermarket chain to buy the property. The offer contained a considerable bonus if the property were free of tenants so that the chain could begin constructing a superstore immediately. Brenner was willing to consider moving, especially because its plans called for an expansion beyond the capacity of its current facility.

On the surface a deal should have been easy to come by. However, both Brenner and the Warrens wanted to get the best deal for themselves that they could. Brenner wanted considerable compensation for moving early, and the Warrens wanted to make no concessions. According to Brenner, the Warrens were about to get a windfall, and it would be a serious inconvenience for Brenner to move earlier than it had been thinking of. The Warren family argued that Brenner would benefit greatly by getting out of its lease early and that if anything Brenner should pay some penalty. The following reconstructed interchanges indicate some of the approaches each group's representatives took to this negotiation.

Brenner: We are willing to move early if that will help you, but it is inconvenient for us to do so, and we will incur significant additional expenses for which we expect to be compensated. If we cannot arrive at a fair compensation, we will be happy to stay.

Warren: You approached us several months ago inquiring whether we would consider negotiating an early lease termination, so don't pretend that this is such a great sacrifice. We are willing to try to negotiate a reasonable deal, but if not, we will be happy to let you stay until your lease expires.

Strategy note: Both are playing the alternatives game here—Brenner says it is happy to stay. The Warren family dismisses Brenner's concerns about leaving and say they are happy to have Brenner stay. Both are claiming that the alternative to negotiating an agreement is just fine for them.

Warren: You were late with your rent twice last year, and you violated the lease provision about parking your vehicles. We think we have a case for terminating your lease. We would prefer to negotiate a friendly solution, and we are prepared to pay some small amount as an incentive to you to find a new location within three months.

Brenner: You failed to maintain the parking area in the condition the lease requires, and we have previously discussed the late payments. You have no case for termination. We are willing to move early if we receive adequate compensation for the inconvenience. We will probably have to go through a period of curtailed production while we move, and this will result in some significant losses. We are sure that any court would recognize this. Also the soonest we could move would be in six months.

Strategy note: Both are continuing to play the alternatives game—this time by arguing that each can force the other to comply. More important, however, they are indicating their willingness to deal and are beginning to reveal their interests, which have to do with timing, amount of compensation, and disruption of production. They are also suggesting principles that might be applied to a solution.

Warren: So we have agreed that we will compensate you the equivalent of four months rent if you move out within six months, and six months rent if you move out within four months, assuming our deal with XYZ Corporation goes through.

Brenner: We would also like you to share in our moving costs, and we need to be told for sure that this deal is on within the next two weeks or we will be unable to conduct essential planning for our business.

Warren: We cannot rush XYZ or it may back off the whole deal, which would hurt us both. Also, there is no way that we can assume part of your moving costs. You were going to have to incur those anyway, if not now, soon.

Strategy note: They are working out a deal that is essentially integrative, although the discussion sure sounds like a distributive and positional negotiation. The closer they get to maximizing the integrative potential, the more they are trying to eke out some further distributive gains. When they run into a distributive roadblock, they naturally look for further integrative options.

And so it went. While Brenner and the Warrens negotiated, the Warrens continued to talk with XYZ to try to get additional assistance in buying out Brenner's lease. In the end, as the deadline for closing a deal approached, Brenner and the Warrens worked out a deal that included a little assistance with moving, a six-month rent waiver, and a two-phased move in which Brenner would move its manufacturing operation in four months and its warehouse in six.

Fractionalization

Another way negotiators reach agreement is through breaking a conflict down into smaller parts. This fractionalization can make a negotiation more manageable and create opportunities for incremental successes. People can then gradually chip away at their larger conflict, and they can develop an investment in preserving agreements that have already been reached. Fractionalizing also creates more opportunities for trade-offs than would otherwise exist and allows some issues to be settled and others to be delayed to a time when resolution is more likely.

Fractionalization carries dangers as well. If issues are inappropriately divided and people try to deal with closely related pieces separately, they can become harder to solve. Sometimes it becomes particularly difficult to settle the last remaining issues because the opportunities for trade-offs diminished when earlier agreements were reached. Also, an issue that seems small and readily resolvable can become a real showstopper if it turns out to represent a fundamental underlying dispute that is not being addressed. The art of fractionalization is to divide a conflict into manageable chunks that are neither too large nor too small and that do not isolate any major issue in a way that makes creative problem solving more difficult.

Agreements in Principle

The flip side of fractionalizing a conflict is attacking it on its most general level. Often general, or in-principle, agreements can be reached on the broad issues, and these agreements can then be refined and specified until the parties reach concrete operational agreements. On the one hand the advantage of this approach is that it defines the overall dimensions of the needed final agreement, it creates a framework in which individual issues can be resolved, and it builds a gradual habit of agreement among people before they have to commit themselves to specifics. On the other hand, often the devil is in the details. People may feel they have an agreement only to see it fall apart when they attempt to negotiate the specifics. We can look at the history of attempts to implement the Oslo agreement between Israel and the Palestinians to see both the advantages and disadvantages of this approach. As a general rule, however, it is useful to start out in a negotiation by identifying the agreements in principle that can be reached and that can then pave the way for the rest of the discussion.

The Fractionalization–In-Principle Loop

As is the case with other sets of approaches, in practice negotiations do not usually follow one or the other of the previous two strategies exclusively. Negotiators loop back and forth between fractionalizing issues and arriving at broader more comprehensive agreements. Often people start with one approach, pursue it until they are no longer making progress, switch to the other approach, pursue that one as far as is practicable, and so on. I have often seen coworkers agree, sometimes almost too quickly, on general statements about respect, teamwork, and open communication. They often become stuck, however, when they try to make these agreements operational by specifying just how workload divisions, performance reviews, and decision making will work. The art of reaching closure often involves making wise decisions about when to go for more specific and detailed agreements, when to work on more general principles, and when to stop pursing agreements for a time in order to delve more deeply into the needs of each party.

The Maturation of a Conflict

In reaching closure, as in so many other steps in conflict resolution, timing is critical. Often negotiators have a pretty good idea from the outset about the kind of agreement they will reach, but until a conflict or issue has matured, it is not possible to achieve closure. Brenner Enterprises and the Warren family probably could have predicted the outcome of their negotiations, but they still had to go through their dance. Trying to reach closure prematurely can harden people's resistance to a solution that they might have been more open to at a later time. Conversely, when people wait too long they may see their potential agreement unravel or fade in power.

When is a conflict mature? When participants have engaged in a mutual educational process; when emotions that have kept people from carefully considering their alternatives have subsided; when the issues have been effectively framed, essential information gathered and shared, and realistic alternatives identified and evaluated; and when the value to people of remaining in conflict has sufficiently diminished, then a conflict has essentially matured. In other words, *complete* maturation of a complex conflict is a rare thing. The fact that a conflict is immature does not mean the resolution efforts are doomed. Immature conflicts can be resolved, but complete closure is likely to be an elusive goal.

Gaining the Inner Part of the Wheel of Conflict

Because resolution requires dealing with the feelings people have as well as the outcomes they are seeking, most closure requires some emotional discharge as well as problem solving. Often we think of these steps as sequential, but this can be misleading. People do not usually get their emotions dealt with first and their problem solved later; these two processes are intertwined throughout. As discussed in Chapter Five, the cognitive, emotional, and behavioral dimensions of resolution tend to develop together and to reinforce one another. Often during closure people revisit each element of the resolution process. They need to try on earlier perceptions of each other or of a conflict, and they need to again experience some of the feelings associated with an earlier stage of the process. As people near closure, many of their earlier fears and resentments are reawakened. Often it is not until people consider a potential agreement that they really face the implications of settling a conflict, including the emotional ramifications.

Successive Reframing

Successive reframing is a common and natural way to articulate operational agreements. It takes the parties through an iterative refinement of a problem statement, during which they gradually define and redefine the issues to be resolved in narrower ways, until the problem statement resembles a solution (see Figure 7.1). This process involves the following components.

Figure 7.1.　Successive Reframing.

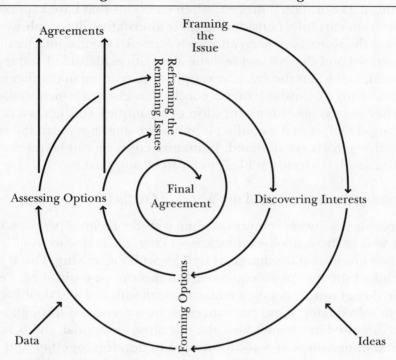

Framing the Issue

Whether artful or clumsy, implied or explicit, an issue somehow is initially framed for discussion.

> *Framing:*　Who's going to have the children when?
> *Framing:*　Something has got to be done about the impact of this factory on this community.

After the issue is framed the search for a solution begins.

Discovering Interests

People go through some process of discovering each other's interests. Often they do not recognize that they are doing this, but each person almost always has some assumptions about what the other parties to the conflict are trying to accomplish.

> *First party:*　I want the children some part of each week and weekend.
> *Second party:*　I do not want the children living out of a suitcase.

First party: We need this place cleaned up because it is degrading our community and threatening our health.

Second party: We can't take responsibility for turning a commercial area into a homeowners' paradise.

Forming Options

Sometimes in a separate step, sometimes interspersed throughout the process, options are generated. Options may take the form of positions, suggestions, demands, possibilities, ideas, or proposals, but somehow negotiators propose alternatives that will at a minimum meet their own needs and may also address the needs of others.

First party: Perhaps the children should spend Sunday through Thursday with me and the rest of the week with you.

Second party: Why don't you take them every other weekend and one night during the week.

First party: Let's just agree that all hazardous emissions will be halted, noise reduced, contaminants removed from the site, and future plant traffic diverted around the community.

Second party: We will gladly comply with all relevant regulations, and we will be happy to demonstrate our compliance to a community advisory panel.

Assessing Options

Options are then assessed in some manner. Sometimes this assessment is formal and purposeful. At other times it is almost unconscious or it is mixed in with the overall process of advocacy and argumentation. During this assessment some options may be rejected, others accepted, and still others carried forward for further discussion.

First party: Sunday through Thursday is a long block of time for me to have no contact with the children, plus I want to see them on some Sundays.

Second party: I want them to have blocks of time with me, not just popping in every other weekend.

Agreements: some school week and weekend time with each parent

Rejected options: visits every other weekend

For further discussion: a smooth schedule with some weekend and weekday time with each parent

First party: "All hazardous emissions" is an extreme standard. The goal of zero emissions is neither practical nor necessary.

Second party: Your version of compliance is very different from what we believe is required by law and necessary for our health.

Agreements: some clean up and reduction of hazardous emissions

Rejected options: zero emissions, simple statement about regulatory compliance

For further discussion: target levels for emission reduction and other clean-up procedures

Reframing the Remaining Options and Issues

At this point one of the most crucial and creative steps in the problem-solving process occurs, often naturally, sometimes intentionally. The issue is reframed in a more specific way, reflecting the evaluation process that has occurred and the interests that have been discovered. Throughout this process, more information has been added to the discussion. It may have consisted of data about issues, options, constraining or enabling circumstances, or other developments. The reframing reflects this new information.

Reframing: Let's figure out a schedule that gives each of us about equal weekend time and the possibility of weekends off as well and that gives each of us substantial although not equal time during the week.

Reframing: We need to identify clean-up levels that are feasible, legal, and healthy.

The reframing is not always as balanced, clear, interest based, or friendly as this. But somehow, the issue becomes more narrowly defined. The entire reframing process is then repeated in some way, often many times. The final framing of the issue resembles a final agreement.

Final Reframing: We need to agree on which two school nights attached to the weekend the children will spend with me every other week, and which single night during the alternate weeks they will stay with me.

Final Reframing: How are we going to know when you have achieved emission reduction to the point where public health risk factors in our community have reached the agreed-upon level?

Sometimes successive reframing converges on an agreement as illustrated here. Sometimes it can only go so far before an impasse is reached and more information must be collected, time must be allotted for the issues to mature, or work in another arena must be done. At other times the process seems almost to reverse itself and come unraveled. Particular agreements that have been reached fall apart, interests that have been taken into account are ignored, and options that have been rejected are brought back for consideration. This is just to say that not all negotiations succeed, and those that do succeed are unlikely to follow a simple, linear path. However, despite the uncertainties and variations of the closure process, I have found the dynamic of successive reframing to be the key to how people zero in on agreements and achieve closure during many negotiations.

We all negotiate daily, and our success in our personal and professional lives is closely related to how effective we are as negotiators. Any effort to analyze the dynamics of negotiation, or of any complex human interaction, must inevitably run up against the reality that every person, situation, and system creates its own process. Furthermore, some of the most important occurrences in negotiation are unconscious, unintentional, or instinctive. People will not become better negotiators by trying to keep all the dynamics described in this chapter in their minds all the time. However, the more people understand the essential dimensions and dilemmas of the negotiation process, the better they will be at handling a wide variety of negotiation challenges. Becoming conscious of these dimensions and dilemmas does not require people to sacrifice their natural skills, their spontaneity, or their instinctive responses. But these skills and abilities need to be built on and refined, just as we work to improve our skills in music, sports, parenting, or any other endeavor that matters to us.

Chapter Eight

The Road to Resolution
Overcoming Impasse

Many conflicts appear to lurch from impasse to impasse, and few disputes follow a straightforward path to resolution. Even the most skillful conflict resolvers are sometimes at a loss for a way to move a resolution process forward in the face of what seems to be an intractable dispute. None of our theories or techniques can force someone to be reasonable, flexible, or wise. Disputants often seem closed-minded, and conflicts can drag on for a long time with destructive results for everyone. This raises an important question for conflict resolvers. How should we understand impasse, and what can we do about it?

The Nature of Impasse

Impasse is a necessary and often useful part of the conflict process. When people are at an impasse, they are not ready or able to move forward through conflict and resolution, or at least not by using their current approach. Impasse is not necessarily destructive, although it can be, and it occurs because in some way it meets the needs of at least one of the parties. We often think of impasse as *being stuck*, but this can be a misleading metaphor. Being stuck can imply that people would like to move forward or that it would be better for them to move forward if only their own inadequacies or the forces entrapping them were less. I do not think this is a helpful way of looking at impasse, even if it is occasionally accurate. Often people are at an impasse for very good reasons, and sometimes they are quite content to be there. The key to understanding impasse is to view it in terms of what it is accomplishing for the parties involved and not to focus solely on why it is a problem.

Tactical and Genuine Impasse

An impasse can be tactical or genuine. Tactical impasse occurs when disputants refuse to proceed with a resolution effort in an attempt to increase their negotiating power, to put pressure on others to make concessions, or to enhance their negotiating position in some other way. In other words, they are intentionally using impasse as a means for advancing their goals. Tactical impasses usually result from a short-term calculation of costs and benefits and do not usually last very long. They are generally indicative of a distributive approach to negotiation. Employing them can be a high-risk strategy because it can escalate a conflict.

One of the most dramatic examples of tactical impasse I have encountered was also one of the least effective. In retrospect, it was not surprising that impasse was used so dramatically in this case. After all, at issue was the future of a theater company.

About forty long-term members of a theater troupe were about to file a suit against the board of directors of the nonprofit performing arts center with which they were affiliated. The actors, directors, and technical staff had accepted lower salaries and donated much time over many years under the assumption that the money saved was being used to sustain and expand the theater facility and an associated school for actors, producers, and directors. Then the central figure in this organization, a well-known theater director and the CEO of the center, was suddenly fired because the board discovered that she had appropriated a great deal of money for her own purposes and that the building fund and endowment were basically nonexistent.

Most of the theater troupe had looked to this director as a teacher, mentor, and friend. They felt personally abused and wanted compensation for the money they had sacrificed. The board had acknowledged that some settlement was appropriate, but the board and the troupe members were far apart in their views of how big it should be. They asked a colleague and me to mediate this dispute.

After several difficult and emotional meetings we were able to focus on a potential settlement formula. Important principles were agreed to and considerable progress was being made in arriving at specific terms when the attorney representing the plaintiffs suddenly announced that they were pulling out of the negotiations and proceeding with their suit in court. He indicated that his group had compromised as much as it possibly could, that he did not believe the board had taken any genuine responsibility for what had happened, and that unless the board was prepared to accept all the terms of the plaintiffs' "last and final" offer, the plaintiffs were going to court.

My co-mediator and I were surprised by the suddenness of this because we had thought that considerable progress was being made. We both suspected that this was primarily a tactic to wrest further concessions from the board, but we were not sure. When we met privately with the plaintiff group, the attorney was every bit as adamant, but the plaintiffs seemed uncomfortable. Clearly, the attorney was trying to convince us that they were in fact ready to go to court, but by then we were quite sure this was a tactical move. Nevertheless it was not an empty bluff. To really pull this off, the attorney had to be willing to carry out the threat—even though to us it seemed contrary to his clients' interests.

The board members were outraged. They felt they had been extremely generous. They also felt they had a fairly strong legal case themselves, but that the process of taking the dispute to court would be detrimental to the organization. They thought that the plaintiffs were not negotiating in good faith, and they were ready to call the bluff—which could have led to a genuine impasse. No one really wanted to go to court at this point, but there would have been no easy way of avoiding the next step, which was to formally file a suit. This would almost certainly have led to considerable negative publicity for the organization, with potentially serious financial consequences.

My colleague and I decided to do two things. First, we wrote up the agreements in principle and the range of outcomes that people had discussed, so that they would not be lost and so that people would have tangible evidence of how far they had come in their discussions. Second, we redefined the impasse as an important time for each group to think through its choices and to see if any other approaches to a settlement might be developed. We did not try to get either group to make any further concessions.

Not surprisingly, the impasse did not last long. A key board member held a series of informal meetings with one of the plaintiffs to examine other options, and they were able to come up with a plan that was acceptable to the vast majority of the plaintiffs and to the board. It involved a few minor concessions to the plaintiffs, but more important, it redefined the settlement offer in such a way that it was not the "take it" or "leave it" set of proposals previously identified, but a new formula entirely. In the end, it became the basis for settlement. Certain additional (although fairly small) gains were probably achieved through the use of this tactical impasse but at a cost of considerably greater stress and anger than the parties might otherwise have experienced.

Genuine impasse occurs when people feel unable to move forward with a resolution process without sacrificing something important to them. If, for example, the board members had felt that their only option besides impasse was to agree to terms that would bankrupt the center (which is in fact how they did feel at times), then they would have been at a genuine impasse. Usually, disputants experience this kind of impasse as beyond their control, and they feel they have no acceptable choice but to remain there. Of course disputants sometimes try to use a genuine impasse to their tactical advantage, and sometimes what starts out as a tactical impasse can become genuine. The tactical use of impasse by the theater troupe came very close to producing a genuine impasse, because what was tactical from the troupe's perspective was genuine from the board's perspective.

The Dimensions of Impasse

The dimensions of conflict and the wheel of conflict offer two approaches to understanding the nature of an impasse. Impasses can occur on the emotional, cognitive, or behavioral dimensions of conflict. Of course many play out in more than one of these dimensions.

When people cannot move toward resolution because their feelings prevent such progress, then they are at an emotional impasse. A divorcing couple who are so locked into their anger at each other that they cannot agree to anything, despite the fact that an agreement would meet their substantive needs, are at an emotional impasse. For some people, arriving at a divorce settlement requires the emotional relinquishment of a relationship, and some cannot move toward resolution because they are not ready for this. At other times a person's level of anger is so great that the act of arriving at any agreement feels like a personal violation. Whenever a disputant cannot proceed down a path toward resolution because of such obstacles, he or she is experiencing an emotional impasse of some kind.

A cognitive impasse occurs when people cannot change their view of the conflict or the other parties in a way that the resolution process demands. The dramatic moment when Yitzak Rabin struggled over and then made the decision to shake Yassir Arafat's hand in the Rose Garden of the White House when they signed their historic agreement was a wonderful illustration of someone making the effort to overcome a cognitive impasse. For most of his life, Rabin had viewed Arafat as a terrorist. To change his perception of Arafat and see him as a partner in peace was a major cognitive switch. Arafat had to overcome a similar cognitive obstacle. That they could achieve this cognitive change was perhaps their major personal contribution to the peace process. It helped many Israelis and Palestinians go through a similar process, an effort that continues to this day. The struggle of Palestinians and Israelis to change their views of each other and to redefine the issues in their conflict may be the most important part of the process for bringing peace to that region. Cognitive impasses are often the most difficult to overcome.

A behavioral impasse occurs when people cannot identify or agree on behaviors, or actions, and therefore cannot move the resolution process forward. Will a dam get built, or will it not? What pay raises or other benefits will people agree to in a contract negotiation? What level of emissions will become the legal limit for a certain chemical? This is the dimension that most people generally focus on when they experience impasse, but it is often derivative of the other two dimensions. When the impasse is genuinely based in the behavioral dimension, people usually feel that moving forward toward resolution at that moment does not meet their needs as well as does remaining at an impasse or pursuing some other route of achieving their goals.

The Sources of Impasse

It is also useful to examine an impasse in terms of the wheel of conflict (Figure 8.1) in order to think about its essential source. Impasse always occurs because one or more of the disputants have needs that they believe or sense will not be adequately met by moving toward resolution. Sometimes this is a very clear and deliberative decision; sometimes it is made instinctively or unconsciously. Often this decision involves choosing among competing needs. For example, if I have made a strong statement that I will not agree to some-

Figure 8.1. The Wheel of Conflict.

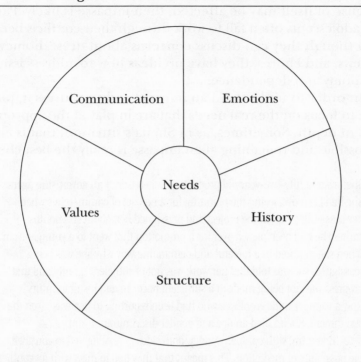

thing unless certain conditions are met, then I have created a need to maintain face by remaining true to this position, even though I might meet other important needs by backing off. This was one of the ways in which the theater troupe nearly created a genuine impasse out of a tactical move. Disputants dig this kind of hole for themselves all the time. Often resolving an impasse is a matter of timing. Have I fought the good fight long enough that I can now gracefully accept a lesser agreement? Moving toward resolution often means accepting that a perfect solution is not possible, that not all of one's needs can be completely met. This is often very hard for people to do, and sometimes it is easier to remain at an impasse than it is to face these choices.

Sometimes resolution efforts are ineffective because they address one level of need but the source of the impasse is at a different level. For example, if negotiations about siting a landfill in a community focus on traffic, aesthetics, emissions, discharges, and land use but fail to address the way in which a community's image or sense of itself may be affected, then impasse is likely. Parents and adolescents often fail to work through their conflicts because, even though they can discuss concerns about dress, homework, curfews, and chores, they have no ideas how to address issues of autonomy and dependence.

In order to understand an impasse and to address it, people have to focus on the real needs that are in play at the appropriate level of depth. Sometimes, as in Sheila's situation, that is almost impossible and remaining at an impasse is really the best choice.

Sheila was a fifty-five-year-old production supervisor at an advertising agency. She had been overseeing the planning for a new set of commercials when her boss pulled her off the project and reassigned her. About six months earlier she had been passed over for a promotion that went to a younger man. When she inquired in a forceful and demanding way why she was being reassigned, she was told that her work was not of sufficient quality and that progress was not being made at a sufficient pace. To add insult to injury, Roy, a younger male employee who had been reporting to her, was given the assignment. Sheila filed an age and gender discrimination suit.

In keeping with company policy, both sides were obligated to consider the possibility of mediation. This meant that they had to meet with a "conflict resolution counselor" to discuss the advisability of mediating although they were not bound to actually enter mediation. Of course by meeting with a counselor they were in a way beginning a mediation process. I was asked to serve as the counselor. Normally, this step would have been handled in house, but the human resource director had been involved in a previous grievance filed by Sheila and felt that it would be advisable to bring in someone from the outside.

Jonathan, the department supervisor, felt that Sheila's work had long been substandard and that it was only because she was seen as "litigious" that she had not been demoted. He felt that he had taken a big risk by assigning her to the project in the first place. He had only done it, he said, because she had campaigned hard for a chance to prove herself after she was passed over for the promotion. In his view she had been in totally over her head, and the only reason the project was not in big trouble was that Roy had been covering for her. He felt he would have been putting the company (and his own reputation) in jeopardy if he had not taken decisive action.

Sheila of course had a very different view. She felt that she was never given credit for what she had accomplished and that the agency was "an old boys' club with a glass ceiling." She felt that she had repeatedly "pulled Jonathan's chestnuts out of the fire" and that he was covering up his own incompetence by blaming her for problems for which she was not responsible. What was really interesting to me was that there was nothing Sheila really wanted out of the grievance procedure other than victory. She no longer wanted the project back. She was not interested in promotion, reassignment, or financial recognition of any kind. On the part of the grievance form that asked her to name the redress she was asking for, she had written some fairly confusing language about wanting "vindication" and a guarantee that "nothing like this will ever happen again." When the company suggested training programs to enhance her skills and other ways to support her in future projects, she dismissed those ideas out of hand.

Sheila confided to me that she thought things would change in the organization only if the management was publicly humiliated in an arbitration or court proceeding. She was obviously very angry about what had happened, and beneath her anger was a significant injury to her pride and self-esteem. She was very clear that she would rather lose in an adversarial contest than work out an agreement, even though she realized that her job could be in jeopardy.

I filed a report in which I summarized and framed the issues and options as best I could, and I recommended that the parties not proceed with mediation. The case went to arbitration. Sheila lost and shortly afterward resigned.

I have often wondered what else might have been done to overcome this impasse. Could Sheila have received the recognition or acknowledgment she needed through mediation to allow her to discuss some realistic agreement? Was there some level at which I was not hearing her or understanding her feelings or needs? Probably, but I also believe that in a way she got just what she wanted. She stood up for herself. She did not compromise on what she felt was an assault on her dignity, and she tried very hard to get full vindication. When she did not, she gave herself an acceptable reason to leave what was in some ways a good job for her but in other ways was a dead end that was contributing to a deteriorating self-image.

As discussed in Chapter One, needs do not exist in a vacuum, and it is important to locate the impasse in the outer circle of the wheel of conflict as well. Are disputants unable to communicate effectively or at all, and if not, why not? Have their emotions overwhelmed their ability to think clearly about ways to address their needs? Are historical forces hindering a resolution process, and are they too powerful for people to overcome? Is the immediate conflict part of a larger dispute from which it can not be separated? Are structural factors impeding progress? Are people unable to move forward because they cannot overcome basic value differences or because it is more important for them to assert their values than resolve the conflict?

A key to understanding impasse is to accept that from some vantage point it makes sense. Often this vantage point is hard to take, but we must try if we are going to understand what is really happening. There are two common shortcuts we often take to explaining both conflict and impasse. We ascribe impasses to disputants' immoral or evil behavior or to their irrational or crazy behavior. How else can we explain, we tell ourselves, Saddam Hussein's behavior in Kuwait, Milosevic's in Kosovo and Bosnia, or Hitler's? But these explanations merely end up begging the question of what is really going on.

The problem with these approaches is that they really explain nothing and they lead to inappropriate or rigid responses. If someone with power is really crazy or evil, then obviously the only way to change his or her behavior is by overwhelming force. Although it may be necessary at times to employ coercive power, it is much wiser to do this as a consequence of understanding the needs that are motivating disputants than as a consequence of a rationale that focuses on disputants' moral or mental deficiencies. There may be plenty of craziness and evil afoot, but they seldom explain why a particular approach to conflict predominates, particularly when we look beyond interpersonal disputes. Depicting impasse as stemming from insanity or immorality is often an excuse, a means for avoiding a serious consideration of the essential needs that are at stake and the real sources of the problem.

Moving Through Impasse

As with so much else about effective conflict resolution, moving through impasse is usually more a matter of attitude than of tool or technique. Seldom will people break a significant impasse by using a clever intervention strategy, unless that strategy addresses the fundamental cause of the impasse or the needs of the participants. Third parties and disputants are more likely to be effective in dealing with impasses if they operate with certain attitudes and beliefs. (For a very practical approach to dealing with impasse, see Ury, 1991.)

Constructive Attitudes About Impasse

Impasse is OK. It is easy to believe there is something wrong with people who are not ready to move forward toward resolution. But this attitude is seldom helpful. It leads to a focus on disputants' behaviors or personalities rather than to an understanding of the nature of the problem that needs to be addressed, and it can easily cause people to respond to an impasse by turning up the pressure for conflict resolution to unproductive levels. The consequences of an impasse can be serious, but it is important not to proceed as if the problem were the impasse itself. It is better to have the attitude that impasses are acceptable in disputes.

People have good reasons for being at an impasse. Everyone who chooses not to move toward resolution is doing so for a good reason from his or her point of view. Sometimes remaining at an impasse is the only choice people feel they have.

Disputants have to find their own way through an impasse. Third parties can help, but if they take it upon themselves to "solve a conflict," "fix a problem," or "break a deadlock" they are missing the point. Third parties help by working with disputants to address the source of the impasse or to find a creative solution to it. But it is the disputants themselves who have to move through the impasse when they are ready. When mediators take too much responsibility for overcoming an impasse, they can actually make things worse by allowing the parties individually and collectively to avoid responsibility for looking at their own situations clearly and courageously.

Anxiety and fear are not helpful. For both disputants and third parties, anxiety is often the biggest problem to be faced in an impasse. Anxiety and fear breed rigidity and shut down communication and creativity. Therefore it is usually important to avoid the temptation to try to move past impasse by increasing people's fear and anxiety. If the situation is really dangerous or the stakes are extremely high, then anxiety can be a natural response, and perhaps a useful warning sign, but it is not normally a helpful tool for overcoming impasse.

Impasse is a natural and often helpful part of the conflict process. Often it is only when people find themselves at an impasse that they begin to consider their choices in a more realistic way. Impasse helps people separate essential from less essential needs, and it can be an impetus to their achieving a better understanding of each other's perspectives. If anxiety is not too high or anger too great, impasse can also be a great spur to creativity and risk taking. Furthermore, sometimes people recognize that a conflict exists only after they find themselves in some kind of impasse.

An impasse may not have an immediate solution, but people can usually find a constructive next step. It is often more useful to think through a helpful immediate step one can take than to struggle with finding ways to "overcome" impasse or "break" a deadlock. Sometimes a problem has no immediate solution, or people are unready to move beyond impasse. At times the best thing to do is nothing. Occasionally, people need to be given permission to stay at an impasse. Sometimes more active intervention is needed. Regardless, it is often better to ask, What is the best thing that can be done now? rather than, How can this impasse be overcome?

In an impasse, slower is usually faster. Many people have a natural tendency to respond to impasse by turning on the pressure and by imposing deadlines. Usually, this does not help. Of course deadlines are sometimes genuine, and people will not always make a choice among unpleasant alternatives until the way closes behind and forces a decision. Sometimes there really is a golden opportunity to reach an agreement, and efforts will unravel if agreement is not addressed in a timely manner. Usually, however, the best approach is to provide more time rather than to impose deadlines. When people can take the time to think through their choices, revisit their concerns, and come to their own conclusions, they usually become more flexible, imaginative, and realistic. Under the pressure of deadlines, compromise often feels to disputants like capitulation, but given the time to make decisions under less duress, they are more likely to see compromise as a reasonable, conciliatory move. Therefore providing more time and space at this juncture often shortens the overall process considerably.

When people are faced with a genuine impasse with significant time pressures, it is very hard to act on the basis of these principles. Yet they are usually disputants' best hope for moving a situation past the impasse. It was very hard for me not to take on Paul's panic in the following case, for example, but it was essential.

The creditors were breathing down Paul and Sharon's back—something had to be done right away, which meant it was time to slow things down. Paul and Sharon had been married for twenty-five years when they separated. Their children were grown, and the major issue they needed to negotiate was the disposal of their ranch in western Colorado. Paul had moved to Denver where he worked as a ranching supply salesman; Sharon continued to live in the family home on the ranch. During the previous two years the ranch had not been worked. Some of the fields were rented out, but they did not generate enough money to cover the payments on the mortgage and other outstanding loans.

Sharon wanted to continue to live in the house and had some general ideas about continuing to operate the ranch. She felt Paul should assume the debts, and she should take over the ranch. Paul wanted to sell everything, pay off the debts, and divide up the remaining assets. He argued that Sharon's proposal was a sure road to bankruptcy and that the creditors would never agree to separate responsibility for the debt from the ownership of the ranch. Sharon had no faith in Paul's ability to maintain a job and felt that this was the only way she had a hope of getting some financial stability in the future. This standoff had been going on for about nine months when they began mediation.

Paul was extremely anxious about the time it was taking to conclude a deal. He said that every day they waited, they were pouring money down the drain and getting closer to financial ruin. If they sold the ranch and the equipment soon, there would be some assets left to divide up; if they waited too long, there would be nothing. He insisted that a decision had to be made immediately. Even waiting until their next meeting in two weeks would be too long, he argued. Paul wanted to reach a solution in mediation because it would probably take at least another nine months to get a court date. Sharon responded to this pressure by disengaging, canceling meetings, and blaming Paul for poor management. In effect she said, "This is your problem, Paul, not mine," to which Paul replied, "We are losing money daily, so it is our problem."

Clearly, there was a time factor that needed to be kept in mind, but the effort to break the impasse by applying this kind of pressure was counterproductive. Faster was slower in this case. So I decided to slow things down to speed them up. I said that regardless of the time pressure, they each needed to be assured that they were making the right decision, and this meant obtaining financial and legal advice and costing out different options. I suggested that they needed to meet with their creditors and that they needed to assess how they might refinance and whether there were any potential buyers available (Paul was sure there were).

Paul and I had a frank discussion about the problems involved in such an approach. Although acknowledging his predicament, I said that there might be no way to avoid bankruptcy—but if there were, it would involve taking the time to assess the alternatives without feeling pressured. I told him that he could not force Sharon to "face reality," as he put it, but he could help her to look at their options.

I asked Sharon whether she really believed they were under the time pressure that Paul had described. She thought Paul was exaggerating, but she did acknowledge that the longer they waited, the more debts they amassed. What did she think needed to happen? She wanted Paul to negotiate a new financial arrangement that would keep her on the ranch. She was not ready to concede that any of the ranch had to be sold, although she understood that this might become necessary. "How would you know?" I asked. This question made her think, but she had no answer. I told her to take the time that she needed to think about these issues and to call me when she felt ready to discuss it further.

After about six weeks, Sharon called and said she wanted to discuss dividing the ranch and selling some of it. In the end they worked out an arrangement that left Sharon with the house, a few acres immediately around the house, and some equipment. The rest was sold. The debt was considerably reduced, and the threat of bankruptcy receded. I suspect a better financial outcome would have been possible six to eight months earlier. And probably they lost some additional assets during the six weeks to two months that the mediation process was on hold. But this was the price they had to pay to work their way through the impasse.

General Questions for Addressing Impasse

When conflict resolvers face an impasse, they will find it useful to ask five simple questions that can help them develop an approach to the situation. These are relevant whether one is a third party or a disputant:

Am I breathing (metaphorically speaking)? The first thing to do in almost all intense interactions is to try to get as centered, focused, and relaxed as possible. All of us will deal with impasses and other crises better if we contain our own anxiety and if we do not internalize the tension of others. Sometimes this means literally concentrating on our own breathing. Usually, it means taking the time we need to think through a situation and our response to it. When faced with very tense and difficult situations, we often feel we must respond instantaneously, but we almost always have a moment to calm ourselves down and think about how to respond.

This lesson was forced on me early in my career when I was confronted with what was perhaps the hardest interchange I have ever had to deal with in a family mediation.

> I was working with a family on a revision of a parenting schedule for a teenage girl who had been living primarily with her father and stepmother while her mother completed a technical training program. Now that the mother had finished this program, both the girl and the mother wanted to change the living arrangements. Although the father was amenable to a change, he was worried that the mother was manipulating the daughter, and he wanted to schedule a meeting with his daughter, wife, and me to talk to her about what she really wanted. With the mother's agreement, I consented to this.
>
> It quickly became apparent to me that there was another purpose for this meeting. The father had been unable to articulate to the stepmother the reasons for the change, and he wanted help in getting the daughter and the stepmother to talk to each other. The stepmother was extremely angry at the mother and was unable to contain herself in front of the daughter. She started calling the mother a "slut" and a "whore." To me, this seemed to come from nowhere. I was flabbergasted and speechless. The girl was crying, the father was acting as if nothing unusual were happening, and the stepmother actually seemed to be enjoying herself. Something had to happen, but what?
>
> I did breathe for a second and then decided that I had to do two things quickly—put a limit on the stepmother's behavior and rescue the girl from this interaction. I was by no means clear about how to pull this off within the mediator's role, but I knew I had to try. So I said that I would not allow that kind of talk in this session. Next, I excused the girl and suggested she take a

walk. When I met alone with the father and the stepmother, I expressed a great deal of concern about what had happened and asked what was going on. Evidently, the stepmother had been waiting for an "appropriate" setting to tell the girl just what she thought of the mother.

We had an intense discussion about this, in which I made my views about speaking like this in front of the girl very clear—perhaps more to satisfy my own needs than for anything else. I also asked the father for his input. He said, rather timidly, that he did not want his daughter to hear that kind of talk about her mother either, and he would talk to her about it. The stepmother fulminated somewhat further about the mother, but then did agree not to explode in front of the teenager again.

Later I talked with the girl, who was extremely thankful that I had gotten her out of the room. She discussed how hard it was to relate to her stepmother, although she said that the behavior I had seen was extreme and unusual. I tried to give her some suggestions for dealing with the situation should it occur again, although I had no magic up my sleeve to offer her. In the end, a very different kind of parenting plan was settled on, which made the mother's home the primary residence.

I still look back at that situation and wish there were something I could have done to prevent the attack from happening or to deal with the interaction more effectively. Perhaps the most important thing I did was to break the interaction and give everyone, myself included, more time.

What is the nature of the impasse? Impasses sometimes look to be simply intransigence, stubbornness, or malevolence, but they are almost always much more complex than that. It is helpful to figure out what is blocking people from moving forward. Whether one uses the wheel of conflict or some other analytical approach, putting words to what one believes is causing the impasse is almost always helpful. It is also useful to ask how the impasse is manifesting itself. For example, are people actively refusing to communicate, or are they avoiding all interactions? Is behavior occurring that is bringing progress to a halt? Are people stubbornly holding on to an unworkable proposal?

What are people accomplishing and risking by remaining in an impasse? From their own point of view, people are accomplishing something by being at an impasse. In some ways they are meeting their needs as best they know how. Gaining clarity about those needs can be enormously useful in trying to work out an eventual solution to the conflict. At the same time, there are almost always risks or costs involved in remaining at impasse. Both the benefits and the costs are often sensed by disputants but not necessarily articulated. Getting them out in the open can help all the parties consider their choices more realistically and creatively.

Can they meet their needs in other ways? Often the only way people can easily see for meeting certain needs is to bring about an impasse. But other ways often do exist, and it is helpful to at least raise the question and attempt to identify them.

Is it better for the parties to remain at an impasse? These considerations lead to this key question, which conflict resolvers usually hate to face but sometimes must. Sometimes it is better for people to maintain an impasse. Usually, this is a matter of timing. There are few conflicts in which a long-term impasse is the best alternative. For short periods, however, people may be making the very best choice possible for themselves by staying in an impasse. Sometimes a creative impasse is the best immediate outcome because it can move a conflict to a more powerful arena. In the following case, people had very strongly held values, which made agreement unlikely.

When a colleague and I were asked to conduct a public dialogue about policies regarding the hunting and trapping of furbearing animals, we knew we were heading into some troubled waters—particularly given the wide-open format of the discussion. Everyone was welcome, and the meetings were attended by a broad variety of groups and individuals representing ranchers, trappers, biologists, regulators, environmentalists, and animal rights activists. Within each group there were a range of opinions and negotiating styles. Many of the people in attendance had a long history of litigation and political struggle with each other.

The process was complicated and intense, leading to a broad consensus on how to approach these policies among the vast majority of the participants but not among representatives of some of the more fervent animal rights organizations or the trappers. Each of these two groups held out for its particular position.

Although this was frustrating for many of the participants, who had worked hard to find an acceptable middle ground, my colleague and I quickly realized that from their own point of view each of these groups was doing exactly the right thing. The trappers believed that they could override any consensus achieved in this process by appealing directly to the state legislature and that holding out was the best way to continue to receive the support of their associates, all of whom were firmly against any governmental regulation. To agree to significant limits on their trapping activities would brand them as traitors. For them it was better to go down as heroes to their peers than to agree to a compromise.

For the animal rights activists the prospect of achieving their goals through a ballot initiative was far more appealing than accepting the results of a policy negotiation. Future administrations or legislatures cannot easily overturn policies resulting from initiatives, and public campaigns could generate support for some of their broader concerns. They believed they could win with a properly worded initiative, and they wanted to try. A negotiated agreement would undercut the appeal of their proposal to the voters.

Both groups proved to be right about their alternatives. Although a broad consensus was reached and much of it was adopted by the relevant administrative agency, the legislature did intervene to weaken the proposed restrictions, thereby justifying the trappers' intransigence. A ballot initiative was then proposed and ultimately passed that codified many aspects of the consensus achieved in the group. Interestingly, it is likely that neither of these two groups ended up with a significantly worse outcome than it would have achieved had it participated in the consensus process, and in many respects the groups' needs were better served by remaining at impasse.

We had come to the conclusion fairly early in the process that there was no very cogent reason for some of the people to get past impasse. Therefore we encouraged all those attending the meeting to focus on achieving the broadest consensus they could but to allow groups to develop their own policy alternatives if they wished, all of which would be presented to the regulating body. In this way the concerns of all groups were articulated, but a broad consensus was also achieved. This was not as satisfying as achieving a complete consensus, but it was a realistic response to the genuine needs of the different participants.

Specific Questions for Addressing Impasse

Once conflict resolvers have assessed the costs and benefits of an impasse and the alternatives to it, it becomes easier and more productive to consider specific questions that may suggest an approach for helping disputants move toward resolution.

Who needs to be involved to move through the impasse? Changing the way a conflict between groups is being conducted often involves changing the people involved, so it is helpful to consider whether the right people are participating in a resolution effort. Are people missing whose input is necessary? Are people involved whose participation is neither helpful nor necessary? Are people trying to solve a problem when they do not really have the power to do so?

What time frame should the parties be considering? By either expanding or narrowing the time frame under consideration, many impasses can be either avoided or at least viewed from a more constructive perspective. Parents who cannot agree on a long-term parenting plan, for example, can sometimes agree on what to do during the next six months.

Are the parties considering the issue at an appropriate level of generality or specificity? The question about the time frame is just one example of the larger question of generality and specificity. One of the ways of helping disputants move through impasses is to either generalize or specify the discussion. For example, during the dialogue about policies toward furbearing animals, finding the right level of generality was critical. The parties could easily have bogged down if they had engaged in philosophical discussions about life or nature, but they could also have been thrown off track by focusing too narrowly on the mechanisms of specific traps. Progress could be made, however, at the level of policy principles.

Are disputants' needs being addressed at the appropriate level of depth? Often, by probing people's needs or interests further and achieving a deeper understanding of them, new approaches to resolution can be identified. Occasionally, however, it is necessary to pull back to a simpler and less far-reaching view of people's needs in order to have hope of making progress.

Do the parties have any uncertainty? Progress is sometimes possible only when people have some doubt about their position or options. Where uncertainty exists, there is often room for movement. Many people under stress do not like to exhibit uncertainty, and they adopt overly firm positions to reduce their anxiety or enhance their power. This makes it all the more important to listen carefully for signs of uncertainty.

How can commitment tactics be avoided or circumvented? Commitment tactics are one of the greatest sources of rigidity and impasse in conflict. Disputants using these tactics lock themselves into a position or demand in an attempt to force others to compromise. When NATO said to Milosevic that the bombing of Serbia would continue until he agreed to a NATO-led peacekeeping force in Kosovo and Milosevic said he would never agree to foreign troops in Kosovo, both were engaging in commitment tactics that led to a major impasse, with tragic results. When disputants can avoid commitment tactics, their flexibility increases, but once commitment tactics have been employed, the question becomes how to help disputants soften their demands or positions or circumvent them without a loss of face. Sometimes this can be done through a reframing process, sometimes through a reinterpretation of the meaning of a position or demand, and sometimes through enlarging the scope of the discussion. Occasionally, conflict resolvers have to help people find a way of totally abandoning a previously strongly held position without a loss of dignity. This sometimes involves working with the other parties so they accept this change gracefully and tactfully.

Has the integrative potential been adequately considered? Have disputants made any real effort to consider their potential for joint gain? Often they will have only given lip service to this concept. Even when there is little likelihood of an integrative solution, the process of considering it can sometimes lead to a more productive negotiation process.

Is there a productive way to discuss distributive issues? The key to moving through an impasse is often to acknowledge the distributive issues in a conflict and to find a nonconfrontational and matter-of-fact means for the parties to discuss them. One approach is to help the parties look for principles that might govern a reasonable distribution of benefits. Another is to look for agreements about the boundaries within which a distributive decision will be made. In a personal injury negotiation, for example, it is sometimes helpful to agree on an upper and lower limit for a settlement before trying to arrive at a particular agreement.

Have people faced their real options and taken responsibility for choosing among them? Frequently, disputants need help in accepting that they have a decision to make and that the need to make this decision will not disappear. At the same time as they are asked to face this reality, it is often important to decrease any pressure on them to make the decision quickly or in a particular manner. In the dispute about the family ranch described earlier, this was in essence the tactic I used. I indicated that a decision would have to be made, and I got both parties to agree on the nature of the decision, but at the same time I worked to decrease the pressure the wife felt about making a quick decision.

Is the right question being asked? Has the issue been framed appropriately, or has it been posed in a way that is causing people to struggle with it and making progress very hard to come by? When we see people struggling with an issue that they genuinely want to resolve, it is often helpful to ask whether an alternative question or framing would offer a more constructive focus.

What is the best next step that the parties can take? Often it is more useful to identify a constructive next step than to try to delineate a path through the entire conflict. I find it is often helpful to point out to disputants that there is no guarantee that any one action or communication will lead to resolution but that if nothing is done the conflict will almost surely continue. Once disputants and third parties focus on a constructive next step, conflicts can seem less overwhelming.

Conflict Within Conflict

An impasse may be viewed as a conflict within a conflict. Thus the same approaches used to understand the overall conflict will help people work through an impasse. It has the same three dimensions—cognitive, emotional, and behavioral—as the larger conflict. The same range of needs drives it, and the elements described in the wheel of conflict also apply to it.

Often an impasse comes to symbolize the overall conflict. Such a transference can make it harder to work through an impasse because the larger picture is then easily lost. The conflict between Israel and the Palestinians is not about settlements on the West Bank, appropriate responses to terrorism, or the status of Jerusalem, although each of these issues is important to the parties. But the conflict itself is about the identity, security, and economic integrity of the Israelis and the Palestinians. The real conflict between divorcing parents is seldom about how many nights a child will spend in each home but about what kind of relationship each parent will have with the child and how the parents will now relate to each other. If we confuse an impasse on a particular issue with the overall conflict, we can close important doors to resolution.

Conversely, working through a key impasse can become a metaphor for working through the overall conflict or can otherwise trigger a move to resolution. Significant progress on the question of Jerusalem will probably not be made until Palestinians and Israelis are ready to move forward on the overall resolution of their differences, but when progress is made on Jerusalem, it might well engender significant progress on the larger conflict. In short, it is important to see an impasse as both a challenge and opportunity, but also important not to equate it with the conflict itself.

Chapter Nine

| **Mediation**

For many, mediation is essentially equivalent to conflict resolution. Mediation is viewed as the central tool of conflict resolution and its primary professional expression. This view is very limiting, both for the field of conflict resolution as a whole and for mediators in particular, but it is also understandable. Mediation is a particularly visible expression of the conflict resolution field. Under its banner, clients can be solicited, training protocols can be established, and practice standards can be set. Although conflict resolution as a discipline provides the professional foundation for mediation, mediation as a practice can be presented in a much more concrete way to the public.

Contemplate these three conversations from a high school reunion:

> *Person A:* Bernie, what are you doing with your life?
> *Me:* I work in the field of conflict resolution. I live in Boulder, Colorado. . . .
> *Person A:* I hear Boulder is a terrific place.
>
> *Person B:* Bernie, so what's happening with you?
> *Me:* I'm a partner in a conflict resolution organization in Boulder. . . .
> *Person B:* Boulder is supposed to be really beautiful.
>
> *Person C:* Bernie, tell me about yourself.
> *Me:* I have a practice as a mediator, and I live in Boulder. . . .
> *Person C:* I'll bet you get some really interesting work. Let me tell you about this conflict I have. . . .

Although the tendency to equate mediation (and sometimes arbitration) with conflict resolution is natural, it is also problematic. Mediation is a role, a skill, an approach, and a practice specialty. I don't think it is useful to view it as a professional discipline. Mediation, like negotiation or communication, is a life skill that everyone must occasionally employ. It is a powerful intervention tool. But it does not stand well on its own as a profession. That does not mean that the practice of mediation cannot be professionalized. It can be—under the aegis of the field of conflict resolution.

Those of us who make our living by offering our services as mediators need to be grounded in a broader and more developed professional and conceptual framework. Like most new fields of practice, mediation is derivative of existing disciplines and should borrow from them as extensively as is helpful. But unless the practice of mediation is thoroughly anchored in a professional discipline that is specifically oriented toward appropriate goals, values, and intellectual requirements, its growth will be limited, its independence constrained, and its conceptual framework simplistic. I believe that field is conflict resolution. That is where mediation's future intellectual and professional development lies. This is also the best long-term answer to the efforts of other professions (law and mental health in particular) to place mediation under their auspices.

This does not mean that every mediator has to have a degree in conflict resolution any more than he or she needs a degree in mediation. There should always be a place for people to function as mediators without making a full-time commitment to mediation as a field of practice. But those who present themselves as professional mediators need to acquaint themselves with the fundamental concepts of conflict resolution. Of course, these concepts are pertinent for other mediators as well. As important as it is for mediators to understand the mediation process, unless they are grounded in a thorough understanding of the dynamics of conflict and resolution, they will tend to view their work as a series of intervention strategies and not as an application of a rich and growing body of knowledge about the various ways individuals engage in conflict and seek resolution.

Having said this, it is important to look at what mediators in particular offer to the resolution of conflict.

What Mediators Bring to the Table

Mediation is an approach to conflict resolution in which a third party helps disputants arrive at a resolution to a conflict. A mediator does not make a decision or impose a solution but rather assists the disputants as they attempt to find their own way through the conflict. Mediation works. Under the right circumstances, it makes a big difference in how well people handle conflicts. This seems clear from the many studies of mediation and from the increasing use of mediators (see, for example, Kressel, Pruitt, and Associates, 1989; Pearson, 1982). But why? There have always been mediators or mediating structures in almost all societies. These people and institutions have sometimes been formalized, neutral, and process focused, but more often they have played a less formal and also less neutral role. Religious and political leaders, elders, and influential community members have all been important sources of mediation services.

However, with increasing social and geographical mobility and the greater institutionalization of community life, these informal mechanisms of community-based conflict resolution have receded. As a result, more formal systems have been needed. The most developed of these formal conflict resolution systems have been the courts and political institutions such as town councils and planning boards. But these have normally been better suited for making decisions than building consensus among potentially competing interests. So it is natural that the use of formal mediation processes and related conflict resolution systems is on the rise. They are fulfilling a need that has always existed. But what exactly is this need, and how do mediators fill it?

There is a big gap between the experience people have when they resolve a conflict on their own and when they turn over entirely the power to resolve it to others. When these are the only choices people have, the likelihood that they will wait for a conflict to escalate to disproportionate levels before seeking or attracting outside attention increases. When people have a significant say in decisions that affect them deeply, they are more likely to feel ownership of those decisions. Therefore they are more likely to make the decisions work, less likely to sabotage them, and more apt to experience a satisfactory degree of psychological closure. Mediation attempts to bridge the gap between resolving one's own conflicts and surrendering the power to do so to others. It helps people maintain their power over important issues in their lives as it also assists them in moving through a difficult conflict process. The need for this kind of assistance seems almost universal.

What is the essence of what mediators bring to a conflict to limit its destructiveness and promote effective resolution efforts? I believe there are four major ways in which mediators alter a conflict dynamic.

They alter the structure of the interaction. Often the mere presence of a third-party neutral changes the course of a conflict, regardless of any specific intervention. The disputants have to alter their approach to the conflict simply to accommodate the participation of someone with whom they are not in conflict. They change the way they present issues, communicate, and express their emotions. Usually, this means that people will tone down their most adversarial behavior when a mediator is around, but the opposite may happen too. That is, sometimes the presence of a third party provides the additional security people need to unleash their more negative behaviors or feelings. Also, the mediator often arranges for new systems of interaction, new types of meetings, new configurations of negotiators, and other structural alterations to the interaction process.

They bring their personal commitment, vision, and humanity to the interaction. Mediators enter a dispute with a set of beliefs about the potential of mediation to assist the parties, a commitment to contribute to the resolution process, and a vision of how to proceed. The energy and optimism of a mediator are often the most important contribution that he or she can make. Mediators also bring who they are as human beings. A mediator's warmth, sense of humor, commitment to the disputants, and ability to establish rapport with them are critical to effective mediation.

They bring a set of skills and procedures. Mediators bring a set of skills and procedures to the process, including abilities in communication, reframing, conflict analysis, problem solving, negotiation, crisis management, maintenance of neutrality, and conflict resolution design. They may have acquired these through formal training or experience; some may be natural talents. Mediators also bring a set of procedures. They usually have a particular sequence of stages they try to take parties through, a set of ground rules, and a specific approach to identifying issues, interests, options, and relevant information. Often the mediator's specific procedures are less important than the fact that he or she has a process. The very existence of a clear approach is comforting to many disputants and adds a certain predictability and definition to the interaction process. It also adds to the mediator's control over the interaction.

They bring a set of values and ethics. Maybe the most important things mediators bring to a conflict are their values and ethical standards. These define mediators' most important commitments to their clients, and they profoundly affect the resolution process. Disputants do not necessarily adopt these values, but by entering into mediation they implicitly acknowledge them and therefore cannot help but buy into them to some extent. For example, a mediator is generally committed to helping parties search for an outcome that adequately addresses each of their key concerns. By entering mediation, disputants in effect commit themselves to searching for such an outcome as well. These ethical commitments are a foundation on which parties can develop trust, respect, and comfort with the mediation process.

Within these four general ways that mediators affect a process, there is considerable variation. Mediators affect the interaction structure in many different ways. They bring many different personal styles, skills, and procedures, and there are certainly many variations among mediators in their values and ethical principles. Specific procedures and tactics are easier to teach and to develop than personal characteristics, but in many ways it is the more complicated or intangible personal traits that are more important. The commitment of mediators; their ability to *join* with each of the disputants; their optimism, integrity, and openness; and their clarity about their value base and their comfort with it are usually the most powerful contributions they have to make. (For a discussion of mediators' different approaches, see Kolb, 1983; Kolb and Associates, 1994.)

What mediators do not normally bring to the process (although sometimes they think they do) is the best solution, the power to make people reasonable, the ability to change the genuine alternatives that people face, or additional resources. Of course, if we are talking about a U.S. Senator mediating an agreement in Northern Ireland, a U.S. President mediating between Israelis and Palestinians, or a city manager mediating a dispute between two city departments, then the mediator does bring significant power and resources. But these are not pure mediation processes, and the mediator's power places its own set of limitations on the mediator's role.

But for most mediators, it is in the limitation of what they can do that their most important resource for contributing to a resolution process lies. Because mediators cannot generally provide additional resources or alter the fundamental approach and behavior of individual disputants, these disputants can more readily turn to them in a confidential and forthright manner. Mediators are easier to trust when they have less power over substantive outcomes. When mediators have greater power over substantive outcomes (say in a mediation-arbitration situation or in advisory mediation), disputants will naturally treat the mediator as a decision maker and approach him or her with more caution.

What Disputants Want from a Mediator

What mediators expect from a mediation and what their clients expect are often at odds and always different. Fundamentally, disputants want mediators to help them get their needs met. Although this usually involves helping the disputants to feel safe, respected, and heard, what they are most likely to focus on is their desire for the mediator to help them achieve a good outcome. How they want mediators to help them and how mediators conceive of the mediator role can be at odds. Disputants often want mediators to figure out a good solution, to put pressure on each of the parties to accept a compromise, and to hammer out an agreement.

Mediators will often do just this, but I believe this is seldom at the heart of the genuine contribution that mediators make to the resolution of profound disputes. In serious conflict, it is not the absence of an effective solution that perpetuates the struggle but the lack of an effective process or structure of interaction. Unless mediators can somehow bring about a change in this situation, their capacity to make a genuine difference will be limited. As a result there is often a tension between what mediators believe their function to be and what clients specifically request. Consider the following thoughts written to me by an attorney very experienced at representing clients in mediation processes:

> Most lawyers prefer active directive mediators—mediators whose mission is arriving at a settlement, who urge the parties to settle, who cajole, who plead, who persuade. We bring our clients to mediation because we want to find a settlement. When a mediator spends the day simply communicating positions back and forth, and then at the end announces, "jeepers, you guys are too far apart," then we feel that we've wasted our money. Lawyers are smart enough to communicate each other's position back and forth. We are looking for an active ingredient, who can give us more than we already have.

Of course, nobody wants to waste a day in a process that accomplishes nothing, but what is interesting in this statement is its description of the way that many attorneys believe mediators can be helpful. The alternatives posed here are "cajoling, pleading, persuading" and "simply communicating positions back and forth." They want mediators to be outcome focused and to commit to arriving at a settlement. They perceive mediators who do not do this as ineffective, patronizing, and naïve. The idea of mediators assisting by delving deeper and helping parties look more broadly at the conflict, for example, is dismissed as "fluff," or as not real. Yet the deeper the conflict, the more necessary such "fluff" is.

Simply put, disputants often want mediators to hear their point of view and then convince everyone else involved that they are right and should get their way. More sophisticated clients understand that some compromise is necessary and that part of negotiation involves looking at new approaches to a problem, but they still want the mediator to help them advocate their interests.

If mediators are to be effective, therefore, they will have to help parties do just that. They will have to listen to all of the parties carefully and give each one an opportunity to present his or her most powerful argument in an effective way. Here is where the real skill and art of the mediator becomes evident, and where the approach of the mediator and the desires of the parties can converge. If the mediator is focused, maybe not on cajoling, pleading, and persuading, but on helping each disputant present his or her views in a cogent manner and on working to ensure that everyone's ideas and needs have been taken seriously, then the disputants and the mediator are working together. Furthermore, if the mediator helps each disputant carefully and realistically think through his or her choices at various points in the process, they are all likely to be working from a complementary set of goals. The mediator must start "where the clients are at" and travel in partnership with them from there.

Mediators' purposes do not have to be identical with those of their clients, but mediator and clients should not be working at cross-purposes either. Mediators would do well to listen to clients when they express not only their goals for mediation but also their ideas about what role they want the mediator to play. Inherent in those ideas will be very significant concerns that need to be addressed. This does not mean that mediators have to be cajolers or arm-twisters, or that they have to focus exclusively on finding a solution. It does, however, mean that they need to be very sensitive to the challenge posed by the differences between their sense of how to accomplish the purposes of mediation and their clients' expectations. In effective processes, mediators and the parties to the conflict are constantly reevaluating and in effect negotiating exactly what they are trying to accomplish in mediation and how.

Of course some mediators view their role exactly as described by my attorney friend. They believe that their job is to get an agreement and that the best way to do this is to confront parties with the weaknesses of their positions, the necessity of compromise, and the merits of the offers that have been made. There is nothing intrinsically wrong with this approach, and in many situations it is more likely than alternative methods to lead to an agreement. However, it is unlikely to achieve a deep level of resolution. For arriving at a dollar amount in a personal injury or patent infringement case, it may be appropriate. For helping people repair a work relationship, achieve a broadly accepted consensus about how to approach a public policy question, or learn how to be effective co-parents, such an approach may not only be ineffective but harmful.

Things get really interesting for mediators when the clients themselves have very different ideas concerning what mediation should be about.

When a group of professionals asked me to mediate the dissolution of their partnership, I found myself caught in their contradictory expectations about what would occur in mediation. On one level this was a negotiation about money and buyout terms, but it was also about hurt relationships, bad feelings, and blame. The professionals who were leaving wanted only to discuss the terms of the buyout, whereas those staying wanted to deal with the relationship breakdown and their anger at the departing partners. There was a sort of chicken-and-egg dilemma here. On the one hand, if we did not address the money issues first, the departing group would have a hard time discussing the relationship or addressing the remaining partners' concerns about future communications. On the other hand, if we did not address some of the anger and hurt that those remaining were experiencing, it would be very hard for them to move on the more substantive issues.

I presented this dilemma to both sides and suggested that we work simultaneously on both types of concerns, but that notion did not fly. The departing group saw it as a way of avoiding the financial issues that they viewed as their reason for agreeing to mediation. They were not here "to kiss and make up" they told me. So I tried a two-prong approach. I focused everyone in both groups on financial issues but acknowledged that it was unlikely we would get closure on these issues until we dealt with the less tangible aspects of the conflict. Then, in separate meetings with each group, I tried to probe more deeply. The partners who were remaining expressed considerable anger about how the departure of the others had come to pass and how unfair they felt any payment to them was. But they also knew that some payment was necessary and inevitable. They also could see that an in-principle commitment to some payment to the departing partners might lessen the hurt and anger all around.

I asked the departing partners why it was so important to nail down a buyout agreement before discussing relationship issues. They offered two reasons. One was money. They felt that if they did not get some commitment of funds quickly, they could not cover the initial expenses of their new organization. The other was their desire for an acknowledgment from the remaining partners that they did have a right to their share in the firm's assets and a right to leave if they chose. After an extensive discussion of these concerns, I suggested that they might be able to get a quicker and greater commitment

of money if they were willing to discuss the relationship issues underlying
the firm's breakup.

In this way, by starting on the more tangible and concrete issues ("where
the client was at"), both groups were able to come around to a deeper level of
discussion about both financial and relationship issues. I felt throughout this
mediation that I was engaged in a tricky negotiation with the clients about my
role and the focus of the process.

The Premises of Mediation

Regardless of the approach people take to mediation, there are
certain implied assumptions that govern how a mediation process
unfolds. These premises exist because of the structure of mediation, and they define some of its greatest strengths and limitations.

Disputants need help (and can benefit from it). A conflict goes to mediation because the parties feel they need help to arrive at a satisfactory outcome. They may have failed in their independent efforts
to reach an agreement, or they may recognize that without mediation the conflict is likely to escalate or be prolonged. Sometimes
mediation is structured into a contractual or legal process, as in
grievances or divorces, but usually there are plenty of opportunities to settle a dispute independently before that becomes necessary. On the one hand the parties' realization that help is needed
is one of the greatest sources of power a mediator has. On the
other hand people are very resistant to acknowledging the need
for help, and therein lies much of the resistance to using mediation in the first place.

*There is an advantage to disputants' reaching a voluntary agree-
ment.* Why not go straight to a third-party decision maker, where
at least some substantive outcome is guaranteed? There are certain
tactical reasons not to do this—uncertainty about the outcome or
the time and transaction costs of going to trial or arbitration, for
example. But beyond this is the notion that people are likely to
reach better, more carefully crafted, and more durable solutions if
they are the primary architects of those solutions. Therefore it is
worthwhile trying to arrive at a voluntary agreement with the help
of a third party before turning the decision over to an external
decision maker. The belief that the best agreements are those

made by the disputants themselves is at the heart of the values and approach of most mediators.

Mediators can help people come to an agreement through intervening in an unproductive negotiation or problem-solving process even though they do not have the power to impose an outcome. Participating in mediation usually implies that there is at least a possibility that a third party with no power over the outcome can make a difference. More than that, mediators' lack of power is part of what allows disputants to engage in the process. The deal disputants make with a mediator in essence is: "I'll give you power to run an interaction (up to a point), and I will reveal things to you and listen to your ideas about how to proceed, but in the end, I get to decide."

Process is important. For the most part, participation in mediation suggests that it is not just the elusive solution that is missing when parties are in conflict but that something about the process of the interaction needs work. How conflict resolution is conducted, how negotiations proceed, and how communication occurs are important. Mediators are called in to alter the process.

It is possible for a third party to be attentive to potentially competing interests. People do not necessarily have to believe a mediator can be neutral, impartial, or even fair. But by entering mediation, they accept the possibility that a third party can at least understand competing needs and views and can conduct a process without exclusively promoting the position of one side.

These assumptions exist regardless of the approach of the mediator. Some additional assumptions will exist that are not automatically implied by the basic structure of the mediation process but are very much dependent on the approach of the particular mediator or the agreement negotiated between the mediator and the parties and are rooted in the culture within which the mediation occurs. For example, there is no automatic assumption that direct communication among the parties is beneficial, and mediators vary widely on how they handle such communication. Many believe that direct communication is critical to an effective resolution process, although it may not always be possible. But I have heard mediators, usually those specializing in commercial cases, state that they would never bring two parties together until an agreement has been reached. Much of international mediation also occurs through so-called shuttle diplomacy, in which the parties communicate largely through the third party.

Mediators also have many different approaches to confidentiality. There is significant legal protection for the confidentiality of mediation in most parts of the United States, and most of us who mediate use confidentiality as an important tool when we are trying to change the dynamics of a negotiation. However, not all mediation is confidential—public policy mediation in particular often has to occur in public. Mediators differ about the confidentiality of private communications, about whether they will reveal what occurred in mediation if the parties give them a release to do so, and about the confidentiality restrictions parties must agree to when they enter into mediation. Confidentiality is a strategic consideration, but not one that is necessarily built into the structure of mediation itself. What is almost always necessary for the credibility of the process is that the ground rules around confidentiality for each mediation are explicit from the beginning.

Impartiality (exhibiting no bias toward one of the parties or the concerns he or she is expressing) and neutrality (having no relationship with one of the parties or stake in the outcome) are not implicit in mediation. Without getting into a discussion of whether there even is such a thing as impartiality, it is clear that most mediators put themselves forward as having no interest in any particular outcome, no special relationship with any of the parties, and no intention of advocating for any one disputant. In this sense they indicate that they are neutral and impartial and offer that as part of what they bring to the process.

But mediation does not demand neutrality or impartiality. In many settings the mediator is not neutral and may have a special connection to one of the parties. In-house mediators in organizations, village elders in mediative roles, and family members who try to reconcile differences among other family members may not be neutral or impartial. What is required is that the mediator tries to help the parties interact with each other more effectively or work out an agreement that they all can accept.

Credibility is established in different ways depending on the values and needs of the people involved. In the middle-class professional world in which most of us operate, the promise of impartiality, neutrality, and confidentiality is usually necessary for establishing the credibility and safety of mediation. But in other settings the community standing and personal status of the mediator may be far more important.

What Mediators Do

What is it mediators actually do to influence a conflict? Mediators work in many ways, and each mediator has an assortment of approaches. Nonetheless, certain actions characterize what most mediators do, regardless of their personal approach. (For the most comprehensive discussion of the processes and interventions that mediators use, see Moore, 1986, 1996. For additional perspectives, see Folberg and Taylor, 1984; Haynes, 1981, 1994; Rubin, 1981; Saposnek, 1983; Williams, 1998.) Here are the key activities that mediators engage in to help parties move through a resolution process.

In the Beginning

- Assess whether and how to intervene in a conflict
- Create or redesign an arena for communication and negotiation
- Get parties to participate
- Negotiate the purpose, structure, and guidelines of mediation with the parties

Throughout the Process

- Help each party to feel heard and to hear others
- Identify the key issues that parties need to address and the needs driving these issues
- Frame and reframe issues, suggestions, and concerns
- Work to create an atmosphere of safety
- Manage emotions and communication
- Explore needs at a useful level of depth
- Deal with unproductive power dynamics
- Help disputants work across cultural, gender, class, and other differences
- Encourage incremental and reciprocal risk taking
- Facilitate an effective negotiation process
- Deal with impasses

During the Problem-Solving Phase

- Encourage creativity
- Help parties develop and discuss options with each other
- Help people think through their choices
- Articulate and solidify potential agreements
- Apply appropriate amounts of pressure
- Discuss implementation

This is by no means a complete list of what mediators do. For example, I have not discussed drafting agreements; designing ongoing systems for conflict resolution; dealing with intraparty conflicts; communicating with such others as lawyers, judges, and substantive experts; following up on agreements; or teaching communication or conflict resolution skills, all of which are common activities of mediators. But the interventions listed here are, in my view, at the core of what mediators generally must accomplish in most disputes.

Most mediators will at some point engage in almost all of these interventions. The most effective mediators are those who can approach each one strategically. That is, they have a variety of approaches to each of these tasks and can choose among these approaches based on their assessment of the needs of the particular situation. This does not mean that they are always aware of doing this. Like any other skilled practitioners, the most accomplished mediators make many of their choices without consciously thinking them through. But I believe that effective mediators, if asked, can nevertheless articulate the thinking behind these decisions. To explore what mediators do further, the following sections discuss several of the interventions I have listed.

Mediators Assess Whether and How to Intervene in a Conflict

Just because mediation is requested does not mean it is appropriate, and even when it is appropriate, there are many different ways of proceeding. The first step in any intervention should be some assessment of the appropriateness of mediation. Often this assessment can be done rapidly, but at other times it requires an extensive effort. The mediator's decision not to mediate or to suggest some other form of intervention is in itself an important contribution to a conflict resolution process. One of the worst situations mediators can find themselves in is the middle of a dispute that is not appropriate for mediation and with all the key parties committed to going through with the process. Several years ago a colleague and I found ourselves in the middle of a dispute feeling as if we were holding a tiger by the tail.

Two teachers at a private school had filed a complaint against the acting headmaster and his assistant alleging intimidation and hostility in the workplace. The headmaster claimed that the teachers were refusing to accept the legitimate decisions of the board and the leaders of the institution and were fomenting "chaos and anarchy," and he threatened "significant disciplinary action." This standoff had found its way to the front page of the local newspaper. Subsequent to the appearance of that article, a large number of teachers and parents signed a letter requesting that a mediator be brought in, which the administration readily agreed to, and my colleague and I were contacted.

We traveled to the school for two days of meetings. During the first day we conducted individual interviews with all the primary parties and with others who had knowledge of the situation. On the second day we were planning to hold joint conversations with the people who were in dispute. However, after some of the meetings on the first day, including several with the headmaster and his associate, my colleague and I both sensed that there was more going on than we were being told, a lot more. The headmaster was uncomfortable with any questions about what would have to happen to improve working relations but very eagerly told us just how "crazy" the teachers were. What was really telling, however, was the headmaster's response to our questions about what he hoped to get out of mediation. There was nothing he could articulate except a desire to show the staff and parents that he had followed through on their request.

Finally, we bluntly asked him whether he had already decided to take personnel action against the teachers and whether this was subject to discussion. After obtaining a reassurance about the confidentiality of our discussions, he said that the board, on his recommendation, had already decided to fire the two teachers and that a letter of dismissal had been prepared and approved by the board and the board's attorney. He and the board members all felt, however, that they had to go through with the mediation because they had promised the rest of the staff that they would do so. He was sure that mediation would fail and that the letter of dismissal would then be delivered.

What really convinced us that this was a hopeless situation was that letter. It was over one hundred pages long! Hours or maybe days of devoted effort had been put into its creation. The commitment of the headmaster and assistant headmaster to this course of action was obvious. We probed for any sign of flexibility from the headmaster and from some of the board members we met with later that evening, but there was none that we could discern. So we stated that it was inappropriate to proceed with mediation.

But there was a problem. How could we stop the process at this point, given that everyone else was expecting and preparing for a joint discussion the next day? We could not break confidentiality, but we also could not proceed with an illegitimate process. We met with the different parties before the scheduled joint session and said that we did not believe the situation was amenable to mediation at this time, but we were unable to give very satisfactory reasons why. We suggested to both the headmasters and the board that there might be a need for mediation after some of the dust settled from the dismissal. They seemed to feel that they just needed to tough out the next step and everything would work out. It didn't.

The letter was delivered, the teachers dismissed. They filed a suit. Eventually, the headmasters were dismissed, and the teachers offered their jobs back. Instead they arrived at a monetary agreement with the board and took jobs elsewhere.

My colleague and I had planned on using our first day of interviews for assessing the situation and planning our intervention. In retrospect we both wished we had done more of this before we ever arrived on site.

Mediators Create or Redesign an Arena for Communication and Negotiation

Often people in conflict have no constructive mechanism for communicating with each other. They may be communicating through formal letters, court filings, public hearings, voice mail, or inappropriate third parties (like their children). Or they may be trying to communicate more directly but with negative results. Mediators try either to create a new forum for communication and negotiation or to bring about a change in an existing one. Often this forum is the mediation session itself, although in many kinds of mediation more complex mechanisms need to be designed. In dealing with discussions of public policy issues, for example, the design of an appropriate negotiating forum is a major aspect of what mediators do.

Mediators are often involved in the challenge of orchestrating a system for interaction among multiple parties, much of which will occur outside the mediation sessions. Sometimes this involves setting up subcommittees, encouraging particular individuals to communicate, making sure that representatives of organizations keep in touch with their constituencies, connecting people with substantive experts, keeping lawyers informed about what is happening, and so forth.

Another challenge facing mediators is finding a way to influence an existing forum that has already fallen into a rhythm of interaction and developed a set of norms and procedures, not all of which are productive. This was my challenge when I was asked to help with an ongoing dialogue on regional development policies in which everyone seemed happily ensconced in a thoroughly dysfunctional process.

The community activists and the developers involved in the policy dialogue were expert at humorous put-downs, but underneath their wit was a great deal of animosity. My first exposure to the group came when I entered a room in which a subcommittee was discussing a draft statement about the goals of the dialogue. A group of developers had just presented their revision of a previous draft, and a representative of a community group was raising certain concerns about it. The following interchange occurred within two minutes of my entrance:

Developer: I suppose you are going to organize a picket line at the local Safeway to protest our revisions. [*Developers chuckle.*]
Community activist: Maybe, but you won't have to face the mob because you will be in your polyester clothes hanging out with your cronies at your country club, which probably wouldn't allow our kind in anyway." [*Community representatives chuckle.*]

As much as I like to use humor to create rapport and remind people of their common humanity, this was out of hand. The group had fallen into a pattern of interaction that was both comfortable and destructive. They did not know me or my colleague, and there was a real danger that our efforts to put limits on such interchanges or to search beneath their surface for the real concerns that inspired them would alienate this rather prickly group. Nonetheless something had to be done. We decided to restructure the way the overall group and its subcommittees functioned so that there was a tighter agenda for meetings and a more active role for the mediators. We also tried to set an example of a gentler form of humor (more self-deprecating than attacking), and we talked about the type of atmosphere that would be productive. New norms slowly developed, and the group was able to make considerable progress. The banter continued, but it was less hostile (and, to my way of thinking, funnier).

Mediators Get Parties to Participate

Often not all the parties to a conflict have agreed to participate in mediation (or even an assessment of the situation). How mediators obtain participation is very indicative of their overall approach to mediation. Some rely heavily on persuasion, guilt, or a hard sell about the advantages of mediation and the consequences of non-participation. I believe that these approaches can easily become counterproductive because the mediator then has a responsibility to prove the value of the process. How mediators get people to agree to participate has to be congruent with the way in which they want them to participate.

It is more effective for the mediator to approach resistant parties by trying to help them think through the pros and cons of mediation for their circumstances than by trying to convince them to participate. One of the greatest services mediators provide is not just getting people to participate but doing so in a way that builds momentum for a collaborative process. Another important service is helping people decide not to mediate when that is the best decision for them.

Mediators Manage Emotions and Communication

This may be the primary tool of the trade. Mediators help people express their emotions or feelings as necessary and appropriate, and they manage the flow of communication. This is also the area that may witness the greatest variation in mediator style. Some mediators place a heavy focus on helping people express their feelings, whereas others shy away from this in the name of avoiding therapy and concentrating on helping people reach an agreement. Some mediators are very relaxed and easy about letting parties communicate directly from the outset. Others conduct the process so that almost all communication goes through the mediator— sometimes to the extreme of not ever bringing the parties together. I have found that the more secure mediators are in their ability to manage emotions and communication, the fewer restrictions on direct interaction they impose.

Mediators Explore Needs at a Useful Level of Depth

As discussed in Chapter Seven, the art of creative problem solving involves finding the right level of depth for exploring people's needs, interests, hopes, and fears. Needs should be discussed at a deep enough level that the real forces driving the conflict can be addressed. Mediators help each person explore the issue at the level of depth that is relevant to him or her and then they try to find a way of discussing everyone's needs that encompasses the different levels that apply to each disputant.

Mediators Encourage Incremental and Reciprocal Risk Taking

Searching for resolution takes courage. Disputants make themselves vulnerable when they raise a conflict, reveal their concerns, provide information, agree to negotiate, express their feelings, suggest solutions, or commit to agreements. If they take too large a risk, they may encourage an adversary to try to exploit a perceived advantage, and this may ultimately lead to an escalation of the conflict. Trust is built by incremental and reciprocal risk taking. As people make tentative concessions or share important data and receive reciprocal concessions and information, confidence is built and resolution promoted. For this process to work, the risk must be large enough to be meaningful but not so enormous that the party taking the risk is made disproportionately vulnerable.

Mediators often have to work with the parties to encourage some risk taking, help them think through just how large a risk is advisable, and nudge them to reciprocate when others have shown a willingness to take a risk. People are usually much more aware of their own concessions and risks than those of others, so mediators have to help them recognize others' concessions or risks and appreciate them. When mediators talk about orchestrating compromises or trade-offs among parties, in essence what they are doing is arranging for an exchange of risks.

Mediators Encourage Creativity

When conflict is intense and emotions are rampant, creativity can suffer. One way mediators deal with this is by trying to create a comfortable, relaxed atmosphere in which different ideas can be put forward and discussed without exposing people to personal attack. They also try to ensure that people feel able to suggest ideas without having to commit to them. Mediators often focus the parties on integrative or joint gain possibilities that they have not adequately explored, and in general mediators try to get people to look at a dispute from a new perspective that will open more creative ways of thinking about the issues.

Another approach is to bring new inputs into a process to provide fresh and hopefully creative perspectives. Sometimes this involves bringing in substantive experts or individuals who represent slightly different points of view or approaches. At other times it may involve referring people to outside resources or having them look at how others have solved similar problems.

One approach that I think is often overused is substituting the mediator's creativity for the disputants' creativity. Mediators often believe that they can find the solution to a problem because of their experience, their communication with the different parties, or their own creative abilities. Although I have occasionally identified a potential solution that nobody else seemed aware of, usually because of the confidential access I had to different parties, the real challenge is always how to bring the parties to the point at which they can identify the potential of a new approach for themselves.

Once in a great while I have found that a simple suggestion I have made will work. But more often than not what has appeared to me to be a particularly clever solution has long since been discarded by the parties because of factors I was unaware of. Furthermore, if a mediator proposes a solution, and it turns out that this solution promotes one party's interests at the expense of another's, then the mediator may well have compromised his or her more fundamental role. There is an art to putting forward ideas at the right time and with the right amount of tentativeness that can help prime the pump of others' creativity or get an option on the table that would be tainted if it were suggested by one of the parties to the conflict. But it is important for mediators to avoid becoming personally committed to a particular approach, especially to the point where they start trying to convince the parties of its merits. More often than not, the mediator's highest value is not in figuring out creative solutions but in promoting an open, relaxed atmosphere and an effective communication and problem-solving process that elicit the creativity of all the parties. Mediators also need to be alert to the possibility that creative solutions will come from unexpected sources.

> Charlie and David taught everyone involved in their parents' divorce a lesson in creativity and flexibility. The parents of these two preadolescent boys had already overcome a lot of animosity as they tried to work out parenting arrangements in mediation. The mother was about to graduate from a professional school and wanted to take on a greater parenting role. Her class schedule had limited her flexibility, but now she had a job with regular hours. The father had resented her entering this program to begin with and blamed it for their divorce. He had been resistant to any change in the arrangements before issues about decision making, church, and education were settled.
>
> These parents were beginning to work with each other in a more constructive way, but scheduling Monday nights became a major obstacle. The boys were active in a Boy Scout troop that met near the father's home. For the parents' tentative schedule to work, however, the boys would need to be at the mother's house, forty miles away, on Mondays. This was too great a distance to manage on a school night. We discussed all sorts of different ideas in our sessions, but nothing seemed to work.
>
> I decided to talk about this directly with Charlie and David, because each parent was worried that the other would manipulate the children in any discussion of living arrangements. The boys came in together, and when I got around to asking about Boy Scouts, they both said how important that activity was to them. But almost immediately they also mentioned a troop some of their friends belonged to near the mother's house that was doing "cool"

things. End of problem. I really wondered why neither of the parents nor I had thought about the possibility of a different troop, but we hadn't. It took the input of the boys to identify a creative solution to the parents' dispute.

Mediators Help People Think Through Their Choices

Mediators sometimes need to nail down potential agreements when the parties are ready to commit to them. At other times they need to slow down the process so that people feel they can make a deliberate and clear choice among what are often less than ideal options. Usually, mediators have to do a little bit of both things at once. Typically, when an agreement seems possible, mediators will articulate it, frame it in a balanced way, ask people whether they are ready to commit to it, and if they are, then write it down. But there is also often an important pause at this point, during which people have second thoughts, doubts, or premonitions of what is sometimes called buyer's remorse. When this pause happens, many mediators want to turn on the pressure. However, what is often the most useful thing to do is the opposite, to decrease the pressure and give people more time or emotional space for considering their choices.

This is often a difficult point in a conflict, one at which potential agreements can fall apart. Seldom, however, have I seen a mediation fail because people took the time to think through their alternatives at this stage. More often I have seen agreements unravel because people were uncomfortable with commitments that they had made under pressure.

Mediators Apply Appropriate Amounts of Pressure

No matter how facilitative or process oriented they are, mediators apply pressure in some form to the parties to encourage them to move toward resolution. They may or may not be aware of or comfortable with this aspect of their work, but it goes with their role. When mediators encourage disputants to make an offer, to respond to concessions, to share their concerns, or to think through their real options, there is almost always some degree of pressure involved. Sometimes mediators put time limits on the process, and this too amounts to pressure on the parties.

There is a fundamental difference, however, between putting pressure on someone to agree to a particular outcome and encouraging them to take a conciliatory step. If mediators believe their role is to identify a reasonable solution and cajole, plead, and persuade parties toward that outcome, then the pressure they put on can become quite heavy handed. If mediators see their role as helping the parties to a conflict engage in a collaborative process to meet their needs, then they are more likely to use their power to assist and encourage parties to communicate and negotiate in a more integrative manner.

When Mediation Works and When It Fails

Assisting Harvey and Laura with their divorce negotiations resulted in probably the most successful failure that I have had as a mediator. Harvey and Laura had left the mediation hopelessly deadlocked and had taken their case to court. In the mediation they had fought bitterly about everything, but they did reach tentative agreement about most of the issues in their complex divorce. I had drafted a comprehensive memorandum of understanding, but as we were reviewing it, they had several disputes about its specifics and broke off mediation, indicating that they would prefer to take their chances in court.

At the time I viewed this as a failed mediation. But about three years later, one of their attorneys called me to say they had some new issues and wanted to return to mediation to "update their agreement." "What agreement?" I asked, and pointed out that they had not reached any agreement. The lawyer told me that I was wrong. In court they had each presented their copy of the memorandum. Though they had some minor additional requests, the judge basically entered the draft agreement as the court order. The couple referred to this as "the bible," and it had become the cornerstone of their postdivorce parenting and financial relations. When I met with them, each had a well-worn copy of the draft agreement, with highlighting, annotating, and underlining.

As it turned out, they had been able to use mediation to negotiate the terms of an agreement, but they had been too angry with each other to accept ·it voluntarily. They needed an outside authority to impose the agreement on them. I was concerned that they would feel that mediation had manipulated them into an outcome that they did not really want, and that the voluntary nature of the process had been corrupted. But they seemed perfectly happy with the way their mediation had played out. Though there may have been aspects of the agreement that each would have preferred to change, they felt that it was as good a solution as they could expect. They had just needed someone else to finalize it.

This case pointed out for me the elusive nature of what mediation really accomplishes, of the times when it works and the times when it fails. I believe that successful mediations do not necessarily end in agreements and that failed mediations sometimes do. People come to mediators because they want help in reaching an agreement. If that end is never achieved, clearly something is wrong with the process. But the equating of success with reaching agreement and of failure with not achieving agreement is very limiting, particularly in complex disputes. The longer, more involved, and more intense a conflict, the less useful it is to see resolution and agreement as the same thing. Agreements are often just steps along the way. Mediators can be particularly helpful in taking those steps, but their larger purpose is to help people engage in a constructive resolution effort.

Mediation has been successful when the addition of a third party has helped people proceed with a resolution process appropriate to their particular circumstances. It is not successful if it does not do this. Sometimes this can be equated with whether or not an agreement has been reached. In most commercial mediations, for example, agreement and resolution go together. But in many public policy and interpersonal conflicts, reaching a consensus, especially one that is premature or overly general, may be less valuable than helping people confront their differences, articulate their beliefs, and frame the issues in a clear and constructive way.

Mediation is a powerful intervention. Societies need mediators, and in almost all cultures there are people who act in a mediative way. All of us, at some time in our lives, take on this role. Similarly, we all sometimes need help that assists us in resolving our differences rather than resolves them for us. But just like any other approach to human interaction, mediation has its limits and is not always appropriate (see Chapter Ten).

Even though mediation is a basic role in human interaction, it is probably an inadequately developed or institutionalized function in much of the world. Historically, most mediation has been provided in the context of less mobile and complex societies. Where community structures were strong, extended family systems powerful, and social networks durable, there were many effective informal mediative roles. But fewer such structures exist now, and the need for formal mediation services has grown.

Something is gained and something is lost whenever formal processes with trained personnel are substituted for informal processes, whether we are talking about counseling, education, medical care, or conflict resolution. When people bemoan the loss of community, part of what they miss is the more personal, familiar, and accessible approaches of smaller and less institutionalized processes. There is a built-in contradiction here that defines mediation's greatest challenge. Mediators are trying to provide a formal and professional intervention to assist people to reach resolution in an informal way and without giving up power to other formal and professionalized procedures. The tension created by this contradiction gives a creative impulse to mediation but also explains much of the resistance to its more extensive use.

Chapter Ten

Other Approaches to the Resolution of Conflict

Mediation may be the role most often identified with conflict resolution, but it is by no means the sole approach of conflict resolvers. As the field of conflict resolution grows, the ways in which its practitioners define their role and conceptualize their work has diversified. Although mediation continues to be an important aspect of the work of conflict resolvers, there is a demand for a much broader set of approaches. Many of these other roles overlap with mediation, even as they bring a new dimension to the practice of conflict resolution. The future of conflict resolution as a profession will be defined to a large extent by its success in developing and integrating a powerful range of approaches to conflict. The growth of mediation and arbitration has been an important step in this direction, but only a step. The field is now in the midst of the next fundamental step in its growth. This step involves a redefinition, as practitioners identify themselves with the broader field of conflict resolution rather than with just the specific service they offer.

Conflict Resolution as a Continuum of Services

The more conflict resolution practitioners can view the field in its broadest dimensions, the more able they will be to make a differential assessment of each conflict situation. That is, the initial question conflict resolvers will ask is not whether or how to mediate a dispute, but what kind of approach is needed at any given time and how that approach can be provided.

Conflict resolution as a field is at the point where it needs to take the development of a *continuum of services* seriously and to begin to identify the essential pieces of this continuum. Right now, new approaches are being developed as particular needs arise, but they have not yet been effectively tied together into a coherent continuum of services for people in conflict, although there is some encouraging movement in this direction. Currently, the field encompasses people who provide mediation, arbitration, training, facilitation, and settlement conferencing, among other services. But concepts of how to link these services; what a continuum of services, or interventions, would look like; and how it might be brought to bear in different conflicts are still primitive.

In order to clarify the dimensions of this continuum, we may consider the types of assistance that people in conflict need. In the last chapter I discussed what mediators offered to a conflict resolution process. However, it is also important to consider the limitations of mediation and specifically what needs it does not address. This will help us identify the characteristics that a continuum of services should possess.

The Limits of Mediation

As versatile and useful as mediation is, it has significant limits on what it can provide to people in conflict. Moreover, these limits are essential to mediation because they are also the sources of some of its most significant capacities to help people cope with conflict. In some respects, mediation is powerful because of what it does not attempt to do. For example, on the one hand, mediators do not generally offer themselves as evaluators of the merits of each party's position. (I am referring here of course to process-oriented mediation and not evaluative mediation or mediation-arbitration, which are discussed later in this chapter.) This is one reason disputants will often share confidential information with a mediator. On the other hand, such an evaluation from a third party is sometimes useful to disputants.

The major limits of mediation as an approach to conflict resolution are identified in the following paragraphs. Each limit suggests conflict resolution approaches that can do what mediation does not do and that might become part of an effective continuum of services.

Mediation is primarily used to intervene in conflict rather than to prevent it. To be sure, mediation can be used to negotiate an agreement before a conflict has developed, but that is not its primary application. For the most part, people employ mediation after a conflict has arisen, and they feel they need help in managing or resolving it. Approaches such as partnering, team building, and systems design are more useful for preventing conflict and are designed to forestall the need for conflict intervention.

Mediation by definition involves a third party who is directly involved in the communication or problem-solving process. Even though a mediator seeks to empower disputants and leave them with the primary responsibility for the conflict outcome, his or her presence at the table changes their role. Frequently, people are reluctant to give up even procedural power to a mediator or to reveal their circumstances or concerns to any outsider. As useful as mediation may sometimes be, most disputes will be resolved by the participants themselves, without direct outside assistance. Thus there is a need for interventions that are designed to help people solve their own disputes without the direct participation of any third party. Training is one such intervention, as are coaching, systems design, and facilitated planning sessions. Working with groups to help them prepare for a negotiation can be a very powerful intervention, as it was in the following case.

> Several years ago a state agency and all the county service-providing agencies it funded were sued by a national advocacy group in a class action to force the provision of additional services to the agencies' clients. The advocacy group presented the action as a "friendly suit," on the grounds that it was actually trying to force the state legislature to provide more money for the agencies' programs. But the agencies felt that the suit could easily lead to their losing control over their programs and to a serious increase in the "bureaucracy of accountability." A colleague and I were asked to assist the state and county agencies to prepare for the settlement negotiations that were about to take place.
>
> We worked with the agencies in three ways. We facilitated a set of planning sessions during which agency representatives discussed their objectives, strategy, and the structure of their negotiating team. This included devising a plan for communicating effectively with each other and for making decisions

during the negotiation. We also conducted a training program in collaborative negotiation procedures for the negotiation team, and we provided consultation to the team as the talks proceeded.

Our hope had been to involve both sides in a facilitated planning session to discuss how to conduct the negotiations, and we also invited the negotiators from the advocacy group to participate in the training sessions. They politely declined, feeling comfortable in their own ability to negotiate and probably wanting to maintain some personal distance at this stage of the process, given the likelihood of litigation. We felt, however, that the offer to participate was critical in setting up a positive and open tone for the negotiations. Furthermore, they said that they were very pleased that the agency negotiators were getting this training.

We took no direct role in the negotiations, which were complex and at times difficult. However, an agreement was eventually negotiated and approved by the governor, the legislature, and the courts. It became the basis of some significant changes in the process by which services were delivered. Although the negotiations were tough, relationships among the key players were for the most part constructive.

How much did our work contribute to this outcome? Despite the favorable comments of the agencies' negotiating team, it is hard to know what impact our efforts had. Whatever effect we had resulted from our roles as the team's advisers, trainers, and coaches. Our ability to fulfill these roles would have been seriously curtailed if we had served as mediators because we would have had to maintain a degree of impartiality that would not have allowed us to give the same kind of advice and feedback. Also, I doubt that the team members would have been quite as forthcoming about their internal differences and their concerns about the weakness of their case if we had been working equally with both sides.

Mediation is usually focused on helping people with a negotiation—that is, helping them to arrive at a mutually acceptable outcome or settlement of issues of concern. Of course mediation may be focused on communication, reconciliation, public participation, and related interpersonal processes, but it is most clearly designed and most frequently employed for assisting negotiations. Most of the procedures, guidelines, confidentiality protocols, training, and marketing associated with mediation are specifically oriented to negotiation assistance. Efforts are being made by some in the mediation community to develop an alternative to an outcome-based approach, but to some extent what they are actually doing is inventing a new form of intervention.

Sometimes people start mediation believing that negotiation assistance is needed, only to discover that they have hardly any issues to negotiate. Instead they may need assistance with reconciliation or healing or simply with communicating. Up to a point mediators can help with these needs, but approaches such as reconciliation, counseling, facilitated communication, and comprehensive programmatic interventions are often more suitable.

Mediation does not necessarily lead to an agreement. It is a premise of mediation that people have the right to decide whether to accept any tentative outcomes developed in the mediation process. Therefore mediation does not automatically produce an agreement. When mediation processes have integrity—that is, when they are conducted in accordance with accepted values and principles— a certain percentage of cases will not result in agreement. I am always suspicious of mediators who claim they achieve an extremely high rate of agreements. Too high a success rate could well be a sign of overly coercive practice (or of statistical manipulation). Of course a low settlement rate is a problem as well.

Yet sometimes the guarantee of a decisive outcome is important, either because the situation demands it or the parties to a conflict want it. For example, organizations often want an alternative to litigation to settle grievances that have not been resolved in mediation. Arbitration, private judging, mediation-arbitration combinations, and more complex dispute resolution systems are some of the approaches used when people want a guaranteed outcome.

Mediation is process focused. Mediators are not normally contracted to provide substantive expertise, and when they are hired for that reason, their process role can be detrimentally affected. Mediators generally do need some substantive expertise in, or at least familiarity with, the kinds of issues with which they are working. But this is to ensure that they understand those issues, can help parties evaluate their alternatives, can detect important unspoken issues, and can understand the implications of different options under consideration.

Often, however, the parties themselves have a need for substantive information and technical assistance. Mediators can offer small amounts of such information on occasion without diluting their role as impartial process facilitators. For example, a mediator might explain the steps in a grievance system or the time schedule for putting together an environmental impact statement. But the more mediators make the provision of substantive information or advice the centerpiece of their work, the harder it will be for them to focus on promoting effective communication, negotiation, and decision making.

Disputants often receive all their substantive assistance from people who are highly partisan, such as their lawyers or technical experts committed to a particular cause. As a result the different parties often operate on the basis of different, inconsistent, and sometimes biased information. In many environmental disputes, for example, the battle of experts is a serious obstacle to resolution. In many circumstances alternative and less biased approaches to collecting, analyzing, and interpreting information are essential to the success of a conflict resolution effort. This has led to an increased use of fact finders, neutral evaluators, evaluative mediators, technical dispute panels, and other methods for providing balanced or impartial substantive information.

Mediation naturally operates at the level of interests. Although mediators sometimes explore the deeper levels of needs, their natural focus is on interests. The mediation process is generally structured to push people to move beyond their focus on what it is they want to a somewhat deeper consideration of why they want it. But mediation is not generally set up to push people to consider their identity needs. To get to this level, it is usually necessary to develop a deeper rapport, spend more time, and work at a greater distance from the immediate conflict than most forms of mediation allow. Furthermore, although mediators have been used to defuse tense situations where lives were at stake, the more common types of mediation are not designed to address immediate survival needs either.

For example, divorce mediation is seldom the best place to deal with an immediate crisis in which the physical safety and well-being of children are at issue. Similarly, the fundamental concerns individuals who are divorcing may have about the meaning of their lives and their ability to sustain an intimate relationship are not best dealt with by most mediation processes. There are conflict resolution procedures that are better oriented toward dealing with issues of identity. Reconciliation processes, counseling, longer-term dialogues, and more programmatic approaches to building relationships are often better suited to dealing with conflict at this level. Survival issues usually require crisis intervention and tangible resources of some kind.

Mediation is a short-term intervention. Mediation is normally structured as a time-limited intervention with a specific focus, and that focus is usually the attainment of some specific and immediate goal. But many serious conflicts require long-term, systemic, and multifaceted interventions. The process of building peace in Northern Ireland or the Middle East, for example, has required multiple mediations, but it has also required many other processes as well, such as economic development, grassroots peace building, institutionalized communication structures, and multiyear strategic planning processes.

These limitations do not mean that mediators cannot or do not adapt to particular conflicts by altering the structure of what they do and the roles they play. Mediators have to be flexible, adaptable, and creative. Many creative new conflict intervention strategies have arisen when mediators or other conflict resolvers have found themselves facing a situation that called for a significantly altered approach. Also, many new interventions first appear as hybrids constructed from the alternative roles that a particular situation demands.

On several occasions I have found myself developing what felt to me to be entirely new roles in response to very specific requests from clients.

Helping siblings permanently sever their relationship was not the business I thought I was in, but that was what I found myself doing. Two adult brothers came to me as a result of a dispute about an inheritance. The terms of their mother's will specified that they should consult a "third party" before taking legal action. The older brother, who had experienced a series of business failures, had received much the larger part of the estate, and his younger sibling felt manipulated and cheated. He confided in me that he did not have the money, the law, or the resilience to take this to court but wanted a chance to state his views in a way that his older brother would have to listen to. After that, he wanted help in saying "goodbye forever." Perhaps not surprisingly this exactly mirrored the desire of his brother. He wanted to make his case and then "wish his brother well."

They both felt that there was nothing to negotiate. The basic damage had already been done to their relationship, and they now wanted help in achieving closure—but not under the guise of therapy. To them, therapy implied a desire to heal the relationship and reestablish better communication.

Probably more to satisfy my needs than theirs I explored with them individually whether any agreements between them might be possible or useful. Although the younger brother would have liked a more equal division of the estate, he believed that this was not going to occur in mediation, and he was right. There really was no outcome that either of them wanted other than this facilitated siblingectomy. In individual sessions I listened to the worst feelings each had about the other, and I explored with them what they needed to say and what they were likely to hear. We discussed how they might present their views and feelings and respond to what they heard with dignity, honesty, and sensitivity.

The joint meeting, in a weird sort of way, was extremely moving. Each brother talked about feeling that the other was the "favored child," and about how much he thought he had sacrificed for the other. Each described how he thought the other had manipulated their mother. Most important, both talked about their need to "end the relationship." They did remember better times between them, and although skeptical, neither ruled out the possibility of contact at some point in the future. Then they both thanked me and with tears in their eyes said goodbye. I checked in with each of them shortly thereafter, and they both said that the meeting had accomplished exactly what they wanted.

Was this some sort of reverse conciliation process? A kind of antimediation? Whatever its label, I felt this hybrid of counseling, mediation, and facilitation had somehow accomplished an important purpose that would allow healing for both parties. They seemed to feel freer to go on with the rest of their lives after this encounter. Maybe they will reconnect someday, and perhaps having been through this process will make that easier, but there is no way of knowing this. I can now think of a number of situations in which facilitated leave-takings could be useful—relinquishment of children to adoption, divorce, and dissolution of long-term business partnerships, to name a few.

Many other new approaches have developed out of the particular circumstances of individual cases. Mediation-arbitration, sometimes called med/arb, arose when clients who could not settle a case in mediation but had invested time in the process and developed a good rapport with the mediator wanted that mediator to render a decision. Sometimes people (or their lawyers) who have an ongoing but hostile relationship (such as divorced parents or hostile but successful business partners) contract with a third party to be available to make immediate decisions, often by phone, as conflicts arise. Lawyers sometimes seek ethical ways to advise parties through mediation rather than take on the responsibility of a client-attorney relationship. This has led to the concept of "unbundled legal services" (Mosten, 1997).

New approaches to conflict resolution are designed constantly. Some of them can be viewed as variations in how a particular service is delivered, but often an entirely new role is being devised. Of course great care must be taken to clarify exactly what this role is. One sure way to create distrust and suspicion of a conflict resolver is to allow a situation to develop in which the conflict resolver and the disputants have inconsistent understandings about the nature of the process or the role of the conflict resolver.

An Effective Continuum of Services

New approaches to dealing with conflict develop because of the limits of mediation or other established means of conflict resolution. The challenge for the field of conflict resolution is to promote an effective continuum of services rather than identifying primarily with one or two types of intervention. The specific interventions selected from that continuum will then vary depending on the type of conflict (CDR Associates, 1996). Environmental, family, organizational, and commercial disputes, for example, all require somewhat different approaches. In general, though, all effective systems of conflict resolution will in some way provide prevention services, procedural assistance, substantive help, support for reconciliation, decision-making assistance, and mechanisms for design and linkage (see Figure 10.1).

Prevention

There are two aspects to prevention. We may attempt to prevent conflict in the first place, or we may attempt to prevent conflict

Figure 10.1. Elements of a Conflict Resolution Continuum.

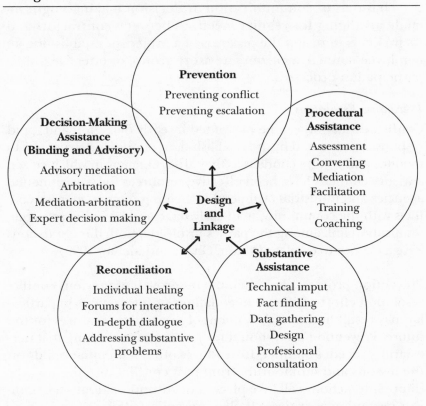

escalation. And for each of these aspects, there are always two approaches—substantive and procedural. People can anticipate the concerns that can cause or escalate a conflict and deal with them before they become problematic, or they can agree on procedures for communication and problem solving to forestall conflict or prevent it from escalating.

Preventing Conflict

Conflict can be anticipated, and agreements can be put in place that address those issues that might later lead to conflict. A prenuptial agreement, a partnership buyout provision, an agreement about what will happen if a contract is not executed in a timely way, and a decision on land use made before there are development pressures are examples of this substantive approach to prevention. The procedural approach of opening more effective channels of communication or decision making might include arranging for regular meetings between contractors and their clients to review the progress of a project or establishing an employee council, a citizen's advisory group, or effective public participation processes.

Preventing Escalation

Conflict escalation can be prevented by early detection and rapid response systems and by the establishment of ongoing structures to monitor and resolve conflicts as they arise. One way in which citizen advisory councils have been effective resources for governmental agencies and industrial facilities is by helping them to identity conflicts with the community at an early stage and by acting as a communication link among the parties involved before these situations have a chance to escalate (Mayer, Ghais, and McKay, 1999).

Prevention processes are often the outgrowth of previous conflict resolution efforts. Difficult negotiations or interactions in particular may result in the establishment of preventive measures for the future. Prevention then should not be seen as something that necessarily precedes conflict. Instead it is often a link that builds on the lessons and momentum from past conflict to redefine how future interactions will take place. The institutionalization of conflict resolution activities is itself a prevention effort.

Conflict resolvers play several roles in prevention. They point out the need for prevention, help parties agree on preventive measures, consult on the design of prevention systems, and facilitate or organize the operation of those systems. They also provide training in communication, teamwork, conflict management, and related topics.

The line between prevention and intervention is a thin one. Often the effort to put preventive processes into place starts by revisiting a previous conflict and dealing with its unresolved issues. Escalated conflicts are often addressed from the point of view of prevention as well. I have frequently been asked to help prepare labor and management negotiating teams for the next round of bargaining. These ostensibly preventive activities almost always begin with an intense discussion of what happened in the last round of negotiations. Before people can focus on the future, they almost always have to revisit their lingering feelings from the past. After processing some of these issues, some genuine preventive planning can take place.

Procedural Assistance

Systems of conflict resolution have usually been built around some approach to providing procedural assistance, usually a form of mediation. In many ways, process is the conflict resolver's specialty. The acceptance and growth of conflict resolution as a field has been fueled by the increasing awareness that trained third parties can significantly assist people in conflict and by a growing understanding of the difference between procedural assistance and decision making.

Although mediation may be the most established form of procedural assistance, it is not the only type. Other procedural roles are being developed or formalized all the time. Some of these are aspects of mediation (for example, situation assessment) that are developing into independent roles. Others (for example, training) are not generally part of the mediation process. Process assistance roles in addition to mediation include the following.

Assessment

When organizations or public agencies are involved in complex disputes, they often find it useful to hire a conflict resolver at the outset to assess the situation and recommend what, if any, type of procedural assistance or other approach to resolution might be useful. Although the assessor sometimes later serves as the mediator or facilitator, there is a potential conflict of interest in combining these roles. Sometimes, therefore, the person doing the assessment is contracted for that task alone.

Convening

Conveners help start a process but do not necessarily assume responsibility for conducting it. They identify potential participants, discuss their concerns about participation, identify an overall set of issues to be addressed, develop a preliminary formulation of the purpose and design of the process, and arrange for the initial gathering of the parties in a suitable forum. The participants may then run the process themselves, or a different third party may be brought in as a facilitator or mediator. Sometimes the convener has an ongoing role during a process, but at other times his or her purpose is served once the dialogue or negotiation begins. Often the functions of situation assessment and convening are combined, and one person or team does both.

Facilitation

The term facilitator is used in different ways, however it usually refers to someone who is conducting an interaction of some kind and whose focus is on guiding and improving the process of the interaction. Facilitators usually do not have a substantive process role but try to help a group accomplish its goals or purposes. Mediation is in essence a form of facilitation where the focus is on helping people to resolve an identified conflict. Generally, mediators facilitate a negotiation process. Facilitators are often used to help people arrive at a consensus decision, an agreement that all participants can accept. So the role of the facilitator is in essence to guide a group process and, where decision making is involved, to orchestrate a consensus-building effort. (For an extensive discussion of the consensus process, see Susskind, McKearnan, and Thomas-Larner, 1999.)

The concept of facilitation is broad and somewhat fuzzy, however, and a great many activities are labeled facilitation. Mediators are sometimes called facilitators, as are trainers, counselors, team leaders, and group therapists. I have sometimes been hired as a facilitator because people did not want a mediator and at other times as a mediator because people did not want a facilitator and in both instances I had to do essentially the same work—that is, help a group communicate about a conflict and arrive at agreements for how to proceed.

To some people, facilitation sounds less controlling or intrusive than mediation but also less powerful. I see facilitation as encompassing a broad category of activities for guiding a group process, and I do not care whether people want to label it mediation or facilitation. Facilitation may help in many different aspects of an interaction, not just in decision making. Any time a person has the task of focusing on the process of an interaction as opposed to the substantive issues themselves, he or she is taking the facilitator's role. (For two different approaches to facilitation, see Doyle and Strauss, 1976; Schwarz, 1994.)

Training

Training is training—it is not in itself an intervention to resolve a specific conflict, but it can play a major role in assisting people to conduct an effective process. The line between training and intervention becomes fuzzy, however, when people or teams who are potentially in opposition to each other participate in joint conflict resolution training of some kind. Some of the most powerful steps that I have seen people take to break an unproductive pattern of interaction have come during such training. The purpose of such training is to impart conflict resolution skills, but as important as this can be it is often secondary to the personal rapport that can be built and the understanding of different perspectives that can develop as a result of bringing people together in an educational forum.

It is not unusual for an organization to ask for training in conflict resolution when people's real need is for a different kind of intervention. This can lead to a great deal of frustration for the participants because real issues seem to be hovering over an educational experience without ever being addressed, or it can be an opening for them to begin to tackle these underlying conflicts. Training is often essential if other conflict resolution processes, such as grievance procedures or policy dialogues, are to function effectively.

Coaching

Coaching or consulting to people about participating in conflict resolution processes is an important service that is often neglected. I have worked with many organizations that have grievance procedures calling for direct meetings between the grievant and a manager as a first or second step. Seldom, however, is there any provision for advice, consultation, coaching, or any other assistance to help make these direct meetings productive. Too often the assistance that is available is either adversarial or focused on the substance rather than the process of the negotiation. Coaches can help the parties think through their own key concerns and goals as well as those of others. Coaches can help the parties consider their alternatives, plan how to frame their concerns and suggestions, and consider how to listen and acknowledge other parties even as they disagree with them. Coaches can also prepare people to deal with aggressive behaviors and to be both powerful and conciliatory at the same time.

Substantive Assistance

Disputants often face the problem that either no source of good substantive information exists or all sources are aligned with a particular party or side of a conflict. There are often no credible and neutral sources of legal, technical, financial, scientific, or other kinds of information. I have often wished that there was a way in which a divorcing couple, early in their decision-making process, could hear the same legal opinions at the same time. Some attorneys are willing to sit down with a couple, especially if they have no attorney-client relationship, and discuss these matters. Some mediators will attempt to provide this information. But by and large, the only real opportunity that couples have to simultaneously hear impartial legal analysis is during a settlement conference with a judge or settlement officer.

Technical Input and Fact Finding

The technical advice available in environmental negotiations usually comes from someone representing industry, environmental groups, or government agencies.

Technical experts tend to view themselves as objective and unbiased, but usually whoever they report to or receive their payment from must ultimately be pleased by the overall pattern of their findings if they are to continue to work for that person. Therefore, over time there is pressure for them to emphasize findings that are favorable to their employer. It is no accident, for example, that studies on the impact of smoking generated by the tobacco industry have results very different from the results of studies produced by health advocacy groups. Even when information really is unbiased and independent, the perception of the parties about the reliability of the information is also important. Finding ways to bring substantive information or advice to the table in a credible and accessible manner is therefore vital in many conflicts.

Conflict resolvers have attempted to meet this need in different ways. They have acted as fact finders, with the mission of producing an objective and unbiased analysis of a conflict and its potential solutions. Technical consultants have worked for a dialogue group as a whole or have been hired by a convener or facilitator rather than by one of the parties. Sometimes, in anticipation of possible conflicts—particularly in large construction projects—potential disputants have put together a panel of substantive experts or have agreed on a consultant who will make technical recommendations or rule on technical issues. Mini-trials have been used in large contractual disputes to lay out both technical and legal information for negotiators. These are a sort of mock trial in which lawyers put on their best case in front of the key decision makers prior to settlement negotiations.

Data Gathering

Conflict resolvers often have to work with the different parties to create meaningful ways for them to gain access to information. In a public policy negotiation that involves important data questions, it is often as important for people to participate in formulating the key questions that need to be answered and in reviewing the methodology for obtaining information from a credible neutral source. Sometimes the data generated by one party to a dispute are accepted as credible if everyone has had a chance to review the methodology and if the parties feel that the technical experts have been open and straightforward in discussing their findings. At other times the input of credible and independent technical advisers is disregarded because they did not work effectively with the group to whom they were reporting.

Often the issue that conflict resolvers face is an imbalance in access to technical information. When one party, perhaps an industry group, has access to a great deal of technical expertise and support and another party, maybe a community group, has none, then providing a neutral expert may not be enough. It is sometimes necessary to find a way for the community group to gain access to technical or other consultants who will be their confidential advisers.

Professional Consultation

Conflict resolvers often assist substantive specialists to fulfill what for them is often an unfamiliar role in a conflict resolution process. Conflict resolvers can offer them training, consultation, practice presentations, and ongoing feedback. Gradually, a growing pool of independent individuals and organizations is becoming experienced in providing impartial, substantive input into conflict resolution processes. I have repeatedly found that the role of these experts can be critical to the success of a consensus-building effort, as it was in this waste management policy dialogue.

I received my first exposure to the concept of Gucci Garbage when I worked with two adjoining municipalities after they had received federal funds to investigate alternative approaches to solid waste management. One of the conditions of the grant was that the municipalities convene an advisory group composed of representatives of the waste management industry, recycling organizations, the communities involved, and relevant public interest and environmental organizations. A colleague and I were hired to facilitate the meetings of this group, and several technical consultant firms were contracted to provide substantive input.

Although its members encompassed many different points of view, the group developed a good internal communication and decision-making process. But it faced very complex issues about which there was very inconsistent information. The initial issue defined by the municipalities was, "Should a plant that incinerates waste and generates energy be built in this area?" This raised all sorts of questions about environmental, economic, and health impacts. The group redefined this question as, "What should be the strategy for managing waste in this region to minimize negative environmental, economic, and health impacts, and is there a role for a waste to energy facility within this strategy?"

The technical consultants were a critical part of these discussions, but the group had very different reactions to the economic specialists and the engineering consultant. On the one hand the economic experts never established a strong personal rapport with the group, and despite receiving suggestions from the group, the other technical consultants, and my colleague and me, they were never able to structure a presentation that seemed accessible and relevant to the participants. As a result the group members never believed that they were receiving reliable economic data, and this inhibited their confidence about making bold recommendations.

On the other hand the engineering consultant was extremely well liked, personable, and responsive to the group dynamics. Participants trusted the information he presented and felt that he was not pushing a particular point of view. One day he showed up with a sack full of typical garbage and laid it on a table in front of the group. He then proceeded to tell a story about what would happen under different scenarios with the different contents of the sack. It was useful, funny, enjoyable, and relevant (even if a little smelly). The group felt a great deal of confidence in using the information he provided in their considerations.

The recommendations of the group reflected their different responses to the experts. They believed the primary tasks to be accomplished in solid waste management were to create a regional waste management strategy, to maximize the reuse and recycling programs, and to make existing facilities more efficient. They recommended against acquiring a large energy-generating waste incinerator because they did not think it was needed, did not believe its economic benefits had been established, and were concerned that it would draw resources away from reuse or recycling efforts. They did believe that a smaller more targeted facility, for example in conjunction with a new airport, to process a more refined set of waste (thus Gucci Garbage—the term the engineering consultant used) was appropriate. Most of this group's recommendations were accepted. The nature of those recommendations was a direct reflection of the quality of the input from the various experts and of the relations group members had had with those experts.

Reconciliation

Beyond agreement are the deeper and more far-reaching elements of resolution that are sometimes called conflict transformation (Lederach, 1995), peacemaking (Curle, 1971), or reconciliation. In Chapter Five, I discussed the three dimensions of resolution—emotional, cognitive, and behavioral. Often conflict resolution processes focus on the behavioral dimension and do not address the emotional or cognitive dimensions. Yet unless there is also progress on these dimensions, it is unlikely that fundamental changes in the relationship among disputants will occur. Although most conflict resolution efforts can contribute to a broad approach to resolution, individual efforts are often limited in how far they can go.

Multiple efforts, over time, and at many different levels are usually necessary to address deeply rooted conflicts and to promote genuine reconciliation. This is true whether we are talking about violent ethnic conflicts, such as those in Rwanda or Cyprus, or bitter interpersonal disputes, such as those between deeply conflicted divorcing couples. But such conflicts can be resolved in profound ways, and for every story of an intractable conflict that has gone on for years, there is a story of how former bitter enemies have made peace. We are witnessing some amazing transformations in the world—in Northern Ireland, the Middle East, and South Africa, for example. Optimism mixed with realism and hopefulness mixed with watchfulness are extremely important traits for conflict resolvers.

Conflict resolvers have been central to many reconciliation activities. Sometimes they have functioned through the more established roles, such as mediation or facilitation. Victim-offender mediation has proven an effective means for bringing a level of reconciliation and a deeper learning to perpetrators and victims in certain kinds of cases (Umbreit, 1994). My own work with child protection mediation in the 1980s convinced me that mediation could be an important step in setting parents and child protection workers on a different path, one on which they functioned more as allies than adversaries.

But reconciliation often requires approaches that are separate from more immediate resolution efforts. Four basic approaches are often necessary. One approach assists people to go through their own individual healing process. For example, groups that help victims of violence confront and share their experiences or that help perpetrators face their own demons can be vital to reconciliation efforts. A second is the development of safe forums for communication and interaction that allow people to get to know each other as human beings. Camps that bring youths from conflicting regions together or programs that encourage different ethnic groups to work together on common problems are examples of this approach. Often the best way to accomplish this is indirectly, through projects that are not directed simply toward bringing disputants together but that address some other interests they have.

One of the most impressive reconciliation efforts I have seen was at a community center in Banja Luka, in the heart of the Serbian section of Bosnia and the site of some horrible ethnic violence during the Bosnian civil war. At this center there were many reconciliation efforts under way—a variety of classes, recreational activities, and discussion groups. But the most interesting was a radio station. It broadcast over only a two-square-mile area, but teenagers from all ethnic groups eagerly worked together to run the station. Most of them had suffered terribly during the fighting, but at the station they worked together, had fun together, got to know each other, and occasionally shared their personal experiences of war with each other.

A third approach brings people together for a direct in-depth dialogue about the conflict and all the feelings and pain that have gone with it. Sometimes this process encourages people both to take responsibility for their own actions and to forgive others for theirs. The Truth Commissions of South Africa are a fascinating effort of this kind, and so are many other efforts to bring people together, not to negotiate but to hear each other's stories and try to understand each other's experiences. The fourth strategy is to address directly the serious substantive problems that make reconciliation difficult (inadequate housing, unemployment, fears for personal safety, and so forth). Unless the ongoing sources of stress that keep people from feeling safe and secure are addressed, reconciliation efforts won't work. In other words, part of the reconciliation process is to address people's survival and security needs first.

The art of reconciliation requires making a constant judgment whether a practical and concrete problem-solving effort will promote a more profound reconciliation process or interfere with it. Whether reconciliation is formalized as a separate approach or incorporated into other activities, the capacity to move people toward reconciliation and healing is a critical component of conflict resolution. (For an approach to intergroup reconciliation in the workplace, see Blake and Mouton, 1984.)

Decision-Making Assistance

Sometimes consensus-based decision-making processes are either inappropriate or ineffective. People are occasionally unwilling or unable to reach an agreement. Sometimes, a decision is necessary, but the conflict has not yet matured to the point where it is in the disputants' interests to agree. Some decisions are not important enough to merit the time and resources it would take to achieve consensus. On other occasions, a decision must be made so quickly there is no time to implement a consensus-based approach. For these and other reasons, people need an alternative to a voluntary, or consensus-based, approach.

The most frequent public alternatives are court rulings, executive or legislative decision making, or within an organization, the operation of a management hierarchy. Using the courts is normally appropriate (although not always effective) when decisions involve basic issues of law or major questions of citizen rights and protection of the general public. But these decision-making forums are often ineffective, inefficient, or unavailable. Moreover, their very structure may escalate a conflict. Therefore conflict resolution structures need to include access to effective and efficient means of decision making for the parties when consensus-based alternatives are not appropriate or practical.

Two fundamental types of decision-making services are needed—binding and advisory. Giving an advisory opinion can be a bit like supplying substantive information, but it is an important option because it can give people a relatively cheap and quick foretaste of what might occur in a more expensive, lengthy, and possibly more toxic binding process. Advisory or evaluative mediation, nonbinding arbitration, early neutral evaluation, advisory dispute panels, and certain types of fact finding are all examples of this approach.

Advisory Mediation

Advisory mediation, for example, is often used in grievances. In advisory mediation, mediators first attempt to facilitate an agreement, but if that fails, they render an advisory opinion, stating how they would rule were they to arbitrate the case. In one study the bulk of cases settled during the mediation phase, and of those that did not settle, the majority settled subsequent to the announcement of the advisory opinion but before going to arbitration (Ury, Brett, and Goldberg, 1988).

Mediators in more traditional processes are often tempted to play an evaluative role, that is to advise people about what is likely to happen in court or what they think is the most appropriate outcome. For all but the substantively and emotionally simplest of

cases, and maybe even for many of these, such evaluation can easily lead the parties to distrust the mediator and then distance themselves from him or her. So a separate advisory decision-making
process is often helpful. Occasionally, the courts themselves will
provide this service, through the services of a settlement judge or
a pretrial conference.

Arbitration

Binding alternatives to court-based decision making are also increasingly prevalent. Arbitration is being institutionalized in an
increasing variety of contracts and institutions. It may be used even
more extensively today than mediation. Arbitrators approach their
work in many different ways. For example, they may take a rights-
based or an interest-based approach. A rights-based arbitrator will
try to decide how a dispute would be dealt with if it were a legal
case, or how to apply a set of legal principles or contractual obligations to a dispute, and will consider the parties' interests only sec-
ondarily or tangentially. An interest-based arbitrator will try to sort
through the key concerns of the parties and determine a way of
addressing these within the framework of the law. In other words,
arbitrators can take a legalistic or Solomonic approach. Of course,
it is important that arbitrators be clear with their clients about the
basis on which they make decisions.

Mediation-Arbitration

Many other varieties of decision making can be brought to bear in
different circumstances. Mediation-arbitration (in which the same
person acts as mediator and arbitrator) and mediation then arbitration (in which disputants are automatically referred from a
mediator to an arbitrator if mediation is inconclusive) are two
increasingly popular alternatives.

Expert Decision Making

Sometimes people in high-conflict relationships contract with substantive experts to be available over a specified period to render
rapid and binding decisions about issues in their area of expertise.
Divorced parents may use child development experts; construction
contracts may provide for decision making from a designated engi-
neer; business partners may use financial management experts.

Several features seem to distinguish these alternative methods of binding decision making:

- They tend to be less legalistic, or hearinglike, than arbitration.
- They are often linked to other conflict resolution mechanisms.
- They try to keep a door open to voluntary resolution.
- They often focus on very specific aspects of a larger conflict.
- They allow roles that are more fluid than the arbitrator's.

Design and Linkage

The continuum of conflict resolution services is expanding with increasingly sophisticated approaches. This has led to important efforts in dispute systems design. Dispute system design is an approach to conflict resolution that is both preventive and systemic. System designers work with organizations or groups that are anticipating a set of conflicts they are likely to face over time, such as grievances, customer complaints, neighborhood conflicts, or citizen appeals of government actions. Together with representatives of the different groups involved, a designer works out a series, or a system, of linked conflict prevention and resolution steps to deal with the most commonly anticipated disputes. Such a system often includes training, communication procedures, process assistance of different kinds, and decision-making assistance. There are a number of principles that designers usually try to incorporate in such processes. (Some of these principles have been described elsewhere; see Ury, Brett, and Goldberg, 1988; CDR Associates, 1996. For other information about dispute system design, see Slaikeu and Hasson, 1998.)

- Emphasize assisting disputants to make decisions themselves, unless matters of overall organizational or public policy are involved.
- Assist disputants to resolve conflicts on the basis of their needs as much as possible.
- Assist disputants not only to settle differences but also to repair relationships and restore effective communication.

- Give disputants as many chances as possible to revert to needs-based decision-making mechanisms.
- Design the intervention of third-party decision makers to minimize stress, expense, and toxicity.
- Make decision-making and dispute resolution processes transparent, accessible, understandable, and easy to use.
- Make sure that the process of designing, implementing, monitoring, and evaluating the conflict resolution system reflects the values and goals of the system as a whole.
- Make sure that the system really is a system—that is, that the connections between its elements are well thought out and smooth in operation.
- Build the system on the strengths of existing conflict resolution mechanisms and with a careful consideration of the existing organizational structure or group norms.
- Build new systems incrementally.

The last principal reflects an important lesson that dispute system designers have learned about working with organizations. Although there may occasionally be circumstances in which profound organizational change or systems breakdown requires and allows implementing a whole new system, it is important not to build cathedrals. Ideal systems are seldom realistic systems. Often the most important question is, What are the key changes that can be made at a given time that will move a dispute system in a more collaborative direction?

Another challenge is to make the dispute system concept itself tangible and accessible to people who are trying to formulate a practical day-to-day approach for dealing with conflict. The concept will seem abstract, theoretical, and ungrounded to practitioners if they cannot translate it into usable everyday actions.

Despite these challenges, the dispute systems approach is at the cutting edge of conflict resolution practice because it seeks to fill in the gaps and create linkages among the approaches on the continuum of conflict resolution services. For the concept of a continuum of services to be more than an abstract idea, there must be a linkage mechanism among its different components and a way of deciding which service is appropriate to a particular circumstance.

Dispute systems designers face these questions constantly and are thus on the front line of the ongoing effort to implement an increasingly sophisticated approach to conflict resolution.

Almost all of us who work as conflict resolvers play several roles, but almost none of us can or should fulfill the whole gamut of roles that make up the spectrum of conflict resolution services. The more conscious we are about the range of interventions needed to develop a continuum that truly serves our client base, the more able we will be to make sophisticated judgments about exactly what services people need in any particular conflict. The more aware we are of what we can and cannot provide, the more responsible we will be in making referrals. The growing richness of the conflict resolution field will enhance the work of each of us by providing links to a more powerful set of interventions than any of us can provide on our own.

Chapter Eleven

Conclusion
Conflict Resolution in Our Lives

This book discusses how we can think about conflict and resolution in a useful and productive way. It is not meant to sell conflict resolution as a field or to tell people how to practice mediation, negotiation, or facilitation. I believe that good practice comes from sound thinking as informed and refined by practice. Our growth as conflict resolvers requires that we become increasingly sophisticated in our thinking, that we learn to apply our concepts and to test them in our practical efforts, and that we use these experiences to reevaluate our thinking. The ability to engage in this reflective process is a characteristic of an advanced practitioner. A clear and accessible conceptual framework not only helps us deepen our work but helps us learn from our experience.

Even more important in guiding our work than our thinking about conflict, however, are our values. A powerful commitment to the values that guide our work is the most important foundation from which we can operate. They are the source of our dedication to our work and the compass that guides us through our most difficult moments. Furthermore, if the concepts we use to understand what we do are not grounded in our values or reflective of them, then their power will be curtailed. Therefore I believe it is very important to ask ourselves what motivates us to be conflict resolvers. Of course each of us will have a different answer, but we can certainly learn from each other.

I enjoy the work, finding it challenging, stimulating, and fun. I also appreciate the fact that there are often (although not always) tangible results. My work has taken me to many interesting parts of the world where profound change has been in the works, and I have had the opportunity to meet some amazing and wonderful people. My colleagues are interesting, warm people with values that I appreciate. Working with them has been a privilege. These are major benefits from working in this field. But none of them are at the core of what has motivated me to devote the last twenty years to conflict resolution. Why am I committed to this work? Because I want to see conflicts handled in a more productive way. Because I want to play a role in making this a better world. Because I want my work to help me grow personally.

A Better Way of Resolving Conflict

When people find themselves in conflict, the mechanisms available to assist in resolution—in keeping with the way society responds to many other crises—tend to take power away from the disputants. Power is ceded to judges, lawyers, government entities, child custody evaluators, technical experts, arbitrators, and so forth. I believe as a practical matter and as a value that professionals should try to ensure that people in crisis remain as empowered as they possibly can. This is especially important because conflict is often generated when people feel disempowered.

For example, parents who abuse their children often do so in response to feeling overwhelmed and powerless. The response of the child protection system is often (and to some extent inevitably) to overwhelm and disempower them further. We must find ways of protecting children as we also empower parents to be parents. That is the point of the burgeoning movement to use mediation and other conflict resolution mechanisms (family group conferences, for example) in child welfare (Mayer, 1984, 1995). The challenge is how to take enough power away from parents to protect their children while helping them maintain or develop enough positive power to become more effective and humane parents.

The essence of what the field of conflict resolution has to offer to disputants is an empowering approach to solving serious conflict. The goal and the value is to help people in conflict maintain as much power as possible over their lives while ensuring that other people's rights and concerns are also respected and protected.

Our desire to fix things for disputants, to take over so that people can be protected from themselves, is at the heart of what disempowers people in conflict. Conflict resolvers have to accept that sometimes people will make very bad decisions for themselves, but that is their right. The consequence of our taking on the responsibility of preventing people from making poor decisions is that we also take away a significant degree of personal autonomy. Therefore it is essential that conflict resolvers trust people's ability to make good decisions for themselves and accept their right to make what may be poor decisions as well. This is a defining belief, in my view, of effective conflict resolution practice.

Related to this is a creative dilemma that conflict resolvers face—the question of whether they are in the business of trying to change people. Does profound resolution require personal change? Is conflict resolution about helping people as individuals grow, "transform," or in some way become better? And if it is, how do resolvers reconcile this with the fact that people do not usually come to them for this purpose? How do we empower people if we also have an agenda to change them? The paradox is that much that resolvers do can and often does have the practical effect of changing people, but this result is also closely connected to the fact that it is not their major motive. I believe that effective conflict resolvers often contribute to profound personal change, but in a way that is indirect and respectful of personal autonomy. As they help people work through conflict on as deep a level as is practical and necessary, they help disputants accomplish their goals, and personal change is a frequent by-product of this process.

Another way in which the field of conflict resolution contributes to a better way of handling conflict is by helping people think about disputes differently. When resolvers can help people step outside of the distributional trap, of the dilemma of whether to act to preserve their relationships or protect their interests, of whether to be nice or to be smart, they have accomplished something significant. Conflict resolvers can help people find approaches that avoid such destructive choices, but to do this, we have to really believe that it is both important and possible. Conflict resolvers have to believe that people can be strong and kind, wise and compassionate, realistic and optimistic at the same time. Our confidence that disputants can both protect themselves and deal with others in a principled manner is one of the most important things we can transmit to our clients.

All people have difficult choices to make in life, and no one can always get what he or she wants. Sometimes, in the name of peace or resolution, disputants have to give up something very important to them. But people can address their most important needs and protect their essential interests with dignity and with compassion and respect for those they are in conflict with, even when they don't like these other people and are very angry. People in conflict can get beyond their anger and fear to make wise choices, even when under great duress. By participating in this field, we help make these beliefs a practical reality in a complicated world.

Changing the World

For most conflict resolvers that I know, the purpose of our work goes beyond finding better ways of solving conflict. It involves a commitment to contribute to a better world. Of course finding better ways of settling conflict is part of making a better world, but I think there are other ways in which most of us see our work contributing to fundamental social change.

Violence and intolerance are major problems throughout the world, and the ability of people to accept differences and resolve conflicts without demonizing each other is a major challenge that will shape everyone's future. As I was writing this book, halfway around the world Serbians were expelling Albanian Kosovars from their homes while NATO was bombing the Serbs, and twenty miles from my home, students were being gunned down by their classmates at Columbine High School. Everyone has been struggling with trying to learn why these things happened, what could have been done to prevent them, and what should be done now. Clearly, there is much that we all have to learn about how to live with one another.

The conflict resolution field spans many different areas of human interaction. By learning lessons across these different kinds of interaction, people can do much to promote new understandings of wiser and better approaches to peacemaking. Too often peacemaking is equated solely with ending violence, just as conflict resolution is equated with achieving agreements. Yet we know that genuine peace requires a significant change in the relationship among the disputants, just as genuine resolution occurs only when progress is made on all three dimensions of conflict. We need to develop better approaches to deep peacemaking and to the deep resolution of conflict. By a principled participation in our field, we learn more about how to achieve more profound levels of resolution, and we help develop new approaches for handling serious conflict. In this way we make an important contribution to bringing about a more peaceful and secure world.

Part of the challenge in dealing with violence is to find ways of building more respect for diversity. Much of what conflict resolution is about is helping people respect differences and learn to see them as potential sources of strength rather than as threats. Conflict resolvers are constantly in the forefront of helping people to understand that for every challenge diversity poses, it presents important opportunities as well. They do not do this in an abstract way, but by helping people deal practically with troubling problems they are having with those they view as different. When people experience success in reaching a significant resolution to a conflict, they begin to break down the walls that have separated them from each other.

Another way in which our field is on the cutting edge of trying to improve the world has to do with the deepening of democracy and the struggle for social justice. When I was a college student in the 1960s, active in various social movements, we were often quite understandably taken to task for having a much clearer idea about what we were against than what we were for. Activists made many attempts at articulating the kind of society they were advocating, but the most durable concept that emerged was *participatory democracy*. Aside from sounding good, this term seemed to capture many people's desire to move away from a hierarchical and patriarchal approach to the governance of society and of the major institutions such as corporations, universities, families, and municipalities in which people lead their lives. The practical meaning of this, however, was never clear to most of us, certainly not to me.

What has become clear, however, is that the call for more meaningful participation reflected an important need that people were experiencing. On multiple fronts, people have been demanding more direct input into the decisions that affect their lives. Citizens demand input on land use decisions, transportation plans, police policies, fire station locations, the siting of almost any public facility, the allocation of public funds, and almost every other issue that government faces. Schools have created school improvement teams, parent advisory groups, and other accountability and input structures. Employers have embraced many variations of employee input processes. They may be called flat organizational structures, team management, employee councils, quality circles, Total Quality Management, or industrial democracy, but whatever the label, they all involve attempts to give employees more participation in decision making and more accountability for those decisions. Corporations now form many varieties of citizen advisory groups and negotiate *good neighbor agreements* with the communities in which they are located. And of course there are all the consensus-building dialogues, town meetings, regulatory negotiations, and policy roundtables with which conflict resolvers are so often involved. All of these structures and many others point to people's desire for more involvement in decision making. In fact this is participatory democracy in action.

Some of these new structures for democracy are faddish. Others are more for show or for discouraging political organizing than for encouraging genuine dialogue and problem solving. But those structures that lack real substance do not usually last. The reason many of these new mechanisms for participation have endured and grown is that they meet a genuine need for involvement and participation, for meaning and community, that people have. They also have proven effective at building better relations among people and finding solutions to difficult problems. The infrastructure of participation is growing and becoming more imbedded in our social institutions because it meets a fundamental need and, though its processes are sometimes muddled, it produces better results.

However, there is a definite down side to all this participation. Policy decisions are sometimes more difficult to make. Decision makers, managers, and the public often feel overwhelmed by process. Government officials refer with sardonic resignation to the "c" word—consensus. On the one hand, for example, deciding where to locate a sanitary landfill was a relatively simple matter thirty years ago. Now it involves many layers of often contentious public involvement. On the other hand many of those older land-fills were not safe or thoughtfully located. In order for participatory democracy to work, to provide meaningful participation, to give people input over the critical decisions affecting their lives, and to assist in solving the major public and organizational conflicts that affect them, the tools of the conflict resolution field are critical. In order to allow democracy to deepen without overwhelming people with process or the "c" word, the contributions of this field are essential.

Conflict resolution approaches are also essential if democracy is to take root in the many parts of the world where it is still a new and untested system. Democracy is at a crossroads in the world. There are many places where people are trying to embrace democratic principles and the freedoms that go along with them, but these efforts are also unleashing serious conflicts. Many people are equating democracy with instability and increasing inequality in the distribution of wealth. Democratic political and economic institutions are being attacked as the cause of personal insecurity and economic deterioration. Ethnic conflict has increased as centralized and authoritarian systems of governance and decision making have collapsed. These conflicts have been used by antidemocratic forces to try to maintain or reestablish authoritarian political structures. If conflict resolution procedures and skills can be introduced alongside democratic political structures, the chances for democratic reforms to take hold will be significantly improved.

The next few years will be critical in determining the future of democracy and civil society in many parts of the world. There are both discouraging and encouraging trends—countries apparently rejecting democratic reforms and countries embracing them. At this juncture it is particularly critical that consensus-building and conflict resolution processes be brought to bear at the level of ordinary citizens' lives in the emerging democracies throughout the world. Ultimately, democracy's strongest safeguard is the expectation of citizens that they are entitled to participate in the decisions that govern their lives.

This cannot be accomplished by simply exporting Western models of conflict resolution and decision making. But as we learn how to deepen democracy in existing democratic societies we can provide an example, a set of insights, a wealth of experience, and above all a sense of optimism to people elsewhere in the world. Others' efforts to create democracy will offer many lessons and ideas to the more established democratic world as well. I believe the knowledge of the field of conflict resolution is vital to the efforts to find an effective avenue for democracy to take powerful and positive root in many societies in transition.

At the heart of many of these struggles is the question of social justice. Can democratic approaches to governance enhance the struggle for social justice? Can democratic structures protect the weak, restrain the acquisitive impulses of the powerful, and balance the distribution of economic and other social benefits in a wise manner? I believe that the democratic framework is ultimately the only way in which enduring social justice can be obtained. However, when we look at the incredible inequalities in the distribution of income in the United States and the deterioration of the standard of living in Russia since the breakup of the Soviet Union, it is easy to become skeptical. I think the answer is more democracy, more deeply rooted, and more genuinely empowering. The more people are empowered to make decisions for themselves, the more they realize that democracy is not ultimately bestowed from above but is taken from below, the more they will find effective ways of demanding a socially just and economically wise approach to the distribution of social benefits.

Conflict resolution is in essence about empowering people to have a greater say over their own lives, particularly, but not only, during times of crises. It is in this sense that I believe the work of conflict resolvers is key to the deepening of democracy and the struggle for social justice in the world. Conflict resolvers are advocates and designers of practical democratic processes. And these processes are key to transforming the world we live in and to addressing fundamental issues of peace, democracy, and social justice.

Changing the Conflict Resolver

In conflict resolution, as in any intense field of work, practitioners as well as clients undergo change. If we are not involved in this business in part because of its personal growth potential for us, we are not fully involved. This is not about being unprofessional, about putting our needs before those of our clients, or about focusing narcissistically on our own development. It is about being fully engaged, present, and committed to what we are doing. Unless we see our engagement as offering something to us personally, to helping us be the kind of people we want to be and to play the role we want to play in the world, our participation in this field will be more mechanistic and calculating than the intensity of the work can ultimately tolerate.

If we are fully present, however, and if we do not create a defensive barrier that shields us from being influenced by our experiences—and I do not think such a barrier is really possible—then we will be profoundly affected on a personal level by what we do. For each of us, of course, the impact will be different. For most of us, participation in the field of conflict resolution will hopefully enhance our ability to communicate, to see the complexities of public and personal conflicts, to empathize, and to be creative. We will also hopefully grow beyond a tendency to see the conflicts in the world and our lives in polarized terms of good and bad, right and wrong, smart and stupid, true and false. And our ability to appreciate differences and to reach across cultural, age, gender, class, and other divides will hopefully be enhanced.

Not all the impacts of practicing conflict resolution are positive or comfortable. Perhaps it is age, perhaps it is the perspective that being a parent and having a career gives, but my clarity of beliefs and ability to be indignant about social ills are not what they once were. Making a continual effort to understand different sides of an issue or to look for the needs that are impelling distasteful behavior on the part of individuals, organizations, and governments can undercut one's ability to take decisive and unambiguous stands about public issues. I sometimes miss my clarity and indignation about people and issues, and every once in a while I look for an area to express this at one time more prominent side of my personality.

The world needs advocates, people who are focused on the struggle for social justice, who defend the unempowered, who strive to protect the environment, and who guard against assaults on our freedoms. It needs people who are focused on promoting the interests of a particular group or cause above the goal of resolving conflict or being collaborative. Without the engine such advocates provide for social change, conflict resolution as a field of practice would be just a means of lubricating the interactions of the powerful. Sometimes such single-minded advocates can be a major source of irritation and frustration. But they play a necessary and valuable role. As conflict resolvers' ability to embrace a larger picture grows, it is important that their appreciation and respect for such advocates does not diminish. Many of us can look at them and see ourselves at one point in our lives.

Something is lost and something is gained by any choice we make about how to lead our lives, and our work in conflict resolution is no exception. For me, the overall direction of the change has been positive. My experience as a conflict resolver has helped me grow as an individual, and it has helped me reconcile my values about human relations and social change. I have felt fortunate to be working in an area that is interesting, challenging, satisfying, and innovative. More important, I have cherished the opportunity to work in a field that contributes to making the world a better place at the same time as it helps individuals with their immediate struggles.

Although most of the roles people play as conflict resolution practitioners require them to act in an impartial way, the field itself is far from being value neutral. Implicit in what we do are very strong beliefs about how to improve the world we live in and about how people ought to relate to each other. Sometimes there is a contradiction between these values and our roles as conflict resolvers. More often, however, these values are the foundation from which we derive our power and energy. A true adherence and commitment to democracy, personal empowerment, and social justice is what allows us to play our roles with consistency, enthusiasm, and strength.

About the Author

Bernard Mayer, Ph.D., is a partner at CDR Associates, an internationally recognized conflict resolution and training organization. He has served as an adolescent and family therapist, a program administrator in mental health and substance abuse treatment programs, and the clinical director of a residential treatment program for emotionally disturbed youths.

Since the late 1970s, he has worked in the conflict resolution field as a mediator, facilitator, trainer, researcher, program administrator, and dispute systems designer, helping people resolve many different types of disputes ranging from public policy, ethnic, and labor-management conflicts to business, family, community, housing, and intergovernmental conflicts. He has assisted Native American governments and associations; federal, state, and local agencies; corporations, public interest groups, labor unions, professional associations, public schools, child welfare programs, mental health services, and universities.

Internationally recognized as a trainer and an innovative leader in applying mediation and conflict resolution to human service issues and particularly to disputes between public agencies and involuntary clients, Mayer holds a doctoral degree from the University of Denver, a master's degree in social work from Columbia University, and a bachelor's degree from Oberlin College. He has taught courses at the University of Colorado, University of Denver, Harvard University, University of Missouri, Windsor University, Colorado State University, University of Warsaw (Poland), the Budapest College of Economics (Hungary), and many other educational institutions. He has consulted on conflict management procedures and has trained mediators, negotiators, and conflict interveners in Australia, Bulgaria, Bosnia, Canada, Moldova, Poland, Hungary, New Zealand, and the United States.

He is the author of many articles and manuals on conflict resolution and the lead author of the *Constructive Engagement Resource Guide: Practical Advice for Dialogue Among Facilities, Workers, Communities, and Regulators,* published by the Environmental Protection Agency in 1999.

Mayer lives with his wife and family in Boulder, Colorado.

References

Axelrod, R. *The Evolution of Cooperation.* New York: Basic Books, 1984.

Bandler, R., and Grinder, J. *Reframing: Neurolinguistic Programming and the Transformation of Meaning.* Moab, Utah: Real People Press, 1982.

Blake, R., and Mouton, J. S. *Solving Costly Organizational Conflicts: Achieving Intergroup Trust, Cooperation, and Teamwork.* San Francisco: Jossey-Bass, 1984.

Burton, J., and Dukes, F. *Conflict: Resolution and Prevention.* New York: St. Martin's Press, 1990.

Bush, R., and Folger, J. *The Promise of Mediation: Responding to Conflict Through Empowerment and Recognition.* San Francisco: Jossey-Bass, 1994.

CDR Associates. *The Mediation Process Training Manual.* Boulder, Colo.: CDR Associates, 1986.

CDR Associates. *The Dispute System Design Manual.* Boulder, Colo.: CDR Associates, 1996.

Coser, L. A. *The Functions of Social Conflict.* New York: Free Press, 1956.

Crum, T. *The Magic of Conflict: Turning a Life of Work into a Life of Art.* New York: Simon & Schuster, 1987.

Curle, A. *Making Peace.* London: Tavistock, 1971.

Deutsch, M. *The Resolution of Conflict: Constructive and Destructive Processes.* New Haven, Conn.: Yale University Press, 1973.

Doyle, M., and Strauss, D. *Making Meetings Work.* Chicago: Playboy Press, 1976.

Etzioni, A. *A Comparative Analysis of Complex Organizations.* New York: Free Press, 1975.

Festinger, L. *A Theory of Cognitive Dissonance.* Stanford, Calif.: Stanford University Press, 1957.

Fisher, R. "Negotiating Power." *American Behavioral Scientist,* 1983, *27*(2), 149–166.

Fisher, R. "Beyond Yes." *Negotiation Journal,* 1985, *1*(1), 67–70.

Fisher, R., and Ury, W. *Getting to Yes.* Boston: Houghton Mifflin, 1981.

Folberg, J., and Taylor, A. *Mediation: A Comprehensive Guide to Resolving Conflicts Without Litigation.* San Francisco: Jossey-Bass, 1984.

Frost, J., and Wilmot, W. *Interpersonal Conflict.* Dubuque, Iowa: Brown, 1978.

Gamson, W. A. *Power and Discontent.* Homewood, Ill.: Dorsey Press, 1968.

Golten, M. M., and Mayer, B. *The Child Protection Mediation Project Manual.* Boulder, Colo.: CDR Associates, 1987.

Hale, K. "The Language of Cooperation: Negotiation Frames." *Mediation Quarterly,* 1998, *16*(2), 147–162.

Haynes, J. *Divorce Mediation: A Practical Guide for Therapists and Counselors.* New York: Springer, 1981.

Haynes, J. *Fundamentals of Family Mediation.* Albany: State University of New York Press, 1994.

Kochman, T. *Black and White Styles in Conflict.* Chicago: University of Chicago Press, 1981.

Kolb, D. *The Mediators.* Cambridge, Mass.: MIT Press, 1983.

Kolb, D., and Associates. *When Talk Works: Profiles of Mediators.* San Francisco: Jossey-Bass, 1994.

Kressel, K., Pruitt, D. G., and Associates. *Mediation Research: The Process and Effectiveness of Third-Party Intervention.* San Francisco: Jossey-Bass, 1989.

Kriesberg, L. *The Sociology of Social Conflicts.* (2nd ed.) Englewood Cliffs, N.J.: Prentice Hall, 1982.

Lax, D., and Sebenius, J. *The Manager as Negotiator.* New York: Free Press, 1986.

Lederach, J. P. *Preparing for Peace: Conflict Transformation Across Cultures.* Syracuse, N.Y.: Syracuse University Press, 1995.

Lederach, J. P. *Building Peace: Sustainable Reconciliation in Divided Societies.* Washington, D.C.: United States Institute of Peace Press, 1997.

Maslow, A. H. *Motivation and Personality.* New York: HarperCollins, 1954.

Mayer, B. "Conflict Resolution in Child Protection and Adoption." *Mediation Quarterly,* 1985, *7,* 69–82.

Mayer, B. "The Dynamics of Power in Mediation and Conflict Resolution." *Mediation Quarterly,* 1987, *16,* 75–86.

Mayer, B. "Conflict Resolution." In R. Edward and others, *Social Work Encyclopedia.* (19th ed.) Washington, D.C.: NASW Press, 1995.

Mayer, B., Ghais, S., and McKay, J. A. *Constructive Engagement Resource Guide: Practical Advice for Dialogue Among Facilities, Workers, Communities and Regulators.* Washington, D.C.: U.S. Environmental Protection Agency, 1999.

Mayer, B., Wildau, S., and Valchev, R. "Promoting Multi-Cultural Consensus Building in Bulgaria." *Cultural Survival,* 1995, *19*(3), 64–68.

McCarthy, W. "The Role of Power and Principle in Getting to Yes." *Negotiation Journal*, 1985, *1*(1), 59–66.

McCrory, J. "The Mediation Puzzle." *Vermont Law Review*, 1981, *6*(1), 85–117.

Mnookin, R. W. "Why Negotiations Fail: An Exploration of Barriers to the Resolution of Conflict." *Ohio State Journal on Dispute Resolution*, 1993, *8*(2), 234–249.

Moore, C. W. *The Mediation Process: Practical Strategies for Resolving Conflict.* San Francisco: Jossey-Bass, 1986.

Moore, C. W. *The Mediation Process: Practical Strategies for Resolving Conflict.* (2nd ed.) San Francisco: Jossey-Bass, 1996.

Mosten, F. *The Complete Guide to Mediation: The Cutting-Edge Approach to Family Law Practice.* Chicago: American Bar Association, Section of Family Law, 1997.

"New Cars: A Buyer's Market." *Consumer Reports,* Apr. 1999, pp. 16–18.

Pearson, J. "Divorce Mediation: Strengths and Weaknesses over Time." In H. Davidson and others (eds.), *Alternative Means of Family Dispute Resolution.* Washington, D.C.: American Bar Association, 1982.

Rothman, J. *Resolving Identity-Based Conflict in Nations, Organizations, and Communities.* San Francisco: Jossey-Bass, 1997.

Rubin, J. (ed.). *Dynamics of Third Party Intervention.* New York: Praeger, 1981.

Saposnek, D. T. *Mediating Child Custody Disputes: A Systematic Guide for Family Therapists, Court Counselors, Attorneys, and Judges.* San Francisco: Jossey-Bass, 1983.

Schellenburg, J. A. *The Science of Conflict.* New York: Oxford University Press, 1982.

Schelling, T. *The Strategy of Conflict.* Cambridge, Mass.: Harvard University Press, 1960.

Schwarz, R. M. *The Skilled Facilitator: Practical Wisdom for Developing Effective Groups.* San Francisco: Jossey-Bass, 1994.

Slaikeu, K. A., and Hasson, R. H. *Controlling the Cost of Conflict: How to Design a System for Your Organization.* San Francisco: Jossey-Bass, 1998.

Stulberg, J. B. "The Theory and Practice of Mediation: A Reply to Professor Susskind." *Vermont Law Review*, 1981, *6*(1), 85–117.

Susskind, L. "Environmental Mediation and the Accountability Problem." *Vermont Law Review*, 1981, *6*(1), 85–117.

Susskind, L., McKearnan, S., and Thomas-Larner, J. (eds.). *The Consensus Building Handbook: A Conceptual Guide to Reaching Agreement.* Thousand Oaks, Calif.: Sage, 1999.

Thomas, K. W. "Conflict and Conflict Management." In M. D. Dunnette (ed.), *Handbook of Industrial and Organizational Psychology.* Skokie, Ill.: Rand McNally, 1983.

Thomas, K. W., and Kilmann, R. H. *Thomas-Kilmann Conflict Mode Instrument.* New York: Xicom, 1974.

Umbreit, M. *Victim Meets Offender: The Impact of Restorative Justice and Mediation.* Monsey, N.Y.: Criminal Justice Press, 1994.

Ury, W. *Getting Past No: Negotiating with Difficult People.* New York: Bantam Books, 1991.

Ury, W. L., Brett, J. M., and Goldberg, S. B. *Getting Disputes Resolved: Designing Systems to Cut the Costs of Conflicts.* San Francisco: Jossey-Bass, 1988.

Walton, R. W., and McKersie, R. B. *A Behavioral Theory of Negotiations.* New York: McGraw-Hill, 1965.

Wehr, P. *Conflict Regulation.* Boulder, Colo.: Westview Press, 1979.

Williams, M. *Mediation: Why People Fight and How to Help Them to Stop.* Dublin: Poolbeg Press, 1998.

Index

Etzioni, A., 62
Experts, 47, 235–236
Expression, desires for, 22–23

F

Facilitation, procedural, 226–227
Fact finding, 228–229. *See also* Substantive assistance
Fairness, 38
Fear, 177–178
Feeling, conflict as, 5
Festinger, L., 99
Fisher, R., 66, 112, 149, 155
Fixes, 28
Folberg, J., 201
Folding, avoidance by, 32–33
Folger, J., 110
Forgiveness, role of, 104
Formal authority, 55
Fractionalization, 161
Framing, definition of, 132–133
Freud, S., 16
Frost, J., 16
Functions of Social Conflict, The (Coser), 22

G

Game, negotiation as, 140–141
Gamson, W. A., 62
Gandhi, M., 57
Generational culture, 72
Genocide, 90–91
George Mason University, 112
Germany, 90
Getting to Yes (Fisher and Ury), 155
Ghais, S., 224
Goals, debate about appropriate, 108–115
Goldberg, S. B., 34, 234, 236
Golten, M. M., 38
Good neighbor agreement, 244
Greece, 85
Grinder, J., 132
Guatemala, 116
Gypsies. *See* Roma people

H

Habitual power, 57
Hale, K., 137
Harmony, 192
Hasson, R. H., 236
Haynes, J., 201
Hispanics, 76
History: as cause of conflict, 13–16; as cultural variable, 84–86
Hitler, A., 176
Hmong, 91
Holocaust, 84, 90
Hopelessness, avoidance through, 31–32
Human needs: at center of all conflicts, 8–9; and community, 20; continuum of, 16–22; and identity-based needs, 19–22; and interests, 17–19; and intimacy, 20–22
Hume, J., 123
Hussein, S., 176

I

"I" messages, 129
Impasse: as conflict within conflict, 187–188; constructive attitudes about, 177–180; dimensions of, 171–172; general questions for addressing, 180–184; nature of, 168–176; sources of, 172–176; specific questions for addressing, 184–187; tactical *versus* genuine, 169–171
Incremental risk taking, 207–208
Indirection, 39–41
Information: as type of power, 55; in negotiation, 150, 151
Institute for Conflict Analysis and Resolution (George Mason University), 112
Integrative listening, 127
Integrative negotiation: convergence of, with distributive negotiation, 158–160; principles of, 151–155
Integrative power, 65–66

Settlement, 217–218

Skills, 192

Slaikeu, K. A., 236

Social change: and changing the world through conflict resolution, 242–246; as purpose of conflict resolution, 108–115, 241

Social justice, 67–70, 111, 243–244

South Africa, 99, 232, 233

Soviet Union, 246

Story line, 137

Strauss, D., 227

Structural inequalities, task of eliminating, 111

Structural power, *versus* personal power, 54–55

Structure: alteration of, by mediator, 193; as cause of conflict, 12–13; as cultural variable, 83–84

Stulberg, J. B., 111

Substantive assistance: and data gathering, 229; and professional consultation, 229–231; and technical input, 228–229

Surrogates, avoidance through, 32

Susskind, L., 111, 226

T

Tar Baby, 39

Taylor, A., 201

Technical input, 228–229. *See also* Substantive assistance

Third-party involvement, 216–217, 225–226

Thomas, K. W., 30, 146

Thomas-Larner, J., 226

Total Quality Management (TQM), 244

Tragic frame, 139

Training, for procedural assistance, 227

Transformation, as purpose of conflict resolution, 108–115

Trimble, W. D., 123

Truth Commissions (South Africa), 99, 233

Turkey, 85

Twain, M., 78

U

Umbreit, M., 232

Unbundled legal services, 222

Uncle Remus, 39

Understanding, deeper, *versus* negotiated agreement, 111–112

United Autoworkers, 45

United Nations, 47

United States drug laws, 91

Ury, W. L., 34, 112, 149, 155, 177, 234, 236

Utah Attorney General's Office, 147

Utah Department of Environmental Quality, 147

Utah Transportation Authority, 147

Utilitarian approach, to application of power, 62

V

Valchev, R., 85

Values: about conflict, 26–29; and acceptability of conflict, 27; and behavior in conflict, 27–28; concurrence of, 82–83; in conflict resolution, 239–240; as cultural variables, 81–83; and mediation, 193–194; and solvability of conflict, 28–29; types of, 81–83

Violence, 242–243

Vision, 192

W

Walton, R. W., 146

Warsaw Ghetto, 85

Way, closing of, 158

Wehr, P., 16

West Bank, Palestine, 20, 187

Western Europeans, 80, 885

Wheel of Conflict, 9; gaining inner part of, 163; and sources of impasse, 172–173

Wildau, S., 85